MULTILINGUALISM
AND
MOTHER TONGUE
IN
MEDIEVAL FRENCH, OCCITAN,
AND
CATALAN NARRATIVES

PENN STATE
ROMANCE STUDIES

EDITORS
Robert Blue *(Spanish)*
Kathryn M. Grossman *(French)*
Thomas A. Hale *(French/Comparative Literature)*
Djelal Kadir *(Comparative Literature)*
Norris J. Lacy *(French)*
John M. Lipski *(Spanish)*
Sherry L. Roush *(Italian)*
Allan Stoekl *(French/Comparative Literature)*

ADVISORY BOARD
Theodore J. Cachey Jr. *(University of Notre Dame)*
Priscilla Ferguson *(Columbia University)*
Hazel Gold *(Emory University)*
Cathy L. Jrade *(Vanderbilt University)*
William Kennedy *(Cornell University)*
Gwen Kirkpatrick *(Georgetown University)*
Rosemary Lloyd *(Indiana University)*
Gerald Prince *(University of Pennsylvania)*
Joseph T. Snow *(Michigan State University)*
Ronald W. Tobin *(University of California at Santa Barbara)*
Noël Valis *(Yale University)*

MULTILINGUALISM AND MOTHER TONGUE IN MEDIEVAL FRENCH, OCCITAN, AND CATALAN NARRATIVES

CATHERINE E. LÉGLU

THE PENNSYLVANIA STATE UNIVERSITY PRESS
UNIVERSITY PARK, PENNSYLVANIA

LIBRARY OF CONGRESS
CATALOGING-IN-PUBLICATION DATA

Léglu, Catherine. Multilingualism and mother tongue in medieval French, Occitan, and Catalan narratives / Catherine E. Léglu.
    p.   cm. — (Penn State Romance studies)
    Includes bibliographical references and index.
    Summary: "Explores the ways in which vernacular works composed in Occitan, Catalan, and French between the twelfth and the fifteenth centuries narrate multilingualism and its apparent opponent, the mother tongue. These encounters are narrated through literary motifs of love, incest, disguise, and travel"—Provided by publisher.
    ISBN 978-0-271-03672-4 (cloth : alk. paper)
    ISBN 978-0-271-03673-1 (pbk. : alk. paper)
    1. Romances—History and criticism.
    2. French literature—To 1500—History and criticism.
    3. Provencal literature—History and criticism.
    4. Catalan literature—To 1500—History and criticism.
5. Multilingualism and literature—France—History—To 1500.
    6. Multilingualism—France—History—To 1500.
                I. Title.

PQ221.L45 2010
840.9'34—dc22
2009047811

Copyright © 2010
The Pennsylvania State University
All rights reserved
Printed in the United States of America
Published by The Pennsylvania State University Press,
University Park, PA 16802-1003

The Pennsylvania State University Press
is a member of the
Association of American University Presses.

It is the policy of The Pennsylvania State University Press to use acid-free paper. Publications on uncoated stock satisfy the minimum requirements of American National Standard for Information Sciences—Permanence of Paper for Printed Library Material, ANSI Z39.48–1992.

This book can be viewed at:
http://publications.libraries.psu.edu/
eresources/978-0-271-03672-4

CONTENTS

List of Illustrations vii
Acknowledgments ix

Introduction 1

PART 1: MYTHS OF MULTILINGUALISM

1
Babel in *Girart de Roussillon* 17

2
Tongues of Fire in *Guilhem de la Barra* 35

3
Acquiring the (M)other Tongue in Avignon and Toulouse 55

PART 2: LANGUAGE POLITICS

4
Translation Scandals 77

5
Languages and Borders in Three *Novas* 99

6
Monolingualism and Endogamy: French Examples 119

PART 3: THE *Monolangue*

7
The Multilingual *Paris and Vienne*   141

8
Pierre de Provence et La Belle Maguelonne   159

9
Travels in the *Monolangue*   177

Notes   195
Bibliography   213
Index   231

ILLUSTRATIONS

1. Peyre de Paternas, *Libre de sufficientia e de necessitat,* MS Paris BNF fr. 3313A, 27v. © Bibliothèque nationale de France.
2. Peyre de Paternas, *Libre de sufficientia e de necessitat,* MS Paris BNF fr. 3313A, 1r. © Bibliothèque nationale de France.
3. *Las Abreujamens de las estorias,* MS British Library Egerton 1500, 3v. © British Library Board. All rights reserved.
4. The Lover besieges the Beloved's tower, *Histoire d'amour sans paroles,* Chantilly, Musée Condé MS338, 11v. © RMN/René-Gabriel Ojéda.
5. *Histoire d'amour sans paroles,* Chantilly, Musée Condé MS338, 4v. © RMN/René-Gabriel Ojéda.

ACKNOWLEDGMENTS

THIS BOOK WAS WRITTEN with the support of the University of Bristol, which awarded me a semester of research leave in 2002–3 and a University Research Fellowship in 2004–5. It was completed with the support of a one-year research fellowship awarded by the Leverhulme Trust in 2006–7. The idea for the book came from Bristol's participation in the Worldwide Universities Network's sponsored project on Multilingualism, and I thank my former colleagues in the University of Bristol Centre for Medieval Studies for ten years of stimulating interdisciplinary dialogue. Finally, I especially thank my family for their help and support throughout this project, but above all in the summer of 2007, when a combination of late pregnancy, a fractured leg, and relocation to a new post at the University of Reading made the completion of this book a task that depended very much on them in countless ways. To Paul, Beatrice, and Josephine, with love.

Chapter 1 is based on my article, "Rebuilding the Tower of Babel in *Girart de Roussillon*," in *Medieval Historical Discourses: Essays in Honour of Peter S. Noble*, ed. Marianne J. Ailes, Anne Lawrence-Mathers, and Françoise Le Saux, *Reading Medieval Studies* 34 (2008): 137–52. I thank Françoise Le Saux for reproduction permission. Parts of chapter 3 are reproduced, with permission, from my article "Languages in Conflict: 'Las Leys d'Amors,'" *Modern Language Review* 63, no. 2 (2008): 388–96. Part of chapter 5 is reproduced, with permission, from my article "Between Hell and a Fiery Mountain: Antoine de La Sale's 'Excursion aux iles Lipari,'" *Studies in Travel Writing* 11, no. 22 (2007): 109–26.

INTRODUCTION

WE OPEN WITH A marginal image in a bilingual treatise, composed and translated around 1350 in Avignon by the Austin friar Peyre de Paternas, the *Libre de sufficientia e de necessitat* (27v; fig. 1).[1] At the top of the left-hand column is the end of a chapter in Occitan. It is then followed by the opening of the subsequent chapter in Latin; Occitan translation follows the Latin text. A large marginal image appears below the two columns of text. It shows an ox standing on its hind legs and guiding a long plow pulled by two men, one bearded and one clean shaven. The ox is shouting in French, "Grizel, avant!" (Move, Grisel!), and prodding the men with a lance that stretches the full length of the plow. The name "Maistre Jehan de Mazeres" has been written next to the heads of the two men.

The marginal image (which dominates the folio and as such cannot truly be regarded as "marginal") is an interpretation of the common proverbial expression for doing things in the wrong order, "Mettre la charrue devant les boeufs," the French equivalent of the English "putting the cart before the horse," except that the cart has been replaced by a plow. The name inscribed beside the men may be that of the illuminator. The manuscript is also signed by its Breton copyist, Guillaume ar Bleiz de Kergoat, and either Guillaume or an assistant occasionally wrote instructions for the illuminator in French. If the illuminator is one of the two men tied to the plow, his companion may well be the Breton copyist. The hybrid human-ox plowman is not identified.

Peyre de Paternas prefaces his bilingual work by describing it to its female dedicatee as a work written "en nostra linga maternal" (in our mother tongue) (1r). Delphine de Belfort was a noblewoman from the Limousin, and the manuscript contains her portrait as well as her coat of arms, which is often set beside that of her husband Hugues de La Roche. The frontispiece of the manuscript contains the coat of arms of Delphine's uncle, Pope Clement VI (the Limousin-born Pierre Roger) and of four cardinals who

Fig. 1 Peyre de Paternas, *Libre de sufficientia e de necessitat*, MS Paris BNF fr. 3313A, fol. 27v. © Bibliothèque nationale de France.

Fig. 2 Peyre de Paternas, *Libre de sufficientia e de necessitat*, MS Paris BNF fr. 3313A, fol. 1r. © Bibliothèque nationale de France.

were their kinsmen (fig. 2). Peyre makes much of the language that he shares with both Delphine and the pope. He claims that he was recruited to the Avignon Augustinian house because there was no other Paris-trained master available who could teach "de lenga ocana." Delphine was from the Limousin and Peyre was from Provence, but he asserts that this *lenga ocana* was a single mother tongue (*lingua materna*) and that this was in demand among the most influential figures in the papal curia.

Peyre's prologue creates two audiences for his book, one reading Latin, the other requiring Occitan either to have access to the Latin or to replace it. The French and Francophone Breton team that produced the book as a physical object construct a third. Peyre's book presents itself as a Latin work supported by an Occitan translation of equal weight and value. It is in the spirit of the prologue of the Occitan *Elucidari*, which describes the young count Gaston of Foix poring perplexedly over Bartholomeus Anglicus's *De proprietatibus rerum*, then exclaiming to a passing translator:

> L'estil del libre m'es salvagge,
> escur, subtil: yeu requier declaragge;
> sera m'util, expres en mon lenguagge.[2]

[The style of the book is aloof from me, obscure, subtle: I need some clarification. It will be useful to me once it has been expressed in my language.]

It would surely be discourteous of Peyre de Paternas to imply that the members of the papal curia were unable to read Latin, so the purpose of the *Libre de sufficientia* has to lie beyond such clarification. Occitan is used in this instance both as a vehicular language for a text in Latin that would (theoretically) remain inaccessible to Delphine and as a prestigious idiom used by Peyre to proclaim his personal usefulness both to the Avignonese papacy and to its geographical and dynastic location in Provence.[3] The young count of Foix demands a linguistic support of his commissioned translator "en mon lenguagge" (my language), the language of his lineage and of his possessions.

I have chosen these two examples in resistance to the prevalent view of late medieval Occitan writing as the last, sad expression of a decadent or politically oppressed minority language. As is well known, Occitan functioned as a vehicular language in some western European poetic circles from the twelfth to the early fourteenth century. It was gradually supplanted in

Italy by Tuscan and gave way more slowly in Catalonia, first to a hybrid Occitan-Catalan narrative poetry and ultimately to works in both poetry and prose that were composed in Catalan. Occitan functions throughout the fourteenth and fifteenth centuries as a literary and cultural go-between. Kevin Brownlee has described the "conflicted genealogy" that is embedded in Italian receptions of French texts, where the anxiety of influence is affected by competition over cultural prestige and dominance: "Dante's notion of translatio is therefore not the progression from Greece to Rome to the France of Chrétien de Troyes and the French literary tradition but rather, from Greece to Rome to Italy, including of course, from Dante's perspective, Provençal as part of the Romance vernacular lyric tradition on the basis of which he (in part) positions himself in the *Commedia*."[4] Occitan (formerly Provençal) is viewed as posing "no threat" to Italian culture (Brownlee's term), largely thanks to its lack of a canonical narrative tradition. It is a lyric mode of expression that could be learned and adapted without the declaration of any political allegiance, one of the few Romance languages that did not eventually become the official idiom of a nation-state and, as such, is reducible neither to the wholly modern concept of "Southern France" nor to a *koine*.[5] As Catalan and French both moved in very different ways toward the position of a national language, Occitan lost its prestige. Where in the twelfth to thirteenth centuries it was a vehicular language for poetry that enjoyed a strong international reputation, by the late fifteenth century it had become the carefully controlled and protected expression of regional and civic identity in certain centers such as Toulouse and Arles. It changed from a deracinated and genuinely international idiom into a minor provincial art form.

The literary context of Occitan in the fourteenth century was mapped more than twenty years ago by Maurizio Perugi in a study that demonstrates the close ties between the Toulousain poetic revival, the less well-known aristocratic poetry of Rodez, and the regions touching on the papal court at Avignon.[6] Occitan narrative works were still being composed in various genres, among them saints' lives, miracle plays, and local histories such as Bertran Boysset's *Roman d'Arles*. The *chanson de geste* was popular in the sense that several Occitan epics survive only in fourteenth-century manuscripts, and the unusual *Guillaume de la Barra* (1318) was written partly from epic models. Perhaps most important is the fact that troubadour *chansonniers* were produced in the mid-thirteenth to mid-fourteenth centuries in northern Italy and Catalonia as well as in the Toulousain and Pyrenees.[7] Occitan-speaking regions became increasingly Francophone after the end of the thirteenth century, through annexation into the French crown of much of the Languedoc, the establishment of a French-based Angevin county of Provence, and the monarch's close political involvement in the Avignon papacy. English political domination was of course marked in Aquitaine and Gascony during much of this period. Contact with both northern and southern Italy was ensured through the Angevin kingdom of Naples as well as Avignon.

However, the dominant view of Occitan literary production remains negative. Despite his sympathetic treatment of this period and region, Perugi uses a number of striking images to condemn what he views as a rhetorical continuity that was marred by lexical and grammatical stagnation:

> La controparte linguistica è costituita dal progressive irrigidimento e imbastardimento della lingua letteraria occitanica, sulla quale agiscono le spinte convergenti di un processo di codificazione imbalsamatrice e carico delle strutture grammaticali, e di un parallelo arricchimento—o piuttosto inquinamento—lessicale con una massiccia intrusione di vocaboli appartenenti ai registri linguistici piú bassi e di forestierismi, in particolare provenienti da oil.[8]

> [The other side of the linguistic equation is made up of the progressive increase in inflexibility and bastardizing of the Occitan literary language, under the converging influences of an embalming process of codification of the grammatical structures, and a parallel lexical enrichment (or rather, impoverishment) by the major influx of words taken from lower linguistic registers and foreign loan words, particularly those from northern French.]

Stiff, embalmed, bastardized, invaded by "low" and "foreign" (French) words—there is little left of the troubadour koine. This mummified yet decomposing corpse stalks the other side of the Pyrenees as well, for Martín de Riquer decried the deadening influence of Occitan poetry on nascent Catalan prose and suggested that its domination until the last years of the fourteenth century compromised promising literary and cultural exchanges with Italy thanks to a style that was "vulgar, bland and prosaic" (vulgar, fada i prosaica).[9] Perugi riposted that the poet Ausiàs March (c. 1400–1459) could not have composed in a Catalan that he sought to free from the language of the troubadours, had he not been strongly influenced by the troubadour tradition, admittedly in part as it reentered Catalonia via Italian lyric poetry.[10] Perugi emphasizes the importance of rejection in reception. He also emphasizes that Raimon de Cornet is one of a number of Occitan poets whose works and career point to a livelier engagement with their times. More recent studies have echoed Perugi's conclusions, but have also emphasized that Occitan and Catalan literary interaction has a more long-standing and richer history than the theory of Occitan precedence would allow.[11] More recently still, the infiltration of Occitan literary culture by gallicisms has come to be viewed as a reflection of fashion rather than decadence, evidence of a dynamic intercultural exchange rather than colonized defeat.[12]

Studies of manuscript production point to substantial levels of multilingualism within courts as centers of patronage, as well as in towns where manuscripts were commissioned, copied, and illuminated. Francophone book production reached far beyond Francophone regions, as is also observed for Occitan manuscripts, many of which are the products of workshops and compilers in northern Italy, "a veritable melting pot" of linguistic interaction.[13] Sermon collections and reports also point to a substantial amount of overlap, as well as some careful marking of boundaries, such as the dissimilar languages used for the same sermon collection compiled in the Pyrenean villages of Organyà and Tortosa and the Catalan prose translation of Matfre Ermengaud's *Breviari d'amor*. Linguistic interference appears in surprising locations too.[14] In the fifteenth century, writers in Provence were more inclined to seek patronage by composing in French, thanks especially to the officially Francophone but polyglot court of René d'Anjou, which also offered patronage to Catalan writers. The Toulousain poetic revival shares the learned basis of Peyre's manuscript, but it coincided with enduring patronage of troubadour poetry in aristocratic courts in both Occitan- and Catalan-speaking regions.

The *Libre de sufficientia* may symbolize the rich linguistic mix of Avignon (admittedly while it suffered a recruitment crisis during the Black Death), a place where friars composed texts in Occitan and Latin and worked harmoniously with French and Breton-French craftsmen to produce luxury volumes that would adorn the bookcases of nobles and prelates alike. Yet the marginal illustration also suggests that someone thought that Peyre de Paternas had muddled his political and linguistic priorities. An Augustinian friar recruited and employed by the pope has, perhaps, placed his Occitan plow before the French oxen that allow the Avignon papal court to produce luxury volumes of this sort. On the frontispiece, the shield of one of the four cardinals is flanked by an ape with an owl perched on its arm, which may be read as a sly allusion to the courtly prelate who goes hawking, "aping" the lay aristocracy, and who makes a public display of his ignorance (one of the many associations of the owl), perhaps by acting as patron to a translation into Occitan of a Latin treatise. The ox may shout orders in French, much as the French king was believed to dominate the schismatic curia, but it is not clear if anyone can understand his words.

Delphine and Peyre are connected, so he claims, by a common "mother" tongue, but should a "feminine" genealogy of this sort be privileged in the context of a court dependent on the paternal protection of the French monarch? Peyre has placed his manuscript under the aegis of genealogy. By highlighting Delphine's kinship with her powerful uncles, the illuminator extends the theme to present a critical gloss on his enterprise. The historiated letter O counterbalances the marginal image with a depiction of the Massacre of the Innocents. In genealogical thinking, the ox should precede the plow; secular men's genitals should plow the fertile earth. The Massacre of the Innocents depicts a crime against medieval views of genealogy, in that the mother's fate should be subordinate to that of her male offspring. It is also a reversal of logic, this time that of lineage. Other literary examples point to a similar dilemma concerning the feminine "mother tongue" (as we will see in Chapter 3) and the connection between lineage and language (Chapters 3, 4, and 5).

If we return next to the count's request in the *Elucidari,* "mon lenguagge" is evidently presented as a clear, unsubtle, and useful medium that is shared by the count and the narrator in the text. This may well seem to be a definition of the mother tongue for a modern reader, but it could just as easily be the image of Latin for an educated reader of that time. If the count is struggling to understand his book, it is not because he cannot read it, as he can make out the words. He lacks the knowledge to see beyond the words on the page, so he requests a vernacular gloss. It is this gap in knowledge that motivates both him and the author of the poem to begin the process of translation. The prologue introduces the count of Foix to a new palace modeled on his own, that of Lady Wisdom (lines 18–26). The narrator overlays the count's castle and his lands with a book that allows him to know (by inference, to own) the properties of all things, mapping vernacular words onto objects and locations that are familiar to him. One layer of vernacular words is placed over aristocratic lands, and the count is urged to gloss the incomprehensible world of a Latin encyclopedia in terms of his home and body, as if these were also "his language." The properties of all living things are mapped onto the valleys and buildings of the northeastern Pyrenees and expressed in an idiom supposedly comprehensible to its inhabitants.

Paul Zumthor traced a vertical relationship between "high" Latin and the "low" vernaculars and a horizontal or contiguous relationship between these less elite languages.[15] Zumthor was not satisfied with this assumption, but it provided a useful working model for his study, as it maintained Latin in its cultural position, as if it were a high tower dominating a plain of vernaculars. Where these vernaculars come into contact, their interaction may not produce a common reference back to Latin or a smooth interpenetration. They may display intense competition. For example, the troubadour Raimbaut de Vaqueiras composed a *descort* (discord), a poem in which each stanza has a different metrical form. Raimbaut wrote each stanza in a different language: Occitan, French, Gascon, Galician-Portuguese, and Tuscan (PC 392, 4; Linskill, XVI).[16] Furio Brugnolo has argued that Raimbaut's song may appear to display a harmonious coexistence of literary idioms, but it also demonstrates to any listener how easy it is to adapt troubadour poetry to other Romance languages.[17] As Raimbaut was one of the first troubadours to obtain extended patronage in Lombardy, his *descort* amounts to a demonstration not of his skill in his mother tongue, but of his role as the provider of a flexible lyric medium to courts that did not speak the language of his songs. Similarly, Miriam Cabré has read Cerverí de Girona's "Cobla en sis lengatges" as part of his persona as a "cultural bridge," transmitting Occitan culture in the Catalan household of Pere el Gran (1276–85), which was also in touch with Sicilian curial culture (c. 1259–85).[18]

Raimbaut de Vaqueiras was a contemporary of the Catalan Raimon Vidal de Besalú, the author of the *Razos de trobar* (c. 1190–1213), the first datable treatise for the acquisition of Occitan as a poetic language. Raimon presents the choice between two vernacular languages in strictly aesthetic terms:[19]

> La parladura francesca val mais et [es] plus avinenz a far romanz et pasturellas, mas cella de Lemosin val mais per far vers et cansons et serventes. Et per totas las terras de nostre lengatge son de maior autoritat li cantar de la lenga lemosina qe de neguna autra parladura. (lines 72–75)
>
> [The French tongue is better and more attractive for composing romances and *pastourelles*, but the one of the Limousin is better for composing *vers*, *cansos*, and *sirventes*. And throughout the lands of our language, the songs of the Limousin tongue have greater authority than any other language.]

This language of the Limousin applies to the dialects spoken in "Limousin, Provence, Auvergne, Quercy, and adjacent provinces" (lines 61–64), a linguistic field now labeled Occitan. Raimon's treatise intends to teach correct usage borrowed from a standardized poetic language (koine) applying it to a neighboring tongue that lacked certain grammatical features that made it suited to complex poetic form. Occitan and French are vernaculars which are part of "las terras de nostre lengatge," but Occitan has greater prestige as a language with *auctoritas*. It is a vernacular with the authority of Latin, one of the languages to which Raimon is offering an alternative. He is probably also countering the prestige within Catalan lands of Arabic and Hebrew as literary and scientific languages, as he says *trobar* is practiced by men of all social ranks, from kings to shepherds, Jews, Muslims, and Christians alike (lines 20–27). Raimon's treatise is composed for an audience of Catalan aristocrats and he is clearly offering them a poetic and historiographical language: "Et tuit li mal e.l ben del mont son mes en remembransa per trobadors" (And all the good and bad things of the world are commemorated by troubadours) (lines 27–28). He adds that "trobars et chantars son movemenz de totas galliardas" (*trobar* and singing are the impulse for all great deeds) (lines 30–31). This koine may structure the narratives of the future as well as the past. Occitan may offer a suitable language, but it needs to be clearly understood by both its authors and its audiences. Raimon criticizes those who pretend that they can understand songs when they do not (lines 32–36) and insists that it is necessary to learn the "saber de trobar" in order to tell the difference between good and bad songs. Acquiring a lyric language is a matter of acquiring intellectual mastery, as well as a certain degree of control over how the past and the future of a lineage or court are narrated.

Raimon may have had some acquaintance with the multilingual poetry that flourished in regions south of Catalonia a little more than a century earlier, such as the *muwashashahat* in vernacular Arabic and Hebrew, which featured refrains (*kharjas*) in a Romance language identified as Mozarabic. While direct contact still remains to be established, a broader intercultural contact has been suggested by María Rosa Menocal.[20] The *muwashashahat* depend on bilingual performers, one masculine voice enacting the erotic material of the main song and the refrain in Romance vernacular placed in the mouth of a woman. Medieval Arabic writers commented that the *muwashashat* were vulgar songs and that their multilingual content associated them with the lowest rank of performers: "gypsies," prostitutes, and those who travel and who are paid for their entertainment.[21] A key figure in the performance of the corpus seems to have been the Mozarabic slave, usually female, who was employed as a musician in *taifa* courts. María Rosa Menocal has made much of a report that an eleventh-century Norman crusader listened to a group of female performers and appeared to understand some of their song. One chronicler claimed that William IX of Aquitaine (the earliest known troubadour) grew up in a court that included "Saracen" women musicians and dancers who had been captured by his father.[22] Both accounts are seductive but neither says that the nobleman did more than exploit the women's skills. The troubadour Marcabru (fl. c. 1130–50), whose early career was at the court of Poitiers, appears to have borrowed both the meter and the rhyme sounds of an Arabic *muwashashaha*, but not the sense of the song. The Arabic piece is a love song, but Marcabru's version is a crude parody of a three-way dialogue between a lover, his lady, and a messenger bird. More intriguingly, a troubadour of the following generation, Peire d'Alvernhe, rewrote Marcabru's two songs as a serious dialogue between a lover, a nightingale, and the lady. Have the Occitan poets done more than borrow an attractive Andalusian melody? It is well known that musical instruments such as the '*ud* (lute) were transmitted across western Europe through the High Middle Ages. Both troubadours take as their central character a messenger bird who interprets the words of the lover to his distant lady. In troubadour poetry, birds are figures that sing in their language (*lati*, "Latin") without being comprehensible beyond the general sense that they are singing about their love. Both Marcabru and Peire d'Alvernhe enjoyed periods of success in the courts of northern Spain, but how much these audiences would have understood the finer points of their often complex poems is clearly debatable. This single instance of direct poetic exchange certainly does not suggest that the *content* of troubadour songs may be traced reliably to Andalusian sources, though instruments, melodies, and styles of performance are a different matter.[23] A troubadour in this context may have been as incomprehensible as a bird.

Troubadour songs were performed in courts that did not speak Occitan, and the songs owed their success in part to the *razo*, what seems to have been an oral introduction or commentary to a song. Indeed, one of the reasons for the success of troubadour poetry is that by the mid-twelfth century it was adopted and translated into several other vernaculars around Europe. The performance of a song in its original form with an explanatory *razo* in the audience's vernacular is an efficient means of diffusing a poem outside its speech community, although it may open up countless new modes of interpreting and (mis)understanding it. Raimon Vidal was addressing a Catalan audience that had already produced some notable troubadours and would continue to do so. His treatise was copied and improved on for another century in Catalan, Occitan, Italian, and Sardinian regions. A number of treatises produced by Catalan poets for collections of Catalan texts also cover the presumed hiatus between the 1280s and 1324, when there is little extant evidence of cultivation of troubadour poetry beyond isolated instances in the Pyrenees.[24]

The language Raimon Vidal sought to teach to Catalan speakers in the 1190s was in such a parlous state in the Languedoc by the 1320s that it was reimported. The new *Consistori de la sobregaia compania del gay saber*, founded in Toulouse in 1323 on the model of northern French poetic Puys, sought to provide an adequate treatise for would-be poets, Occitan speakers who would have been trained in Latin prosody. In 1341, the Consistory member Joan de Castellnou added refinements to Raimon Vidal's original theory, in the light of ample evidence of nonstandard usage in the Occitan-speaking regions:

> Tug li vocable de Limosi ni d'Alvernha no son abte ni covenable a far dictatz. E qui vol allegar Raimon Vidal, pot hom respondre que ço que il ditz deu hom entendre quant al cas, no pas qant a tots los mots singulars.

> [Not all the words of Limousin and Auvergne are either apt or acceptable for making poetry. And if anyone brings up Raimon Vidal as evidence, one can reply that what he says should be understood in terms of the case system, not in terms of individual words.]

The long process of composition of the *Leys d'Amors* manuscripts reveals two dominant impulses. The first is a drive to create a standardized form of poetic expression that would place the Occitan *parladura* on a par with Latin. The second is a strong sense that the standardized language is already dead.[25] The Catalan language starts to develop in literary and cultural terms from the time the Occitan lyric tradition dwindles, and nonlyric authors such as Ramon Llull and Arnau de Vilanova are key figures in this transition, which the present study is too limited to cover. In Part 2, I will examine texts that are composed in octosyllabic rhyming couplets in a hybrid blend of Occitan and Catalan. This was the standard vehicle for narrative expression in Catalan-speaking regions until the late fourteenth century, when Catalan prose writing developed its distinctive identity, largely through a strong curial culture that devoted funds and energy to translating Latin, Italian, and French works into Catalan. This phenomenon is the subject of Chapter 6.

Medieval literature is intercultural in the sense that lyric poetry, Arthurian tales, or *chansons de geste* provided a singularly coherent basis on which many culturally specific variations could be played.[26] These dialogues have been readdressed as medievalists have moved toward what might be termed a postcolonial view of literary culture.[27] Sociopolitical context is important when reading different versions of the same story in different languages. It is evident, for example, that there is a cultural and political gap between Catalan royal patronage (focused on a colonizing and expansionist international policy, developing a "national" language, associated with military Christianity) and the claims that have been made concerning troubadour poetry even up to very recently as a proto-heretical, subversive, and individualistic genre.[28]

In this book I examine the literary use of competing Romance vernaculars in the later Middle Ages. A porous borderland has produced striking examples of multilingual interaction, especially between French, Occitan, and Catalan,[29] which I believe are worth exploring in an awareness of cultural differences as well as sociopolitical pressures.[30] In Chapter 1, I will examine an earlier text, usually dated to the late twelfth century, because it provides an exceptionally good illustration of multilingualism and contrasts very fruitfully with the text from 1318 that I study in Chapter 2. I have included several works from the mid- to late fifteenth century and do so in deference to Lola Badia's point that there is no distinction between "Renaissance" and "medieval" in Catalan literary works produced between 1380 and 1500.[31] One point is in my view axiomatic, that every text is to be read individually, on its own merits, rather than as part of a grand metanarrative of what happens to the literary vernaculars in this region and period. Each chapter explores one or more texts in its or their own terms and linguistic, geographical, and (if possible) historical context.

In the three chapters that make up Part 1 of this book I reassess representations of interlinguistic tension (Babel, Pentecost, Soloi) in three Occitan works: the twelfth-century epic *Girart de Roussillon*, a *roman d'aventures* of 1318, an Occitan translation of a universal history that was probably produced in Avignon about the same time, and the Toulousain *Leys d'Amors*. In Part 2, I explore the possibility that what we now regard as the fairy tale of Sleeping Beauty may function as a secular allegory in which linguistic and geographical boundaries are figured. I look at treatments of the same motif, first in hybrid languages (Occitan-Catalan and Franco-Venetian), and second in monolingual texts (Old and Middle French). This second part of the book ends with a chapter that is devoted to the clash in Catalan literature around 1400 between monolingual writing produced through translation, and multilingual writing. In Part 3, I turn to the period when Occitan had given way to French. In Chapters 7 and 8, I analyze two fifteenth-century French romances that are believed to originate in Provence. *Paris and Vienne* is a work that enjoyed extensive diffusion in many translations. *La Belle Maguelonne,* by contrast, is the product of translation, including that of the French *Roman de Troie*. This section ends with a chapter in which I explore the complex ways in which a French-speaking author from Provence, Antoine de La Sale, navigated the Angevin domination of Naples.

Part 1

MYTHS OF MULTILINGUALISM

1

BABEL IN *Girart de Roussillon*

A SUMERIAN MYTH SAYS that all humans spoke one language until Enki, the god of wisdom, "changed the speech in their mouths / [brought] contention into it, / Into the speech of man that (until then) had been one."[1] The cause of this ancient confusion of tongues is not clear, but it is clearly a precursor of the biblical tale of Babel. It may well be explained as a punishment for human ambitions to touch the divine realm or possibly for the reason given by Flavius Josephus, punishment for builders' refusal to populate the earth with their offspring out of their fear that separation would weaken their population (1.4.1, § 110). In the book of Genesis (11:4), the builders' motivation for their project is their fear of being scattered across the earth, and in an ironic twist, the thing they fear becomes reality.[2] Much has been written about medieval beliefs concerning languages, summarized here by George Steiner: "The tongue of Eden was like a flawless glass; a light of total understanding streamed through it. Thus Babel was a second Fall, in some regards as desolate as the first. Adam had been driven from the garden; now men were harried, like yelping dogs, out of the single family of man. And they were exiled from the assurance of being able to grasp and communicate reality."[3] As we will see in Chapter 3, this pessimistic narrative is only one interpretation of the myth of Babel, but it is nevertheless the most persistent. Isidore of Seville describes the standard history of language, as it remained until the early modern period.[4] Hebrew was the universal language granted by God to Adam, but when men built the tower out of a prideful wish to get closer to Heaven, they brought their division upon themselves (*Etym*. I.1).[5] These languages cause the descendants of the tower's construction teams to be eternally at odds with one another, unable to regroup forces in order to challenge divine power again.[6] Isidore notes that for his own time, some languages have retained a connection with divinity: "There are three sacred languages, Hebrew, Greek, and Latin, which shine over the whole world" (I.3). However, Isidore's three sacred languages are not monolithic, and some are more authoritative than others. For example, Latin has four varieties, each corresponding to a historical period: "Priscam, Latinam, Romanam, Mixtam." The "mixed" Latin of the fourth, post-imperial period is characterized by its corruption by solecisms and barbarisms (I.3–7). Even sacred languages, it would seem, have their colloquial and demotic varieties. It is interesting that Isidore singles out the Latin of his own time (and of his text) as a corrupt, post-imperial shadow of its predecessor, the expression of *romanitas*. His Latin is not a sacred hymn, nor is it scripture. Rather, it is a corrupt writing idiom designed to allow the reader to begin work on any language with proper levels of distance and skepticism. Isidore points to his *Etymologies* as an attempt to build a vision of languages from corrupt fragments, sifting through the ruins rather than the archaeology of Babel.

According to Isidore of Seville, "Peoples come from languages, languages are not drawn from peoples" (*Etym.* IX.I). Spoken and written idioms identified their users in both geographical and political terms, as well as in terms of religion and learning, and only did so in a context in which several languages coexisted. Christian intellectuals of the Middle Ages tended to focus on four biblical events related to language. In addition to the Creation (the gift of language) and Babel (the "confusion" of language) came the trilingual writing on the cross, a sign that the three sacred languages, Hebrew, Greek, and Latin, enjoyed a closer relationship between themselves than with any others. Fourth came Pentecost and the gift of tongues to the Apostles, who were able to preach in all vernaculars across many lands.[7] Pentecost did not resolve the disaster of Babel, but it provided one remedy for it. This was glossed typologically, citing the Pauline epistles that proclaimed the abolition of divisions between religions and peoples, but emphasizing conversion. Conversion and languages are important concerns in two texts that also illustrate the hybrid linguistic and generic nature of Occitan narratives. The *chanson de geste* titled *Girart de Roussillon* (after 1160) was popular in northern French regions, but its complete text survives only in three redactions that show that it was composed, or rewritten, for an audience that understood both Occitan and Old French. *Guilhem de la Barra* (1318), the fourteenth-century hybrid epic romance (*roman d'aventures*), appears to be an isolated product of the Languedoc after its absorption into the French crown. It is the work of a man who might have been trained as a lawyer, educated and probably working in Toulouse. *Guilhem de la Barra* is preserved in only one manuscript and seems to have had no impact on any other writers of its time. Both texts explore questions of language and conversion, Babel and

Pentecost, and do so in ways that shed light on their literary and spiritual contexts. In this chapter I will examine *Girart de Roussillon*. *Guilhem de la Barra* is discussed in Chapter 2.

Mainstream writings on the confusion of tongues preserved the idea that scattering, separation, and ultimately war were the inevitable results of linguistic divisions. Several versions of the vernacular Alexander romances (the earliest fragment of which survives in a Franco-Provençal dialect) include an account of the Tower of Babel related to the city of Babylon. Babylon emerges as the ultimate goal of Alexander's campaigns, largely thanks to its association by the High Middle Ages with the goal of crusaders, as well as with the eschatological identification of Babylon with sin. The lists of languages that illustrate these narratives of the Tower of Babel seem to crystallize Alexander's empire building, as they emphasize the connection between languages and peoples. The Venice redaction of the Old French *Roman d'Alexandre* (usually known as the B text, copied in the fourteenth century) recounts God's decision to punish humanity for its pride (*orgoil* [line 7792]) by ensuring that building work stops (when a man asks for a stone, he gets a loaf of bread; when he asks for mortar, he receives knives), and that the fathers grieve as their children scatter across the earth (line 7805), to become members of new nations:[8]

> Li uns devient caldeus, li autre yndians
> E li autres mesopotamians,
> Li autres fu turqueis, e l'autre elemitans.
>
> (B, lines 7806–8)

[One became Chaldean, the other Indian, and the other Mesopotamian; one became Turkish, the other Elamite.]

The list of fifty-two languages (approximating to the traditional seventy-two) (lines 7806–32) includes Western vernaculars:

> Li autre fu romans e li autre toscans,
> Li autre fu lombars e li autre musans,
> Li autre proënsals e li autre tolsans,
> Li autre fu gascuns e l'autre alvernans,
> L'autre fu espaneis e li autre marmans,
> Li autre erupeis e parla bien romans,
> Li autre fu franceis e li autre loërans,

Li autre fu bretons e li autre venecians,
Li autre fu flamens e li autre loarans.

(lines 7819–27)

[One became Roman, another became Tuscan, another Lombard, another *Musans;* another Provençal, another Toulousain, another Gascon, another Auvergnat. One man was Spanish and another *Marmans* [?]; another was from Hurepoix and could speak in the Romance language. Another was French and another of the Lorraine; another was Breton and another Venetian; one was Flemish, the other from the Loire.]

Once again, languages and peoples are associated, so that a language becomes a lineage both geographically and politically. These lists find an echo in the armies that are enumerated in *Girart de Roussillon:*

Gen devit ses escales Carles lo res,
E met el premer cap ses Erupes,
Ces d'entre Leire e Seine, vassaus cortes;
Furent i cil de Cartes e de Bles,
O les lances trencanz, auz arz entes.
E gide les Arbez, uns cons de Tres.
Mancel e Beruer e Aucores
E la premiere escale ferrunt manes, (Manes)
(E) en l'autre Peitevin e Bretones,
(E) en la carte Normant e Flandines
Poherenc e icil de Vermendes.

(laisse CCCXXIV/323, lines 4929–39)[9]

[King Charles led his companies well. He put in first place his men of Hurepoix, the ones from the region between Loire and the Seine, courtly vassals; then came those from Chartres and Blois with sharp lances and taut bows, under the leadership of Arbert, a count of Troyes. Manceaux, Berruyers, and Auxerrois in the first company attacked the men of Le Mans. In the other came Poitevins and Bretons, in the fourth company, Normans and men of Flanders, men of Picardy and those from the Vermandois.]

The Castilian *Libro de Alexandre* derives from the Old French romance but also uses Arabic sources and Walter of Châtillon's *Alexandreis.* It has a long digression when it describes Babylon; provides a geography of the region; and appends the tale of Babel and of the multiple languages, it claims, of Babylon (sts. 1505–17).[10] Here, all humanity speaks Hebrew, human beings' "natural speech" (MS P, st. 1508), until God scatters them into seventy two linguistic groups (I have kept the orthography used by Willis for his edition):

> Los vnos fon latinos los otros fon ebreos
> A los otros disen griegos a los otros caldeos
> A otros disen araues e a otros fabeos.
>
> (st. 1513)

[Some are Latins and some are Hebrews; some are called Greeks and others are called Chaldeans. Others are called Arabs and others are Sabeans.]

The northwestern European groups are particularly tied to specific regions: "Otros disen jngleses otros son de Bretañja / escotes e yrlandos otros de Alemaña" (Others are called English; others are from Brittany, Scots and Irish, others from Germany) (st. 1514). Babylon itself is multilingual (sts. 1518–32), and the narrator concludes that it would be a great achievement for a mortal to learn all the languages of the earth (st. 1521). In the Alexander romances, fathers (in fact, giants, as the texts confuse the biblical tale with that of the Titans) witness their sons' double alienation from them, for they forget both their original language and their skills. If a man who asks for building blocks or mortar is handed knives or horses, he is given substitutes for the tower that imply survival, but also warfare and travel. Linguistic confusion cuts off the direct connection between fathers and sons, at the very moment that it inaugurates the lineages of the various nations on earth.

In Christian art of the Romanesque period, one of the most interesting artistic explorations of the links between Babel and Pentecost appears at the Burgundian abbey of Vézelay, on the portal through which the laity entered the abbey church (built between 1120 and 1132).[11] This abbey also plays an important role in the final part of *Girart de Roussillon* (after c. 1160). This last section of the poem stages a penitential conversion predicated on preaching by example. I will argue that the relationships between languages, and the preaching association of Pentecost, play a crucial role in closing the narrative.

Synopsis

The Frankish emperor Charles Martel and his vassal Count Girart de Roussillon are betrothed by proxy to the two daughters of the emperor of Constantinople. But Charles prefers Elissent, Girart's intended wife. Girart is awarded his fief as an allod in compensation for agreeing to marry Berte. He and Elissent secretly swear to love each other. Charles later invades Girart's lands. This war ends when divine fire destroys the standards of both armies. The ensuing truce ends when a long-standing feud is reignited, and a more destructive war starts. Defeated, Girart and Berte hide in the forest of Ardenne, working as a charcoal maker and a seamstress, respectively. Twenty-two years later, in the cathedral of Orléans, Elissent obtains a reconciliation between the two rival lords. Later, Girart thinks about starting another war on behalf of his young son. One of his men kills the boy to protect the peace. Berte encourages Girart to penitence. Secretly, she builds a shrine to Mary Magdalene at Vézelay. She overcomes slander and attempted rape to promote peace and penance. A lasting peace is proclaimed by the pope at Vézelay.

The poet endows Berte with formidable linguistic skills:

> Premerement Bertan o le vis clar,
> O le gent cosïer, au bel esgar,
> Sos paire li a fait les ars parar;
> Sat caudiu e gregeis e romencar,
> E latin e ebriu tot declarar.
> Entre sen e beltat e gen parlar,
> Ne pout nus om el munt sa par trobar.
>
> (lines 235–41)

[First, Berte of the bright face, noble bearing, and sweet gaze. Her father has taught her the arts. She knows Chaldean and Greek and can translate into Romance, and she can discourse on both Latin and Hebrew. Between her good sense, her beauty, and her lovely turn of phrase, no one could find her equal on earth.]

Berte's ability to translate sacred languages into the vernacular, as well as her interpretative command of both Latin and Hebrew, denote her as someone who can overcome the confusion of tongues. Her skills are crucial to her peacemaking role in the second part of the poem, where she enacts an extensive *translatio studii* by teaching that she has built the abbey of Vézelay with her own hands, on the model of the Hagia Sophia of Constantinople.[12] Berte's skills are shorthand in other texts for wisdom, for example, that of an elderly adviser in the Venice (B text) *Roman d'Alexandre:*

> Un sage clerc apelle, qui fu de sa contree,
> Qui sot gres e caldeu e sot lenga ebree
> E sot tot les lengages d'outre la mer betee.
>
> (B, lines 7638–40)

[He calls for a learned clerk of his lands, who knew Greek, Chaldean, and Hebrew and knew all the languages from beyond the seas.]

However, the narrative of *Girart de Roussillon* draws attention repeatedly to the political and sacred values of languages of conflict, as well as their salvation through languages of peace, and Berte's status as a feminine *sage clerc* in a Christian setting is evidently one that demands comment.[13]

Medieval multilingualism was an inevitable and complex cultural phenomenon as, contrary to Isidore's claims cited above, peoples were only rarely drawn from languages. Those universal claims that were made for Latin Christendom ran against the fact of regional linguistic diversity, one that meant that the vernaculars were an inescapable source of alleged corruption. Nor was it possible to assert that Latin could be combined smoothly with the other two sacred languages. Intriguingly, the languages of the surviving manuscripts of *Girart de Roussillon* also draw attention to the conflicts and reconciliations that may be worked out between languages. Of the five surviving manuscripts of *Girart de Roussillon* (only two of which are complete or near complete), one is written in a transitional dialect between Old French and Old Occitan that has been variously identified as Poitevin or Franco-Provençal (MS O), another has been identified as a translation of this text into Old French (MS L), and another is a translation of the same text into Old Occitan (MS P). Simon Gaunt has devoted a recent article to reassessing the issue of the language of *Girart de Roussillon,* especially the long dialogue on this subject between the linguist Max Pfister and the poem's editor, Mary Hackett.[14] Gaunt has rejected the label "hybrid" for the language of O on the grounds that the Franco-Poitevin text is not an artificial literary language. Rather, he suggests it is an example of code-mixing between a dominant and subordinate language, in this case, epic French poetry (dominant in generic terms) and an Occitan idiom that seems to owe little to troubadour poetry of the time. The code-mixing imposed on Occitan aimed to, as he states, "emphasize its irreducible foreignness" rather than acculturate it, with the result that that the poem's language became "a marker of difference" of considerable self-consciousness.[15] This hypothesis rests, as Max Pfister suggested, on the principle that what the author(s) of O attempted to do was to blend core elements of Occitan expression into the formulaic patterns of Old French epic poetry. Such a strategy would demand some explanation in terms of the intended audience, but none has as yet been suggested. Hackett favored the view that the transitional dialect of O, like the simplified Occitan of P, was intended to make the tale comprehensible to a wider audience, and it would seem that the two "translations" into French and Occitan reflect a desire to enlarge the poem's audience.

It is unlikely that the composer(s) of O would have sought to impress their audience with a poem composed in an obscure, challenging language, as had they wished to do so, they could simply have written in Latin. It should be pointed out that it is accepted that the author(s) of *Girart de Roussillon* was or were learned in monastic and clerical matters, although the poem's much discussed anticlericalism imposes some caution in that respect.[16] Instead, it seems apposite to explore what the O-text says about language and, specifically, how multilingualism is associated with the typological opposition between Babel and Pentecost.

The poem opens with a court festival at Pentecost. Charles and Girart are called upon to assist the emperor of Constantinople against a Saracen invasion because they are already betrothed to the emperor's two daughters. Subsequently Charles forces Girart to break his betrothal to Elissent and exchange her for Charles's bride, Berte. In an illustration of her linguistic skills, Berte overhears the men's negotiations and runs away to weep:

> Partit de lor plorant soz une aulivie,
> E denant a ses piez magistre grive;
> Non [a] tant saive ne melz escrive.
> La donçele se claime sovent caitive:
> "Maldite seit de Deu ca mars undive,
> E li porz e la naus qui[m] mes a rive.
> Mel vougre lai morir que cai fu[s] vive."
>
> (laisse XXX/27, lines 407–13)

[She left them to weep beneath an olive tree, and at her feet, before her, was a Greek governess: none is wiser or writes better than she.

The girl repeatedly laments her wretched state: "May God curse the waves of the sea, the harbor, and the ship that brought me to these shores. I would prefer to have died there than to be alive here."]

Berte's learned governess makes her only appearance in the text in this comparatively short laisse, to support the rejected princess as the latter curses the ship, the sea, and the harbor that brought her to her humiliating predicament. It may be a learned allusion to the abandoned heroines of Ovid's *Heroides* (the name of Berte's sister, Elissent, moreover, is a transparent allusion to Ovid's abandoned Dido/Elissa).[17] In the O-text of *Girart,* the first figure, an equally fleeting one, to be found seated beneath an olive tree is its purported author:

> Sestu, mongres corteiz, clerz de moster,
> S'estaveit desos l'onbre d'un aulivier,
> E fermat en son cuer un cosier.
>
> (laisse III/3, lines 24–26)

[Sextus, a courtly monk, a clerk of a church, sat in the shade of an olive tree and formed a desire in his heart [to compose a poem].]

The silent *magistre grive* echoes the meditative *mongres corteiz*. One inaugurates the poem, and the other witnesses Berte's learned allusion, but neither figure has any further part to play in the poem. Berte's first independent speech is both implicitly Ovidian (by extension, pagan) and associated with her Greek learning. It affirms her literary and cultural dissociation from the feudal epic rationale that determines her rejection by Charles. Her fleeting display of pagan learning set aside, Berte engages in linguistic activity that is almost exclusively sacred, unlike her sister Elissent, whose actions and words tend to be both erotic and political. The two women, as Sarah Kay and Simon Gaunt have argued, are treated in the narrative as gifts, and the gifts they embody are the learned cultures of Constantinople and Rome.[18] Berte's Greek literacy, symbolized by her nurse, is invoked at the poem's close when one of Girart's men recalls her telling him the story of a woman penitent at Constantinople (lines 9678–9700).

The troubled status of sacred languages in *Girart* may shed light on the way liturgical Latin is mixed into the poem. Charles's bastard brother, a bishop, has his head hacked off by Boson, who calls to him contemptuously to "sing his *saeculas saeculorum*" (line 6034). Charles's men, their armor covered in blood, clamor for the host as the "Corpre Dome" (*corpus Domini* distorted as the "body of a man," *d'ome*) (line 6037). Church Latin, the lowest-ranking of the three sacred languages, is jarringly placed outside its usual context. However, in the closing sections of the poem, translations of scripture are woven into the text (lines 9930–31, 9981–84). The O-text closes as if it were a reading in the divine office, with the words "Tu autem, Domine."[19] Liturgical Latin is the object of corruption, translation, and (finally) incorporation into a text that has by the end turned into a hagiography.

The war between the king and his rebel baron is peppered with allusions to the conflicts between languages after Babel. When Charles decides to reclaim his lands, he attacks Girart in two successive campaigns, which culminate in the battle of Vaubeton, where God strikes both standards with lightning. Charles's army is bilingual: its noblemen converse in both Romance and *Tiois* (a southern German dialect) (line 1860), and outside Girart's palace they pitch sixty-two pavilions (lines 680–85), a number that echoes the seventy-two languages after Babel. Girart's castle, the inanimate target of Charles's lust, is dominated by a tower, made of cemented stones adorned with red marble, that boasts an outside gallery built by Saracens. This detail implies that there has been sufficient harmony between Christians and Saracens in the recent past to enable them to build a tower together (lines 1015–17). Charles's men capture Girart's proud tower and plunder the treasures it contains. They also abduct and rape Girart's kinswomen, illustrating more forcefully the connection between Charles's political and sexual aggression against his vassal (lines 1020–29).

Despite the emphasis on the territories of Aquitaine, Limousin, and Burgundy, there isn't a clear geographical division between the two multilingual sides (laisse CCCLII/349). Girart's army regroups noblemen from Catalan, Italian, and southern French lands, who speak "in their language" (lines 2437, 4892–99), as well as Bavarians, "Allemani," and Burgundians (line 4707). We are told that about a French-speaking Breton lord, "uns romanz Bret" (line 7101), but shared language does not guarantee loyalty: Gascons and Provençaux defect to Charles's side, which also includes lords of the Limousin.

At the battle of Vaubeton, both sides are equals in strength and words: "Li Breton el Gascon sunt per egance" (The Bretons and the Gascons are equals) (line 2505). This is partly because their battle cries are drowned out by the thunderous noise of lances clashing against shields. The battle is ended when (wordless) divine fire strikes both standards. Charles's standard, decorated with letters of gold, bursts into flames, and Girart's crumbles to ashes (laisses CLXXI–II/168–69). The armies scatter as their men exclaim, "Segles feniz" (The world is ending!) (line 2888). These men are wrong, as Vaubeton marks the conclusion of only one kind of "world," the one that was produced by the overweening pride of two men. One lord accuses his king: "Par Deu, Carles Martels, molt mar i fais, / Quan cuides tot un segle metre en pantais" (By God, Charles Martel, you are doing harm by wishing to put one whole world into confusion) (lines 2038–39). Vaubeton is presented as a battle that a century earlier was prophesied to make martyrs of a fifth of the men who took part in it (laisse CLXIX/166), but their martyrdom is solely at the service of their masters' pride (lines 2840–43). Charles's letters of gold are glittering but fallible signs, while Girart's standard, which has no words ascribed to it, simply disintegrates. At another point, Girart's standards are also said to be embroidered in gold (line 4950). Regardless of their inscriptions, moreover, neither battle standard can withstand wordless and unexplained fire.

As the feud progresses over the years from truce to broken truce, from one warring May and Easter to the next, it becomes evident that the "world" of Charles and Girart is one of confusion and vice, limited by an arrogant belief that their world is the only one that exists and that their word, as it is only made of words, can easily be broken. Both sides are knowingly in a state of sin, as both have broken sacred oaths, stolen each other's property, murdered kinsmen, and wreaked revenge.

The second stage of the campaign continues this depiction of two armies that map much of Europe. At the battle of Verdonnet, the narrator announces sonorously, "the Burgundians wage war on the French," but Charles's army draws troops from the Loire Valley, Chartres, Brittany, the Vermandois, and the Poitou (lines 4926–43). His court comprises Lorrains, Germans, *Tiois,* Franks, and Normans (lines 3351–55). When Saracens invade these territories, we are told, they are equipped with a *mappa mundi* to guide their journey to the banks of the Gironde (lines 3286–87). The Franks do not resort to maps, as their languages appear to localize them in terms of political and geographical alliances. Where the Saracens can depict the world pictorially in terms of boundaries and territories, the Franks are mired in a network of interpersonal connections and conflicts, dominated by the spoken word. Charles resents his reliance on Girart's assistance in this short-lived crusade (lines 3296–97), but it illustrates that the disunity between the two sides can find common ground only against an enemy that is defined not by language or place, but by religion (laisses CXCVIII–CC/195–97).

When Girart's tower falls to Charles for a second time, it is undermined from within by the porter and his wife, the latter of whom is also Berte's chambermaid. The porter delivers the keys to the fortress to the king. His men hurry in silence, without uttering so much as a cough, up to the tower's uppermost wall, whereupon they light a fire and yell, "Traït!" (Treason!) to alert both the king and Girart's men (laisses CCCCXXI–XIV/418–21). The whole of the fortress of Roussillon is then pillaged and consumed by flames. Girart's tower is betrayed at its gate and its marital chamber, and it is declared the object of treachery from its highest wall. As the *Imago mundi* declared that the Tower of Babel could be dissolved only by women's menstrual blood (see Chapter 3, p. 61), so Berte's bedchamber proves to be the weakest link in the structure of Roussillon. As he escapes barefoot and nearly naked, thinking that Berte has been abducted, Girart cries out to his three remaining men, "Seinor, or esgardas confusion!" (My lords, look at the disaster/confusion!) (line 6346). Girart enters his exile mourning the loss of his "castel antis" (ancient castle) (line 6388), and Charles boasts—erroneously—that he has finally reduced his enemy's pride (line 6416). Charles resorts to the advice of his men on rebuilding and strengthening Girart's tower, with the assistance of Folc's Jewish vassal, Baufadu. The narrator at this point inserts an attack on Jews and states that Charles's subsequent defeat is caused by his decision to employ Baufadu, something that is not borne out by the rest of the narrative (lines 6455–58). This puzzling insertion may be explained in terms of the theme of Babel, as Baufadu's first action after his introduction into the text is to write in Hebrew.

If Greek is relegated to literary allusion, Hebrew, the most sacred of the three sacred languages, is marginalized still more. Baufadu writes to Folc to warn him about Charles's treacherous plans: "escris un breu / En ses letres cui sat, en lang'ebreu. / Tramet le dun Folcon per un corleu" (He wrote a letter in the letters he knew, in Hebrew. He sent it to Sir Folc via a messenger) (lines 6467–69). Baufadu sends a verbal message with his written letter, and it is this spoken warning that Folc hears: "E Folco, quan l'ouit, loet en Deu" (And Folc, when he heard it, praised God) (line 6474). Baudafu's mastery of Hebrew script circulates as an unread guarantee of purely secular authenticity, as if it were his seal or token. Furthermore, it is likely that his letter is written in a Romance dialect encoded in Hebrew script, a multiscriptural writing process known in Spain as *aljamiado* that is attested in medieval Provence.[20] In *Girart de Roussillon,* the original language shared by the builders at Babel subsists only as a visual code (a script) emptied of both its sacred and linguistic content. By way of contrast, Berte is noted for her skill in interpreting (explaining form and sacred content) both Greek and Hebrew. When Roussillon's tower falls for the second time, Berte leaves it, and the shattered remains of the structure symbolize a world that is more distanced from the divine than ever.

In this secular world divided by speech, where even the three sacred languages have lost their power, the anti-Jewish content of the first and central parts of the poem is striking. Both Girart and Charles are criticized by other characters in terms borrowed from Christian polemical texts that accused Jews of refusing to see or hear Christian doctrine. Thierry de Scanie accuses Charles: "Escoutes e esgardes, e rien ne ves / Plus que judeus Mesie qu'eu en croz mes!" (You listen and you look and you can see nothing, like the Jewish people who put the Messiah on the cross!) (lines 1813–14). Thierry is Charles's brother-in-law. Folc, his enemy, makes a similar attack (lines 4464–66).[21] What is striking is that this polemical attack is aimed by both sides at each other, as Folc also accuses Girart in the same terms: "Oz e vez e escoutes e non entenz" (You can hear, see, and listen, but you do not understand) (lines 4216–17). He also states that Girart has "lowered the worth of Christianity" through the latter's inability to interpret events (line 5323). Each side also calls its opponents Jews, Saracens, Judas, and Satan (lines 4654–58, 5540–43), mixing different registers of invective and religious prejudice. Charles expresses his exasperation with the confused perceptions and loyalties that dominate the text:

> "Ja non aurant tan dur car ne cuiram
> El ni Bos ni Folchers, li trei satam,
> Se pois de lor aicir, ne lor en dam.
> Per hoc soli' um dire parent eram;
> Nos hoc, quo m'es aviz, de linz Adam!
> S'en podie un tener en mon liam,
> Ferie la parer quant fort les am!"
>
> (lines 5558–61)

[No matter how hard their flesh or hide might be (him, Folchier, and Boson, the three Satans) if I get near them, I will do them harm. Nevertheless, it was once said we were kinsmen; well, yes, I think we're all members of Adam's lineage! If I had one of them tied up before me, I'd show him how much I love him!]

Here, Charles's words pinpoint the tragedy of a human lineage that believes itself to be commonly descended from Adam but that is divided by arbitrary linguistic (and, by extension, religious) confusion to the point that *love* is a synonym for *hatred,* and "the three Satans" can also be his kinsmen.

Fallible language is a source of political confusion at several points in the poem. The fabled council scenes in *Girart de Roussillon* are notable for confusing the protagonists with contradictory advice.[22] Human verbal encounters lead to misinterpretation, especially in the embassy of Pierre de Mont Rabei, which collapses into accusations that the interlocutors have childish or misguided minds (lines 4363, 4420). Pierre's own account of his embassy draws attention to the importance of his opponents' misleading words (lines 4600–4604), but ends with his lies (lines 4688–92). Yet again, neither side is shown to be different from the other in terms of its control, in this instance, over speech.

Other scenes show that language itself is drained of what symbolic content it may once have contained. Councilors appear to struggle to find appropriate terms for their rhetoric. In one scene, Andefrey inveighs against Girart's treachery: "Deus confunde vaissel o taus vis plante" (God confound the vessel in which such a vine grows) (laisse CCCLXVI/363, line 5591). Girart's emissary Begon evidently does not grasp the sense of his enemy's words:

> Beget ot Andefret k'eissi desruche,
> Que cubici Girart viel fole rusche,
> [Con s'el er]e vaisels plens de lanbruche.
> (laisse CCCLXVII/364, lines 5593–95)

> [Begon heard Andefrei grow so angry he called Girart a piece of dried-up old bark, a vessel filled with wild vine branches.]

The narrator reports the content as it is understood by Begon, who appears to miss the sense of the curse and focus only on the words. Andefrey is punished for a far more compromising word during the battle of Civaux. He challenges Fouchier by saying that Charles's army will prove Girart to have been a traitor ("Ui proveren Girart a trachor tot" [laisse CCCXCVII/394, line 5958]). Fouchier takes suitable revenge for something he immediately calls a lie ("Mintez i glot!" [You lie, glutton!] [line 5959]):

> Folchers fert Andefret en l'oberc blanc,
> Que tot li fest vermeil e teint de sanc;

Que li trencat lo cor, lo fege el flanc,
E crabentet lo mort a denz el fanc.
E dis: "Querez proveire e queus estanc.
Lo parlar del traïr mar vistes anc;
Eu [en] defent Girart, lo conte franc."
(laisse CCCXCVIII/395, lines 5962–68)

[Fouchier struck Andefrey on his white halberk and made it red and stained with blood; for he sliced through his heart, his liver, and his sides and threw him down dead into the mud. And he said: "Look for a priest and someone to staunch your blood. Your speaking of treason brought you harm; I have defended Girart, the noble count."]

Andefrey is now a vessel that leaks wine-red blood rather than words. It would seem that despite the verbal confusion of some of Girart's men, others are capable of glossing and avenging the sense of specific (and secular) words such as *traitor*.

The "hagiographical" closing sections of the poem stage a recuperation of some sacred dimension to speech, in preparation for the inauguration of the shrine of Vézelay. As an act of penance after the murder of their son, Berte builds a church at Vézelay to house the relics of the Magdalene. She does so in secret, by night, helped by an old man (laisses DCXLIII–DCXLIX/640–46). Her actions are misinterpreted by gossips. Only Berte's verbal interpretation of her actions can lead her husband into identifying and supporting her penitential activity. She is rebuilding the Hagia Sophia of Constantinople (the site of her betrothal to Charles) at the site of Vézelay, a *translatio* of one sacred building and sworn promise into another. Berte's action highlights the importance of her learning, as she is not rebuilding Jerusalem, the enterprise of many cathedrals and churches. Rather, her ambition is to translate her place of origin and her multilingual learning into Girart and Charles's realm. She refuses to have the miracles attending her work preserved in writing, on the grounds that this would draw crowds of pilgrims to the shrine that she wishes to preserve as a personal monument (lines 9803–9).

Vézelay is also the commemoration of a disastrous betrayal, as Charles and Girart broke the betrothal oaths they swore at Constantinople. Elissent attempts to reconcile her public and secret husbands in the cathedral of Orléans without attempting to commemorate the betrothals. Berte's Vézelay, by contrast, transforms her learning into a monument that alludes to the site of her betrothal and subsequent rejection. Elissent's Orléans is a location where ritual gestures cannot bring about a lasting peace. Elissent acts through posture and gesture, but Berte acts through *translatio* and *interpretatio:* she transfers the Hagia Sophia to Burgundy and recasts her personal humiliation as a spiritual triumph.

Above all, Berte's linguistic action is modeled on preaching, something that is particularly important in a *chanson de geste* composed in a transitional language. As a woman, she is not allowed to preach through sermons, but her actions are exemplary: first, in her obedience to her two husbands' political maneuvers; second, in her loyalty to Girart; and third, in her secret construction of the abbey. She resorts to speech only in her long exile in the forest of Ardenne. Her first lengthy verbal action is her *consolatio* to Girart on their exile. She recites several verses from the Psalms, the story of Job, and a saint's writings to her husband (lines 7667–69). From this point onward, Berte's actions and words are combined in a mission of spiritual guidance that raises further questions. Girart is both *illiteratus* and a lay nobleman confronted by the Pax Dei preached by a secular noblewoman to whom he is married, and by whom he has a son. This is no spiritual or chaste marriage, yet Berte's multilingualism makes her a living example of the preacher's connection to Pentecost, the necessary "abundance of language" that included *vulgaris loquutionis*.[23]

Berte's ability to work between sacred and vernacular languages also necessitates evidence of her exceptional virtue, as *Girart de Roussillon* is contemporary with the circulation in intellectual circles of the same period of such necromantic treatises as the *Ars notoria*. This treatise depicts itself as the translation and exposition into Latin by Solomon and Apollonius of tablets written and "subtly distorted" in Greek, Chaldean, and Hebrew ("quae est ex Hebraeo, Graeco, et Chaldaeo sermone subtiliter distorta"). It served to concretize the belief that translating sacred languages one into the other could unlock necromantic powers.[24] Berte's multilingual education in Constantinople is connected with her father the emperor's harmless necromancy, but once it is transferred to Frankish lands, her long silence and twenty-two years of penitential activity appear to prepare her reemergence into rhetoric as a saintly noblewoman. In keeping with other scenes discussed above, this moment is depicted through a semi-allegorical scene. Berte's penitential activity is misinterpreted as an adulterous affair by her chamberlain Ataïn, whose name derives from the feminine noun *ataïna*, "an irritation" or "an obstacle" (laisse DCL/9598).[25] Ataïn attempts to rape Berte as she lies asleep clad in a white linen nightshirt, her flesh as white as a hawthorn flower

("Ot tan blanche la car cun flor d'espine" [line 9620]), but she fights him off with her nails, much as the hawthorn would repel its aggressor. Ataïn takes revenge by telling Girart that Berte is committing adultery, but her reported actions are glossed by an uninvolved figure (Bedelon) in terms of an anecdote she has told him of a poor woman's exemplary actions in Constantinople (lines 9678–9700). Bedelon is rewarded for remembering her *exemplum* by a dream vision of Berte dressed in clothes that are as white as parchment and covered in more flowers than a hawthorn bush (laisse DCLVIII/9709, lines 9710–16).[26] The descriptions of Berte's body shift from something that has been likened by a lustful observer to the hawthorn flower, to something that far exceeds that plant ("plus covert de flors d'un aube espin" [line 9713]). It represents, in that short description, both the power of the written word (*flores rhetorici* set on parchment) and the divine aspects of the transferal of materials from one state to another, a form of *translatio*. If Susan Eberly is correct in suggesting that the hawthorn symbolized carnal love in medieval love allegory, there is here a *translatio* (interpretation) in the proper sense, in that the flower is turned from an image of Ataïn's lust into a metaphor for Berte's holy words.[27] Through two visual descriptions, Berte's body and words are transposed from a shameful object of lust to a dream vision of interpretative and linguistic authority.

Girart de Roussillon ends with the proclamation of peace by papal authority, above the jeers of those poor knights who would rather continue their lucrative warring careers (laisse DCXXXVI/633). The peace also points to the poem's connection with the visual program of the abbey of Vézelay, specifically the main narthex portal, through which the laity entered the abbey. According to Peter Low, this portal's subject is Pentecost as a reversal of the confusion of Babel. Low has suggested, partly in reflection of the shared Pentecost theme between the portal and the Latin *vita* of Girart de Roussillon, that the Vézelay portal may depict the Pauline idea of building a new "church" through conversion (Eph. 2:1–22), the coming together of people from many lands to listen to multilingual preaching: "Ergo iam non estis hospites, et advenae: sed estis cives sanctorum, et domestici Dei . . . in quo omnis aedificatio constructa crescit in templum sanctum in Domino, in quo et vos coaedificamini in habitaculum Dei in Spiritu" (Thus you are no longer aliens in a foreign land, but fellow citizens with God's people, members of God's household . . . In him the whole building is bonded together and grows into a holy temple in the Lord. In him you too are being built with all the rest into a spiritual dwelling for God) (Eph. 2:21–22).[28] The exile of Babel is reversed; humanity is reinvented as a "whole building" bonded together and re-created as a community of individuals. Berte's building work at Vézelay reverses the fall of the tower of Roussillon and the exile of the protagonists from her betrothal onward in a world of confusion.

In the poem, Berte's multilingualism also reverses the confusion of Babel through spiritual conversion into a single language. Ironically, the poem that contains it is in two vernaculars combined, doomed by the historical accidents of language to remain firmly located in the margins of literary history. If *Girart de Roussillon* is read as a poem that is multilingual in content as well as in language, it ceases to be an aberrant object of scholarly scrutiny and becomes the site of a sophisticated exploration of communication and of the pervasive medieval idea that vernacular and sacred languages were in equal measure the source both of harmony and of conflict in the secular world.

2

TONGUES OF FIRE IN *Guilhem de la Barra*

IN MANY WAYS, THE *Libre de Mossen Guilhem de la Barra* (1318) may be read as a back-to-front rewriting of the key narrative features of *Girart de Roussillon*. It opens with a lengthy, violent conversion narrative that addresses the questions of interlinguistic communication, one that has attracted substantial critical attention.[1] A Saracen lady persuades her husband to convert with *belas messonjas* (beautiful lies) (96) and is accordingly baptized with the somewhat ironic name of Constance "en el nom de Dieu que venir / volc en lenguas de foc ardent" (in the name of God who wished to come in tongues of burning flame) (lines 1612–13).[2] The conversion episode appears to be important for the narrative, but it has no further purpose, as neither the converted Saracens nor Guilhem's muscular piety reappear in the main part of the story. Indeed, Guilhem's religious fervor seems to disappear. The main body of his story concerns itself with the consequences of the queen's lust for and aggression toward both Guilhem's family and her kingdom. In this respect, the ethical crisis that determines the bulk of *Guilhem de la Barra* resembles the first part of *Girart de Roussillon* with the aggressor role shifted from the king (who remains a weak and treacherous figure) to the queen. The queen's love for Guilhem, like Elissent and Berte's for Girart, is the product of a proxy betrothal. The king betrays Guilhem twice, first, by failing to remember his service and, second, by privileging his wife's written accusations over Guilhem's silent refusal to appear at court, another echo of Girart's contumacy. Tongues of fire play a thematic role in the remainder of the text, as the queen's false accusation of rape sends Guilhem into exile. In early fourteenth-century Toulouse, those who made false accusations of heresy could be punished by public exhibition wearing red tongues sewn on their clothing, while real tongues of burning flame punished those whose accusers found sufficient support to ensure that they were condemned to death.[3]

It has long been fashionable to describe Occitan chivalric texts as ironic readings of French models. This claim has been made for *Blandin de Cornualha*; *Jaufre*; and, less tentatively, *Flamenca*.[4] I would propose to read *Guilhem de la Barra* in such a light, not because I wish to revive a tired view of Occitan narrative as both derivative and secondary to more canonical (French) literary models, but because it appears to dissolve the moral and spiritual content of both its secular and its spiritual sources. While the manuscript tradition of *Girart de Roussillon* points to its diffusion across both Oïl and Oc domains, *Guilhem de la Barra* seems to be an isolated linguistic and literary experiment that survives in only one manuscript. If *Girart* owes its failure with audiences to its hybrid language choice, *Guilhem*'s hybridity lies in its apparent narrative incoherence and its equally apparent uniqueness. I shall argue that it is neither a unique nor an incoherent work. Additionally, Arnaut Vidal's rewriting of the tale of Joseph and Potiphar's wife echoes Ataïn's failed seduction of Berte, but also provides the ethical core of this troubling and far from trivial work.

Synopsis

Guilhem de la Barra is sent to England by the king of La Serra to fetch his wife, the princess Englantina. He acts as the proxy spouse in a betrothal ceremony and impresses Englantina further when they are abducted on their journey to La Serra by the Saracen lord of Malleo. Guilhem converts Malleo and his subjects to Christianity through several spectacular and violent miracles. During her husband's absence at war, Englantina tries to seduce Guilhem. He rebuffs her. She cries rape and makes a formal accusation against Guilhem, who flees to his castle. The king besieges La Barra. Guilhem flees and hands his two children to a female recluse and a shepherd. His son is adopted by the king of Armenia, and his daughter becomes a noted seamstress whose embroidery wins her the admiration and the hand of the count of Terramada. Guilhem spends seven years with a physician and travels the earth for a further fifteen, until he becomes the tutor to Terramada's children and his champion against the king of Armenia's champion, his own son. The father's war cry ("Barra!") provokes a grand recognition scene. Guilhem decides to reclaim La Barra, Englantina is persuaded to admit her crime, and Guilhem is reconciled with her as well as the king. He is restored to his lands, but lives in the English court for seven years. The king of England eventually makes him the first duke of Guyenne, and he dies after twenty-one years of untrammeled rule.

Guilhem de la Barra was completed in late May 1318 by Arnaut Vidal de Castelnaudary, who was also one of the first laureates of the Toulouse poetry contest in 1324 (lines 5326–44). Its only surviving manuscript is externally dated to 1324 and may show some connection with the Toulouse Consistory, but the poem is dedicated with a fulsome panegyric (evidently in the hope of employment as well as unspecified legal assistance) to a nobleman, Sicart de Montaut, whose seat was at Auterive (Haute Garonne), some thirty kilometers to the south of Toulouse (lines 5290–5325). By 1324, in Arnaut Vidal's prize poem (that date is also inscribed on the manuscript's cover), he says he is a member of the collegial church of Uzeste (Gironde), where the Gascon pope Clement V had been contentiously buried in 1314. He may well by then have been enjoying the patronage of Clement's nephew Arnaut de Canteloup (cardinal of the province of Bordeaux), or of any number of other Gascon relatives of the powerful de Got lineage, who held benefices in that region, including the see of Bazas.[5] The *roman* of 1318 in all probability reflects leaner years, but it has the transparent aim of ensuring that Arnaut Vidal, clearly an ambitious man, would establish links from a powerful network of both secular and religious fellow speakers of Occitan. The poem offers intriguing echoes, however, for Clement V (Bertrand de Got) was connected to the lineage of Mauléon, which is theoretically behind the monolingual, piratical, and pagan lord of Malleo in the opening section of *Guilhem de la Barra*.[6]

The poem is modeled both on *chansons de geste* and on the French *roman d'aventures*. It may derive from a lost original, as much of the narrative (with the exception of the opening conversion narrative) reappears with slight differences in Boccaccio's *Decameron* (*giornata* 2, *novella* 8).[7] *Guilhem de la Barra* also resembles fourteenth-century works such as Jehan Maillart's *Li Romans du comte d'Anjou* (c. 1316), another poem in octosyllabic rhyming couplets.[8] Arnaut calls his poem a *roman* (lines 5304, 5315, 5338) in another nod to the fashions of his time and, like Maillart, eschews the supernatural except in a strictly Christian context.

The text echoes several aspects of *Girart de Roussillon* in its depiction of an underlying sexual rivalry between king and vassal produced by a proxy betrothal, which expresses itself less figuratively through Englantina's accusation, the king's attacks on Guilhem's castle, and the betrayed vassal's lengthy exile. The poem is framed by an explicit association of its narrator/author with Guilhem. In the closing lines, Arnaut Vidal depicts himself as a wronged and isolated man who requires Sicart's legal assistance against the abuses of certain barons (lines 5308–11), hoping that the nobleman will also take him as his servant and reward him suitably, "qu'estat ay un temps encantatz / ab tot jorn prometre ses dar" (for I have been bewitched for a time by endless unfulfilled promises) (lines 5322–23). The betrayed service offered by Guilhem to the king of La Serra is set in a frame that identifies the author with his sufferings, and Sicart with a divinely sent protector (line 5308). Arnaut also affirms his Christian beliefs, as he avers that he believes in the Incarnation "segon ques a mi m'es a vist, / per cartas, et es veritatz" (as it seems to me, through charters, and it is the truth) (lines 5330–35). Such an explicit assertion of orthodox Christian (indeed, Marian) belief, and of reliance on written authority, seems to have been necessary for the poets who participated in the Toulouse Consistory, where the devotional prize poems were scrutinized by masters of the university for any hint of incorrect (by which they meant, heretical) belief. Accordingly, Arnaut prays as he closes the poem that he might be rid of any harm, obstacle, or wicked thought, "cuy Dieus defenda de tot mal / e que.l gar de tot encombrier / e.l tuelha tot mal cossïer" (lines 5340–42).

It is hard to read any literary product of early fourteenth-century Toulouse outside the filter of the repressive religious scrutiny that still dominated the city and its surrounding regions, and it seems essential to do so when we read a poem that foregrounds its French literary influences while using the poetic Occitan that was learned and practiced in the Consistory. Betrayal by powerful rulers and exile are invoked by the poem in both its narrative and its frame; their explicit association with assertions of religious belief would, in my view, point to a further concern with the orthodoxy of its sources. Dispossession and exile were used by Inquisition and French military authorities throughout the thirteenth century as the most palpable aspect of their harsh repression of heresy in the Languedoc (both Cathar and Waldensian). In the first decade of the fourteenth century, it was still possible to seize lands on the suspicion that a deceased family member had had dealings with a heretic. Indeed, the inquisitor Geoffroy d'Ablis, working from nearby Carcassonne, gathered depositions from young lawyers who shared Arnaut Vidal's education at Toulouse that cast doubts on the orthodoxy of both students and masters.[9]

The tale of Englantina's failed seduction of Guilhem derives either directly from the biblical story of Joseph and Potiphar's wife (Gen. 39), or from parabiblical vernacular traditions, which I will discuss below. I shall resist the temptation to dismiss it as a stock tale because its role in this particular narrative is too important, and its surrounding sources too multiple, to overlook. It resembles but does not reproduce the frame narrative of the Occitan-Catalan version of the *Seven Sages of Rome* (c. 1350) (an empress fails to seduce her stepson and accuses him of rape), which was known to members of the Toulouse Consistory.[10] There is nothing commonplace about Arnaut Vidal's use of an Old Testament narrative in an early fourteenth-century Occitan text. The Old Testament was rejected by the Cathars, along with much of the New Testament, so his inclusion of the tale might have been received as an assertion of an approved religious education, but it might also have opened Arnaut to further pressure, because Jewish communities of early fourteenth-century Languedoc were also subjected to aggressive campaigns on the part of both royal and religious authorities. The Toulouse inquisitor Bernard Gui supervised the confiscation and destruction of copies of the Talmud in 1310 and 1319.[11] In 1306, King Philip IV (Philip the Fair) ordered the seizure and sale of all Jewish property, and according to Cyril Hershon, the royal officers in Toulouse declared "that this property was held direct and allodially [*en franc alleu*], and so it could be sold directly for the king's benefit."[12] The Jewish communities of the Languedoc and surrounding regions were systematically dispossessed from 1306 onward. A decree passed by King Louis X in 1315 permitted a difficult return that ended in 1322, but Jewish property in Arnaut's birthplace of Castelnaudary was still being seized by the crown in 1320. Arnaut's assertion that he believes in the Incarnation is especially interesting in this respect because Bernard Gui's *Practica inquisitionis* (1323/24) held that Jews denied the virginity of Mary in their prayers. Denial of the Incarnation is a topos of anti-Jewish, rather than anti-Cathar, polemic from the thirteenth century onward.[13] Arnaut's prize-winning Marian poem of 1324 also mentions the Incarnation quite graphically: "per la virginal porta / intret Dieus dins vostre port" (Through the virgin door God entered your harbor).[14] While there are no grounds for assuming that Arnaut Vidal de Castelnaudary was a converted Jew (the name Vitalis/Vidal is both a Jewish and Christian surname in the Languedoc), his romance focuses on false accusation, dispossession, and exile at a time and in a region in which several religious communities lived under that threat.

Guilhem de la Barra's fortress seems to be the mirror opposite of Girart de Roussillon's tower, but its geography is fantastical: "En una terra lay d'Ungría / Ac .I. rey qu'era de Suría / ques ac nom lo rey de la Serra" (In a country, over there, of Hungary, there was a king from Syria who was known as the king of La Serra) (lines 1–3). La Serra (in Occitan, "a hill or a strait") echoes the nouns that derive from the verb *serrar* or *sarrar*, "to lock, close, or enclose," such as *serradura* (a lock). Guilhem is associated with his wish, in this enclosed land, to lock himself in the nearby fortress of La Barra: "El ha nom Guilhem de la Barra, / el sieu castel que gent se sarra / de murs de marmet tot entorn" (His name is Guilhem de la Barra, in his castle that is attractively enclosed all around by marble walls). "La Barra," or "Barra!" (Guilhem's war cry) may refer to a wooden staff, a barrier, or a barrage.[15] It alludes to Guilhem's repeated attempts to create protective ramparts around himself. This enclosed haven in a "locked" kingdom contrasts sharply with the twenty-four years that Guilhem spends in exile, as well as with the travels he undertakes to England at both the start and the close of the poem. This king of Syria has, for unexplained reasons, established a kingdom in Hungary, so his son's kingdom of La Serra, despite its name, is anything but securely grounded.

Access to La Serra from England (line 116) is further compromised by the presence at the one harbor of the Saracen lord of Malleo (lines 122–37), who exacts tribute and a forced abjuration of Christianity from every traveler. Malleo owns a handsome fortress, "d'obra talhada / espes de torrs e ben dechatz / Malleos" (of carved stonework, thick with towers, and well named Malleo) (lines 154–56). In what way is it *ben dechatz* (well named)? This is usually assumed to be a play on the toponym Mauléon, which would make *mal-leon* (evil lion) a coherent but unsuitable etymology for a well-built fortress, especially as Malleo takes the Christian name Leon on baptism. In any case, Malleo's language is incomprehensible, as Guilhem and his companion quickly realize, for although the first Saracens they encounter speak their language, their lord does not: "E.l bar senher de Malleo / non entendec las lors paraulas, / mas que cujec que fossan faulas" (The noble lord of Malleo did not understand their words and thought that they were *faulas*) (lines 220–22). Malleo thinks that words that he does not understand are fictions and fables; *faulas:* empty words. His *latinier* (interpreter) speaks to him in their shared *algaravic* (line 248), the term for Arabic (*al-fiarabiyya*) that eventually became modern Castilian *algarabía* or French *charabia* (nonsense). The *latiniers* addresses Guilhem and Chabertz in "pla lingage" (clear language), in other words, their own tongue, the Occitan of the poem (line 277). In the *Leys d'Amors, pla* (clear) language is one of the four necessary virtues of the vernacular rhetor: "Lenga per veritat / plana per parlar pla / Per qu'om no parle va" (a smooth tongue truly, for speaking clearly, so that one might not speak in vain) (Anglade, I.85).[16]

The religious conflict is played out through competing statues and actions; both the Saracen idols and the crucifix nailed to a laurel tree move their heads and change position to enact a conflict that cannot be pursued through either spoken or written words, as the *latinier* comments in frustration: "dyabli son / aquelh crestia en lor parlar" (These Christians are devils in their speech) (lines 556–57). The trilingual inscription on the cross is here presented monolingually, in gilt Latin writing, "Jhesus Nazarenum, rex Judeorum," and then glossed orally by Guilhem in Occitan: "e.l sieus noms, qu'es ab letras d'aur, / fon escrit per Pilat desus: / de Nazaret ha nom Jhesus, / reys que fo et es dels Juzieus; / aquel crezem qu'es verays Dieus" (His name, which is in letters of gold, was written by Pilate: "of Nazareth, named Jesus, who was and is king of the Jews"; we believe him to be the true God) (lines 384–85, 429–33). Guilhem ensures that the crucifix is accessible only through Latin (the other two divine languages clearly having been forgotten) and his vernacular gloss, with Pilate and his own voice as respectively the (pagan) Latin *auctoritas* and the Christian interpreter. Malleo's *latiniers* translates this sermon to his master as an invitation to see "lor dieu qu'an mes us .I. laurier / qu'es pens en .I. pauc de papier" (their god, which they have placed in a laurel tree, painted on a scrap of paper) (lines 457–58). He acknowledges the authority of the written inscription in identifying this foreign deity, but denies the value that Guilhem has attributed to it. In Malleo's uncomprehending eyes and ears, it can be no more than meaningless signs on a scrap of paper.

The lengthy conversion conflict stages the violent defeat of the Saracen images by the Christian image: the statues explode, stink, and fester in ditches. Written words and uttered prayers appear to be less effective than the physical actions of warring deities, something reminiscent of the story (often used in iconography) in which Saint Dominic ended a disputation with Cathar *perfecti* by casting both sides' books of arguments into the fire, so that the Christian booklet could fly out unharmed from the flames.[17] The conflict ends when the interpreter converts (lines 714–69), closely followed by Malleo's wife (lines 909–29). The wife manipulates her husband into conversion through what the rubric calls her "beautiful lies" (*belas messonjas* [96]), a foreshadowing of Englantina's lying words later in the text. Malleo, his wife, and their subjects are baptized by the nobleman Chabert on pain of either death or confiscation of their wealth (line 1515), in a ceremony that the rubric terms the most novel and the most pious baptism ever seen ("lo pus novel e.l pus devot babtisme" [108]). It is novel only in that coerced baptism was deemed to be irreversible by inquisitors of the early fourteenth century. In 1320, Jacques Fournier stated that a baptism could be nullified only if the person undergoing it protested or struggled, even in the case of a Jew, Baruch, who had been forcibly baptized in Toulouse's Saint-Étienne Cathedral by a mob. He concluded that baptism bound Baruch either to stay a Christian or to become a "heretic."[18]

In this novel and allegedly pious ceremony, the layman Chabert baptizes Malleo in the name of the Trinity, "senes carta e ses escrit" (without letter or written document) (line 1560). This could be read as an allusion to the Cathar ritual of *consolamentum,* which required the *perfectus* to hold a copy of the New Testament or the Gospel of John over the believer's head.[19] Chabert and Guilhem, laymen both, have already improvised a Eucharistic host from laurel leaves and focused on the crucifix more as an object adored or affixed to a tree than as an image of divine Logos (lines 345–65). Their spectacular gestures have proved more successful than the preaching words that the *latiniers* initially described as "vostre gran no sen" (your great nonsense) (line 281), the mere hearing of which should have provoked Malleo to have them put to death (lines 280–85). Malleo's lady echoes the men's spectacular tactics. She arranges with the interpreter for the collective baptism to take place in a huge circular vat made of a single piece of marble that cannot be harmed by either hammers or clubs (lines 1465–71) and that is sheltered from dirt, dust, and wind by layers of textiles and a surrounding rim of worked gold ("una sentura d'aur obrada") (line 1484). This secure marble circle in turn foreshadows the marble enclosure of Barra.

The conversion episode sets up an uneasy relationship between language and actions. Coerced baptism masquerades as piety; lies and preaching are the flimsy adornment of violent confrontations. If Guilhem's conversion of Malleo and his townsmen claims to be the high point of his spiritual career, it is followed by a brutal fall into far more worldly concerns. Deceitful words (*belas messonjas*), in fact, not pious deeds, are the agent of the ethical crisis that follows the king's marriage. Guilhem inspects the princess of England's naked body, as part of his task of approving her as the king's wife, and brings her to La Serra. He promptly falls sick and goes to La Barra to recover, and the king forgets to inform him of his wedding. The king inadvertently makes an enemy of him (lines 2316–25, 2358–59, 2622–29). Englantina and the king of La Serra spend the first month of their marriage locked in a strong sexual attraction that surpasses even the terrestrial Paradise, and they kiss during Mass before the assembled court (lines 2492–99). It would seem that the court of La Serra does not set a great example of religious piety. The king decides to assist a besieged city in Hungary and he tells the queen that he has decided to entrust both her and his kingdom to the most virtuous and handsome of men (lines 2534–47). The king's description sparks a secret passion in Englantina for this exemplary vassal (lines 2550–53), and she asks to know his name (lines 2554–65). Englantina's lust for Guilhem is then the product of her husband's admiring words: "tant fort fon son cors enflamatz / del cavalier que l'a lausat" (So much was her heart aflame for the knight, because he had praised him) (lines 2570–71). The king's words inadvertently cause Englantina to transfer her erotic desire from her husband to the man whom he has chosen as his substitute in everything but the marital role. This is already an ambiguous role for Guilhem to assume, given his compromising position as the king's proxy in Englantina's chamber in England. On that occasion, Guilhem praises Englantina's beauty as an index of her virtue:

> La.ifanta fo cum causa muda
> De vergonha no poc parlar.
> Guilhem de la Barra intrar
> Vay en la chambray totz soletz,
> E vic son cors c'ayssi fo netz
> E clars e nous cum .I. cristalh.
> Guillem Barra diss: "Ges no.us falh,
> Per ma fe, deguna beutat."
>
> (lines 1920–27)

[The princess was like a dumb thing; she could not speak for shame. Guilhem went alone into the chamber and saw that her body was as unmarked, bright, and fresh as crystal. He said, "By my faith, you are lacking in no aspect of beauty."]

Guilhem can look at Englantina's body without feeling erotic desire, as if she were made of translucent stone, but she cannot listen to the verbal description of his beauty without being provoked into lustful feelings. Guilhem is re-presented to her, no longer as her husband's virtuous proxy, but as a potential lover who has been carefully kept enclosed and inaccessible by the king, "El ha nom Guilhem de la Barra, / el sieu castel que gent se sarra / de murs de marmet tot entorn." Guilhem initially refuses to set foot in the king's palace on the grounds that his children had lost their mother a few days before, and are too young to be left alone (lines 2630–33). He is a widower, enclosed in his stone circle, suddenly endowed with the king's temporal powers. After letting the king's messengers admire the crenellations of his castle, Guilhem consents to his new role (lines 2640–41), as if the fortress of his own counsel had already been breached.

Englantina hides her feelings with hypocritical sighs (lines 2738–43) and ensures that Guilhem's proxy legal authority is endorsed by charters before her husband departs (lines 2724–29). The rubric announces that at this legally charged point, the "diverssas adventuras" of Guilhem de la Barra truly commence (Gouiran, 170). He takes immediate precautions by surrounding the king's palace with a palisade of wooden stakes (lines 2760–65) to ensure that no one can enter it save through a single *port* (entry point), on pain of death. Guilhem's attempt to re-create his secure circle at La Barra is in vain, as the queen (whose heart is sufficiently aflame to burn down any palisade) is already set on undermining his security. A month later, she attempts to seduce Guilhem:

> La regina li vay mandar
> Qu'ela volia parlar am luy,
> E que no fossan mas amduy
> E sa cambra tot per privat.
> Le cavaliers venc de bon grat
> Vas la dona quan lo mandec;
> En sa cambra totz sols intrec
> E vic la sola ses donzela,
> E va.s gent sezer delatz ela
> Sus la colça le cavaliers,
> E fon guays e fon plasentiers;
> E la regina que.l regara,
> E va.l dir: "Senher de la Barra,
> Si.us platz, vos mi daretz .i. do,
> E no m'en vulhatz dir de no,
> Senher, per la fe que.m tenetz."
> "Dona, digay me que voletz,
> Qu'ieu faray per vos tota re,
> Sol que gardetz ma li̇al fe,
> E que no.y capía tracïo."
> La dona diss: "Mot mi sab bo,
> Et yeu diray vos mo voler,
> E no.us tengatz a desplazer,
> Senh'en Guilhem, so que.us vuelh dir.
> El cor m'avetz mes .i. desir
> De fin'amor qui.m ven de vos,
> Qu'ades vos dic tot ad estros

Que fassatz de mi que.us vulhatz,
E que tant sïatz mos privatz
Cum fora mos maritz si.y fos."

(lines 2774–2803)

[The queen had him come to her, saying she wanted a word and that they should be alone together in her chamber, in secret. The knight came willingly to the lady when she called for him. He entered the chamber alone and found her on her own, without a woman servant. The knight sat down next to her on the cushion, both gaily and attractively. The queen gazed at him and said, "My lord of La Barra, please grant me a gift, and do not say no to me, by the faith you owe me." "My lady, tell me what you wish, for I will do anything for you, as long as you respect my loyalty and do not demand any treason from me." The lady said, "That seems good to me, and I will tell you what I want, and please do not be displeased, Sir Guilhem, by what I want to say to you. You have placed a desire in my heart for *fin'amor,* which comes to me from you. I say to you unreservedly that you may do whatever you want with me, and you may be my intimate man [*mos privatz*] as much as my husband would be, were he here."]

Guilhem is horrified by Englantina's proposition, looks into her face to reject her, and receives a "close" kiss on the mouth for his pains (line 2806). He replies:

Madona, per re
Non o faría, quar la fe
Qu'ay mandada a mo senhor
E la lïaltat e l'amor
Li vuelh tenir e la.y tendray;
Perque.us dic, dona, ses tot play,
Que mais voldría esser mortz.

(lines 2809–15)

[My lady, I would never do this for anything, because I want to maintain the faith, the loyalty, and the love that I have pledged to my lord, and maintain them I shall. So I tell you, my lady, without any discussion, that I would rather die.]

If Englantina has until this point been enacting a narrative of *fin'amors,* she is rudely introduced to Guilhem's contradictory interpretation of her words as the lustful advances of Potiphar's wife. The dialogue is strikingly similar to a section of the Catalan *Genesi de Scriptura,* a digest of biblical narratives that is described in one manuscript of 1451 as a translation from Occitan by a certain Guillem Serra:[20]

> E com Josep era bell hom e sert, donali lo dit rich hom les claus de la sua casa e feulo majordom: e quant vench per temps la muller de Phutifar, la qual hauia nom Meuphitica, enamoras de Josep. E un dia quel senyor fon anat a cassa crida la dona a Josep e feulo entrar en la sua cambra e dixli: tu, Josep, vols hauer be e honor? Respos Josep: madona, si volria en bona manera. Ara, dix ella, tinme secreta de tot ço que jot dire e fe aço que jot manare. Madona, dix Josep, totes coses qui sien fehedores fare. Adonchs dix ella: vull que hages affer ab mi e hauras totes coses que demans. E Josep respos e dix: no ho vulla Deus, madona, que jo fassa aytal cosa, que gran traycio seria; que mon senyor se fia en mi e en mon poder ha mes tot ço del seu. No ho faria, dix Josep, ans ne sofferria mort. (35–36)

> [And as Joseph was a handsome and knowledgeable man, the nobleman gave him the keys of his house and made him his chamberlain. And eventually the wife of Potiphar, who was called Meuphitica, fell in love with Joseph. One day, when the lord was out hunting, the lady called for Joseph and made him come into her chamber and said to him, "Joseph, do you want to have possessions and honor?" Joseph replied, "My lady, I would indeed." "Then," she said. "Keep secret everything I will say to you, and do whatever I ask of you." "My lady," said Joseph, "I shall do all the things that may be done." Then she said, "I want you to 'become involved with me,' and you can have anything you ask for." Joseph replied, "God does not want me to do such a thing, my lady, because it would be treason; because my lord has put his trust in me and has put everything he owns in my power. I will not do this." Joseph said, "I would rather suffer death for it."]

The *Genesi de Scriptura* text is quite different from the Vulgate:

> Post multos itaque dies iniecit domina sua oculos suos in Ioseph, et ait: Dormi mecum. Qui nequaquam acquiescens operi nefario, dixit ad

eam: Ecce, dominus meus, omnibus mihi traditis, ignorat quid habeat in domo sua: nec quidquam est quod non in mea sit potestate, vel non tradiderit mihi, praeter te, quae uxor eius es: quomodo ergo possum hoc malum facere, et peccare in Deum meum? (Gen. 39:7–9)

One husband is away fighting the Saracens, and the other is hunting; both tales set the dialogue in a courtly environment and emphasize that the wife has invited the servant into her private bedchamber; Englantina invites Guilhem to sit on her *colça,* and Meuphitica's marital bed is in the room. This is not said in either the Vulgate or the Qu'ran, but the Vulgate alters the Hebrew text (rendered most often as "Lie with me") to order less directly, "Dormi mecum" (Sleep with me). In the Qu'ran, the wife traps Yusuf by closing the entire house, while in the Vulgate, they find themselves alone together in an unspecified location within the house. The *Genesi de Scriptura* tale has Meuphitica fall in love with the slave, "enamoras," but she requests that he "hages affer ab me," which translates clumsily (perhaps quite crudely) as "concerning" himself with her. Englantina unveils her *cors enflamatz* in terms of courtly *fin'amors* and offers Guilhem a privileged status as her *privatz.* Neither woman is as direct as the wife in Genesis, who simply issues twice her command: "Lie with me." Both Guilhem and Josep interpret the wife's words as a betrayal of their role as the husband's proxy in everything but the sexual sense. Guilhem is acting as regent and has been granted judicial powers, while Joseph may be a slave, but he has been entrusted with the husband's household, and as Mieke Bal points out, a house in biblical terminology signifies both the household (*familia*) and the lineage of Potiphar.[21] Both men protest, quite unlike the Joseph of the Vulgate, that their loyalty and love (*amor*) for their master or king must take precedence. In Genesis, Joseph's relationship is primarily with God, and his belief that it would be sinful to take his master's wife. Neither man expresses or feels any reciprocal desire for the woman.

The *Genesi de Scriptura* and *Guilhem de la Barra* diverge at this point. Meuphitica threatens Joseph with a false accusation: "Sapies, dix ella, que si no ho fas, jo dire al senyor que tu m'has volguda forsar e fare en guisa que ell te auciura. E lauors dix Josep: jo per pahor de mort no fare tan gran engan a mon senyor" (The lady said, "Know that if you do not do it, I will tell the lord that you tried to rape me, and I will make sure he kills you." Then Joseph said, "I would never shame my lord out of fear of death"). Englantina, however, immediately tears her clothes and hair, and cries rape to assemble her men as Guilhem tries to escape from the chamber (lines 2816–27). Her torn clothing also echoes the next part of the Joseph narrative. In the Vulgate, it is some time after this dialogue that Potiphar's wife finds herself alone again with Joseph and reiterates her request, "Lie with me," grasping his garment (Gen. 39:11–16). He tears himself away from her, leaves his clothing in her hands, and she shows it to the men of the household as evidence that he has attempted to rape her. She also keeps the garment as evidence for her husband's eyes: "And she laid up his garment by her, until his lord came home" (Gen. 39:16) The *Genesi de Scriptura* translates this detail into a more dramatic accusation:

> E ell, volentse desempatxar de ella e essir de ses mans, desempara son mantel e lexalli e exis de la cambra, e romas elle molt irada e gita lo mantell de Josep sobre lo seu lit e de son marit. E quant lo senyor fon vengut de la cassa troba la dona molt irada e demanali que hauia. E ella dixli: aquel vostro catiu, en que vos tant vos fiats, entra en la mia cambra e volch jaure ab mi per forsa, e quant hoy que vos veniets exi corrent de la cambra: e veus lo mantell que romas sobre lo lit, que nol li lech pendre. Quant lo rich hom hach aço entes, feu metre Josep en la preso. (36)

> [Wanting to extricate himself from her grasp and from her hands, he let fall his cloak, left it behind, and left the room; she stayed behind, very angry, and threw the cloak on her, and her husband's, bed. When the lord returned from the hunt, he found the lady very angry and asked her what was the matter. She said, "This captive of yours whom you trust so much came into my chamber and wanted to lie with me, by force, and when he heard that you were coming, he ran out of the chamber. Look at the cloak that was left on the bed, because I did not let him take it." When the nobleman heard this, he had Joseph put in prison.]

It is very likely that the *Genesi de Scriptura* has expanded on the Vulgate text, because the corresponding narrative in the Qu'ran (sura 12:24–35) says that the lustful wife tears the back of Yusuf's shirt as he flees, and it is the evidence of Yusuf's torn clothing on his own body that persuades the husband of his guilt.[22] However, there may well be other sources, for Potiphar's wife is given the intriguing name of Meuphitica, rather than the more common Zuleikha.[23] In the Vulgate, Potiphar's wife accuses Joseph first before the assembled men of the household (as does Englantina) and, second, before her husband.

Guilhem flees to his castle and attempts to close its gates securely (lines 2836–37), but its walls can no longer afford him the same protection. He relates his version of events to his men, omitting the queen's talk of *fin'amors* in favor of a direct reference to the text of Genesis (39:8): "A ma dona venc en plazer / qu'en sa cambra mi fey intrar, / e va.m preguar e va.m mandar / tot obra qu'ab liey mi colques" (My lady saw fit to have me come into her chamber, and she asked and ordered me openly to lie with her) (lines 2858–61). He states that as soon as she began to tear at her clothing and hair, he realized that this was no joke ("yeu no m'o tengui a gab"), and made his escape (lines 2864–69), upon which she ran after him crying rape. Englantina sends word to the king by letter (lines 2874–2907). The king abandons his siege (the narrator comments that the city promptly falls to the Saracens, lines 2908–9) and applies legal process to his attempted prosecution of Guilhem (lines 2910–47).

The Joseph tale functions as an important structural device, in that it separates Guilhem definitively from his king without compromising his loyalty to him. It also should provide the opportunity to reconcile the two men at the poem's close by condemning Englantina for her lies and disruptive sexual advances; after all, Arnaut's fellow Consistory members were familiar with this outcome to the parallel story of the *Set Savis de Roma*. In keeping with this expectation, Guilhem tells his long-lost daughter that he was the victim of attempted rape:

> La regina, de gran plaser,
> me vay en sa cambra sonar
> de guiza que.m volia forssar,
> e vau me tost de liey partir;
> vas la Barra m'en vau fugir,
> et ela diss qu'ieu la forssava
> e son dan que li demandava;
> qu'ieu era senhors de la Barra,
> et ay nom Guillem de la Barra;
> e.l reys me venc essetïar
> e jugar que.m fey a penjar
> sus al portal de mon castel.
>
> (lines 4574–85)

[The queen took pleasure in calling me into her chamber in order to try to rape me, and I tried to escape from her, to run away to La

Barra. And she said that I was trying to rape her, and asking her to do something harmful to her, for I was the lord of La Barra, and my name is Guilhem de la Barra. The king besieged me and condemned me to be hanged above my castle gates.]

The two terms "que.m volia forssar" and "qu'ieu la forssava" show that Guilhem narrates Englantina's allegedly pleasurable actions (to her) as sexual violence. He flees to his castle but it in turn is taken by force by the king. Guilhem's association of the castle with his chastity becomes explicit at the poem's close. He returns to La Barra to admire the "vila d'obra talhada, / al noble castel de la Barra, / le quals de nobles murs se ssara / totz de marmetz espessamens" (the town built from carved stones, the noble castle of La Barra, which is enclosed by noble walls of thick marble) (lines 4696–99). He tells the assembled bourgeois that in his opinion such a fine marble fortification, with such fine crenellations, should belong to one lord alone, not to two (lines 4716–25). The townspeople have gathered, it seems, partly because these foreign visitors are of a foreign tongue ("foron de estranh lingage" [line 4715]), so Guilhem's description of his own castle, disguised as a foreign visitor, allows them to express opinions they have concealed. Accordingly, one of the bourgeois delivers a lengthy panegyric to the castle's lost lord (lines 4732–61), as he agrees that the king of la Serra has merely appropriated the castle through war (lines 4730–31). Guilhem's virtues (including his good looks, amorousness, loyalty, and charming conversation) make him the rightful lord of such a fine fortress. However, it is not Guilhem's described attractions that win his cause, but the threat delivered by messengers to the king of la Serra that if he does not restore this "little castle" (*castelet*) to his former vassal, his subjects will be massacred by foreign troops (lines 4852–71). Guilhem's beauty and virtues are described once again, this time in terms of nostalgia, and provoking only the chaste *amor* of his subjects. The bourgeois' description allows the queen's misdeed to be revisited and brought to an end, "quar per liey se moc l'ataïna, / e per liey se fara la patz" (for the quarrel arose through her, and through her peace will be restored) (lines 4878–79).

However, the poem does not end quite as neatly as this may promise. Far from denying the erotic bond that was established at the opening through Guilhem's role as the king's proxy in the English court, and far from punishing the queen for her false accusation, Arnaut Vidal binds the two into an adulterous relationship that goes beyond *fin'amors*. Both the bourgeois and the king ask Englantina to forgive Guilhem for his presumed crime, and she agrees to see him, because she still loves him (lines 4916–17). This allows her to confess that she made a false accusation purely in order to test his loyalty to his king (lines 4969–83) and to see Guilhem to ask him for his forgiveness, even though she still desires him (lines 5116–25). Again, there is no sign that Guilhem feels the slightest desire for the queen. The erotic desire is purely hers. The two are reconciled and ride into la Serra together, "speaking about both the present and the past" (line 5130). Finally they process into La Barra, back to Guilhem's castle, and the narrator notes with irony, "Latz e latz venc ab la regina / e dic vos que fo bel parelh" (Side by side he went with the queen, and I tell you, they made a fine pair), as the queen, "joguan rizen" (playfully smiling), invites the king to make his public gesture of affection in restoring the castle to his vassal by receiving the collective oath of the townspeople. La Barra is given commune status by the king. In an ultimate gesture of ironic reversal, Guilhem's son leaves to take up his role as the adoptive son and heir of the king of Armenia, and Guilhem, now childless and freed of his responsibility toward La Barra, leaves for England to become a favored champion and, eventually, duke of Guyenne. No sooner is Guilhem's beloved fortress restored to him than he appears to lose control of it, as both it and his son free themselves from his authority. He appears to return to his own *enfances* as an unmarried knight in the court where he first gazed chastely on Englantina's then uncorrupted body, and it is there that he wins both knightly honors and eventually a duchy of his own, much as he would have done had he won Englantina's hand for himself as a knight errant. Except, and this appears to be the point, he has never desired Englantina's love.

Arnaut Vidal closes *Guillem de la Barra* with an ironic twist that makes this fourteenth-century Languedocian Joseph ultimately the recipient of the lands and near-marital love of Potiphar's English wife, while her husband simply disappears from the narrative. If, as I suggested, the tale of Joseph and Potiphar's wife was one of the sources for the tale, it is altered and rewritten in terms of other narratives. One of these is Guilhem's cherished fortress of La Barra. La Barra is not associated with pride. Rather, it symbolizes Guilhem's virtues, their physical (aesthetic) strength but also their fragility. Joseph's beauty (which was important in both Jewish and Islamic exegesis as a sign of his high spiritual status) is both a guarantor of his high status in Potiphar's house and the cause of his momentary downfall at the hands of the wife. La Barra's marble walls appear to ensure Guilhem's chaste distance from the corrupting environment of La Serra, but they do not resist the queen's manipulative influence, and they cannot protect him when the false accusation is formulated. When the fortress is said to be designed for the rule of a single lord, not two, it proclaims the virtues of loyalty and monogamy that Joseph and Guilhem seek to defend. However, the castle is restored to the equally handsome Guilhem only in order to become affranchised, ruled by the bourgeois who have ensured that Guilhem, and not the king, should own it.

The morality of the kingdom of La Serra disintegrates throughout the narrative, until by its close, the characters appear to have no grounding for their actions except in their collective nostalgia for the actions of the past and a belief in beauty as an index of virtue. As Mieke Bal has said in her recent thought-provoking book, *Loving Yusuf,* Potiphar's wife is received in almost every tradition and every literature as an emblematic misogynous stereotype: she is a predatory, lustful object in Potiphar's house, who endangers Joseph's secure position in his master's love and trust. Englantina adopts a quite different position by being caught in an ambiguous erotic relationship with Guilhem at the outset and developing into his consort in every sense but the sexual one by the end of the romance. It is through her continued and unreciprocated love that Guilhem ends the romance as the first duke of Guyenne. Arnaut associates himself with Guilhem, and implicitly with Joseph, as the wronged victim of unspecified accusations, and this narrative of dispossession and partial restoration of lands has a powerful political and religious dimension for both him and Sicart de Montaut. Ultimately, it seems to conclude that allying oneself cautiously with Potiphar's wife may well provide the necessary route to peace and to other lands, while the lost castles of the present remain forever in the hands of other rulers.

Finally, how does the use of the tale of Joseph and Potiphar's wife connect with the treatment of languages at the start of *Guilhem de la Barra*? According to Shalom Goldman, in some Jewish postbiblical texts, Joseph pretends to be unable to understand the Egyptian woman's words (this may be a source for the stepson's mute refusal of the empress's advances in the *Set Savis*). In others, Joseph's status as an interpreter of dreams includes his knowledge of many (sometimes all seventy) of the languages of the world; as Goldman points out, "A knowledge of many languages was seen as a sign of holiness and power" throughout the ancient Near East.[24] However, Guilhem de la Barra remains monolingual, despite his twenty-four years of exile. At the start of the poem, he converts through actions because he can only gloss a Latin inscription in the vernacular, and cannot enter into direct dialogue with the lord of Malleo. He travels through England and other far-off lands without interpreters, perhaps because the poem presents Christendom as a monolingual environment. Yet these monolingual words in the kingdom of La Serra prove misleading, seductive, and unreliable, and the nonnoble citizens of La Barra identify their Armenian visitors as a curiosity because they are people "of another language." Guilhem may play at being Joseph through his narrator's intertextual work, but he cannot emulate his later career as a powerful interpreter either of languages or of dreams. Guilhem remains tied to an unreliable overlord, striving to maintain and to re-create a protective enclosure for his lineage in a Christianized world that seems bereft of any ethical grounding, where conversion is the product of force and deceit, and false accusations may never be punished. His only resort is to ally himself with his worst enemy, the queen, and to seek an alternative home in exile. While the confusion of Babel has apparently been canceled by the tongues of fire at Pentecost, these tongues would seem to be those that were associated with the spectacular punishments that were organized by Bernard Gui in Toulouse in the years during which the poem was written: not the fiery tongues of multilingual preaching, nor the fires of *fin'amors,* but burning tongues of real flame and the red cloth tongues of false accusation.

3

ACQUIRING THE (M)OTHER TONGUE IN AVIGNON AND TOULOUSE

THE PSYCHOANALYST MARIE BALMARY has argued that it is possible to use a long-established interpretation of Babel, in terms of Freud's writings on the dangerous collective aspects of monotheism, as a critique of monolingualism.[1] The narrative opens with the verse "The whole earth was of one language, and of one speech" (Gen. 11:1). At this point in history, the three sons of Noah (Japheth, Shem, and Ham [Gen. 9:18]) have already produced many lineages. Their reproduction produces diversity among individuals, peoples, and languages ("These are the sons of Shem, after their families, after their tongues, in their lands, after their nations" [Gen. 10:31]); Balmary notes that there are already more than seventy names. There is in fact no monolingualism before Babel, and the tale of the tower must contain a different message to one that celebrates an original linguistic uniformity. When the different lineages join forces to construct the tower, their diversity is lost in the cause of their impossible attempt to prevent their own tendency to disperse into lineages and idioms. They urge each other to work "lest we be scattered." Their language is "confounded"; the builders are struck by linguistic difference and scattered definitively across the world.[2]

This reading of the myth of Babel derives from parabiblical Jewish tradition. Flavius Josephus argued that the confusion of tongues was punishment for the refusal by the descendants of Noah to colonize other parts of the world (*Ant.* 1.4.1).[3] From these men's fear of being weakened by territorial expansion springs their collective submission to the tyrant Nimrod and derives the foolhardy project of the tower reaching up to the skies. Balmary concludes that this slippage from harmonious cohabitation into a totalitarian project stems from the builders' distorted relationship with language, as if monolingualism were tantamount to a denial of the other's status as an autonomous subject. In Balmary's reading, linguistic uniformity destroys the relationship between self and other and denies the differences that are crucial to the construction of an autonomous individual. She calls this a process of *désaltérisation,* the destruction of alterity in the fallacious pursuit of uniformity and power through the collective. As language is constructed by a system of differences, so speech can only be possible between differentiated subjects.[4] Difference between subjects is the motor behind linguistic difference, and it is crucial to human communication. She notes that if "we" all speak the same language and articulate the same thoughts, there is a corresponding loss of awareness that the term *we* is no more than a temporary and illusory unit composed of individuals who will at some point seek to express themselves not as "we" but as "I."

One Occitan manuscript of the early fourteenth century interprets Josephus's account of the downfall of Babel as a positive moment for the constitution of both speech and human society. The manuscript is an Occitan translation of the *Compendium,* or *Chronologia magna,* composed by the Franciscan Paolino Veneto, or Minorita (c. 1270/75–1344),[5] a universal history constructed on a visual model as an illustrated series of tabulated genealogies and lines of succession. Paolino's vertical genealogical tables are interrupted almost at the start by a depiction of Noah's ark above the *Turris Babel* (*sic*) and a *mappa mundi* (3r).

The glosses that comment on the images (citing both Josephus and Jerome) state that Nemroth (Nimrod) wanted to rule over three of the tribes that descended from Noah, so he persuaded them to build "una auta tor perral" on the plain of Shinar (*Ant.* 1.4.2). The tower is so high that even the winds and the rains do not reach beyond its middle, but it is so wide that it seems wider than its already considerable height (*Ant.* 1.4.3). Paolino's scheme is visual, and there is a striking visual gloss on the tower's impact on languages. Words are squeezed into the gaps that remain in the left-hand side of the column that has been assigned to the images of the bottom of the tower and the world, to the extent that they disintegrate into fragments (transcription mine):

> Dieus cofō
> det qui
> las lengas
> de lor.
> E en
> ayshi
> coma dels filhs de
> noe ero ys
> hidas.

sen.ge
nerati
os.tot
enai
shi
la
lẽ
=
ga
hu
m
nal
es
devi
za en
lxii.len
gatges.

Dieus cofondet qui las lengas de lor. e enayshi coma dels filhs de Noe ero yshidas. sen. generatios. tot enaishi la lenga humanal es deviza en lxii.lengatges.

[God confounded their languages, and just as one hundred generations have come from the sons of Noah, so human language has been divided into sixty-two languages.]

Visual scheme and glossing vernacular words are placed here in a striking dialogue. The Tower of Babel dominates the tiny, schematic world map. It is a solid object, four labeled stories high, with a sturdy base of three layers of stones. Far from being demolished by the "confounding" of tongues, vernacular words are compelled to weave and break up around the tower's intact stones. There are no inhabitants or builders on this completed tower. The margins of the folio are damaged, but it is still possible to read on the far left column, a little below the image of the tower, a repetition of the story in which the number of the languages is given as the more conventional number of seventy-two.

As the manuscript's scheme demands that a vertical alignment indicates direct lines of succession, the monstrous tower produces a world that is divided into three regions (Asia, Europe, and Africa). However, this small

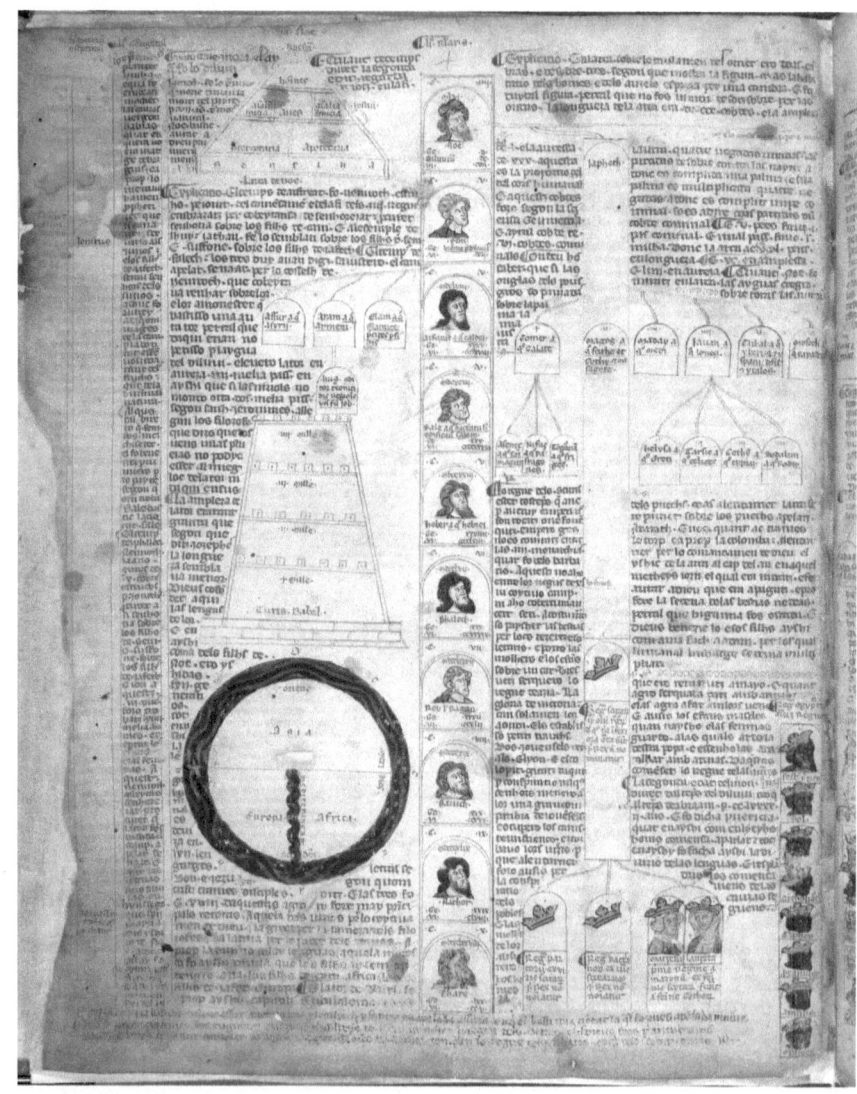

Fig. 3 *Las Abreujamens de las estorias*, MS British Library Egerton 1500, fol. 3v. © British Library Board. All rights reserved.

world is not dominated by its *predecessor*. Those three divisions are subdivided into provinces in a much later note (61r). Europe has fourteen geographical subdivisions. At the base of the same left-hand column, we find that this subdivided world has allotted a geographical location to the remains of the tower: "E la tor de babel. fo en babilonia" (The Tower of Babel was in Babylonia). It would seem that it no longer looms over the world with its extraordinary height and width. Why this should be the case may be explained by a gloss in red ink in the right-hand column (red rubrics in the text signal *explicatio*):

> La seconda edat del mon. duret dal temps del diluvi troq al temps de Abraam. p. cc. lxxxx.ii. ans. E fo dicha puericia. quar enayshi com enlyeyhs homs comensa. a parlar. tot enayshy fo facha qyshi la divizio de las lenguas.

> [The second age of the world lasted from the time of the Deluge to the time of Abraham, for 292 years. It was called childhood, for as every man begins to speak, so was made the division of the languages.]

The *Abreujamens* glosses the division of tongues as humanity's entrance into language in *pueritia,* the apprenticeship period of life that stretched from the age of seven to the entrance into a socially recognized maturity that might start at the marriageable age of fourteen or be delayed well into adult life.[6] This is no longer a disaster, and there is no sense of an exile, for the tower's builders have been freed from the attempted tyranny of Nemroth and allowed to populate, name, and map the entire world. At this point, the text diverges quite markedly from Josephus, who gives a list of the peoples of the world and criticizes the Greeks for imposing alternative names on them (*Ant.* 1.5.1, 1.6.1–5). As the *Abreujamens* consists of a world history composed of genealogical tables, its binding of language, lineage, and human history appears to depend on the multiplication of tongues.

There are few hints of the manuscript's intended recipients; its frontispiece is lost and the prologue mentions no dedicatee. However, Paolino's later draft of the *Compendium,* now in Paris, was a luxury copy presented to Pope John XXII in 1328, and Degenhart and Schmitt conclude that the Occitan translation, being a richly illustrated work, may well have been produced at the same time. The Venetian author of the *Abreujamens* or an associate ensured that an illuminated Occitan version of the Latin text was made available within Avignonese papal court circles. This multilingual environment appears to have persisted, because a number of later hands corrected the text in Latin, Occitan, and occasionally Italian. If the tower indicates the *pueritia* of humanity, it must be associated with the language acquisition that was enabled by education. The sketch of the Tower of Babel loosely resembles the mnemonic visual scheme of the Franciscan John of Metz's *Turris Sapientiae* (*Tower of Wisdom,* c. 1250), in which every stone is a mnemonic locus designed to teach an ethical or religious precept to a child.[7] The *Turris Babel* in the *Abreujamens* is also a *turris sapientiae*. It marks the text as simultaneously a work of translation, translating words into visual schemes, Latin into Occitan.

Pueritia appears to be an entrance into many languages, rather than the primary acquisition of language, which was believed to coincide with the emergence of first teeth at the end of the infant's first year.[8] It fits Giorgio Agamben's theory that infancy can be conceived of as the limit of language, a period before unmediated (prelinguistic) experience is destroyed.[9] A reading of Babel as a dramatic entrance into multiple languages on a par with what the Occitan translators call *pueritia* underscores Balmary's emphasis on this version of the story of Babel as the abolition of monolingual tyranny. Here, the seventy-two languages (or sixty-two, or even fifty-seven, depending on how the faded words are read) are so many "sons" of a lost father, either the tower or their ruler Nemroth, who spoke a single language and who sought to keep his *pueri* locked in a single infertile and unproductive location. Languages and lineages are freed by the confusion (which is not ascribed to divine agency on this folio) to found their own families and idioms. Agamben interprets infancy as the site of a division between animalistic *langue* and the human *parole* that Aristotle identified as the foundation of both household and city. Ethical judgment, and according to Agamben, a sense of history, are associated directly with the primary acquisition of speech.[10] Paolino's world history owes its inception to an extension into childhood of that division, as Agamben would have it: "It is infancy, it is the transcendental experience of the difference between language and speech, which first opens the space of history. Thus Babel—that is, the exit from the Eden of pure language and the entry into the babble of infancy (when, linguists tell us, the baby forms the phonemes of every language in the world)—is the transcendental origin of history."[11] Paolino's *pueri* have lost their original babble. Their acquired languages, like their later history, are strictly patrilinear, but have they swapped one first father (not God, but their self-appointed ruler Nemroth) for a series of fathers and sons? Medieval theories of infantile language acquisition placed the emphasis on the child's mother or nurse, but here, there is not even the conventional feminine personification of Grammar to lead the *puer*'s way into (not out of) the Tower of Wisdom.[12] It would seem that this original tongue is not the mother tongue, because the *Abreujamens* strives to suppress maternal agency. Paolino's genealogical tables run awry whenever they confront feminine succession or foundations, and they resort to complicated diagonal lines or to legal concepts such as adoption that restore patrilinear lineage through purely social means. An introductory note, probably composed by the translators, strives to explain the strange tabulation of the Virgin Mary's lineage (17r) on the grounds that "negus evvangelista no *pauia* la genealogia de la vergena car no es costuma de la escriptura *pauiar* la genealogia de las femnas" (no evangelist gives [?] the genealogy of the Virgin because it is not the habit of the Scriptures to give [?] the genealogies of women) (1v–2r).

The hostility toward feminine genealogy evinced by Paolino may also be connected to Babel. In Honorius of Autun's *Imago mundi* (and its vernacular translations) the Tower of Babel is said to have been built with a mortar made of bitumen, a mineral that could be dissolved only by women's menstrual blood.[13] Josephus is a source for the bitumen mortar, but not this detail (*Ant.* 1.4.3). Women's dissolving blood undermines the tower before God intervenes to sow linguistic confusion among its builders. The confounding of tongues leaves the tower incomplete, in the hope (however vain) of a return to unmediated communication. However, women's fertile blood has already undermined the building's stability. The empty structure is built out of a masculine fear of being scattered by the effects of procreation, and it risks being returned to its original state as a meaningless pile of rubble by women's contribution to that process. No such statement appears in the *Abreujamens,* but Paolino's genealogical fantasies in the service of Crusade ideology appear to be shaken by the intervention of maternal succession. His history depicts a patrilinear world irrevocably divided on religious, geographical, and political lines by firmly drawn borders, where women may occasionally play a disruptive role without undermining its essential workings. Yet the very basis of language, the very start of human history, is potentially compromised by feminine agency. It is a monument to the anxieties of both him and his patrons: a treatment of history and of disciplinary boundaries that constructs false certainties without making allowances for alternative voices or narratives. Were it in Latin alone, it could be described as monolingual, even monologic. As the *Abreujamens* furnishes a vernacular translation, it is at odds with its stated aim, but in harmony with its association of history with the division of one single speech into many.

Language choice is important, as Paolino's text is translated into an idiom that is not the "mother tongue" of its Venetian author. It is not obvious if the clumsy Middle Occitan of the several hands that wrote and expanded the *Abreujamens* between the fourteenth and fifteenth centuries constitutes an attempt to emulate the literary koine of a previous generation, or if it seeks to reproduce the everyday speech of intended readers who were born and possibly educated in the geographical region of Avignon. As such, it illustrates the interpretation of Babel that was offered at the same time by Dante in *De vulgari eloquentia,* that the confounding of tongues was no more than evidence that languages, like all human actions, are subject to space and time. Dante proposed to read the poetic vernaculars as evidence that humans have reconstructed their languages after Babel to their liking, for the confusion of tongues was "no more than the forgetting of the previous language" (1.9.6–7). Daniel Heller-Roazen has proposed that Dante's remark should be read as a radical departure from conventional medieval views of language: "The great 'confounding' of Babel involved neither addition nor subtraction, creation nor destruction, but, instead, a loss of memory, which destined speaking beings to forget their 'one language, and . . . one speech' and, in their oblivion, to develop the many idioms in which they would henceforth be scattered." Heller-Roazen extends this to imply that "confusion" would remain a constitutive element of all human languages thereafter: "It would constitute the invariable core of the variable being we call a tongue, the inalterable kernel of every alteration of speech."[14] This interpretation chimes perfectly with the treatment of Babel in the *Abreujamens* as the release of humanity from the tyranny of an infantile babble that is identified with a tyrannical first parent's attempt to wield localized power, into a "scattered" polyglot, procreative, and yet coherent world. Dante's builders forget a language that remains only as the trace of its confounding, the moment that it was lost. I would suggest that one missing element in this process of forgetting is the maternal. Paolino's builders are embedded in a text that works hard to forget the maternal and, by extension, it would seem, to erase the concept of the mother tongue.

The key to this problematic treatment of the mother tongue is furnished by Gary Cestaro's detailed work on Dante's treatment of language acquisition.[15] According to Cestaro, medieval authors borrowed a classical view of language acquisition as the task not of the mother, but of the nurse: an enslaved, often foreign woman. Milk and language were delivered by a surrogate who would not necessarily (if ever) have been a "native" speaker of the Latin she taught the infant Roman citizen. For medieval and early

Renaissance writers, Latin was irredeemably "foreign," but in such civic centers as Florence, Barcelona, or even Avignon, the wet nurse was often a poor woman, or even a slave who had acquired the vernacular she taught her charge through a painful process of losing her freedom, her religion, and her first language.[16] Cestaro has made a persuasive argument for the *nutrix* tongue to be viewed not as "mother" tongue but as "other" tongue, associated explicitly with the abject, reflecting a "paradigm that dictates the rejection of the nursing body as a prerequisite to rational language and selfhood."[17] Dante's *De vulgari eloquentia* (1.1.2–3) distinguishes between the mimetic acquisition of language in infancy and the more distant learned acquisition of grammar, but Cestaro points out that Dante also credits Adam (the first speaker) with neither a mother nor milk (1.6.1). The peaceful early language acquisition with the mother is forgotten (if it ever happened at all) as the child enters the violent, disciplinarian realm of the "quasi-mother" Grammar who offers milk while brandishing a governess's scourge. As Valerie Fildes has commented, employers of wet nurses who did not share their language or religion were nervous about the linguistic imprinting of infants through lullabies, stories, or milk, but this tension reflects a broader association of nurturing femininity with "horror," the abject physicality that demanded the nursing woman's exclusion from the human (masculine) society of the schoolroom. Cestaro comments: "Lacan is, in a sense, very classical in his insistence on the barring and exclusion of maternal desire as constituent of the ego."[18] In this spirit, I would comment that when Agamben discusses a prelinguistic, infantile "experience" as something that precedes and is destroyed by language acquisition, he appears to be suppressing the maternal too, even by evading any mention in so many words of its role. The nursing mother who imparts language is both visible in medieval piety and invisible, even horrifying, in medieval society. Her milk is viewed as an altered form of menstrual blood, a source of considerable anxiety. Just as in the early modern period, the idealized dyad of nursing mother and her infant would be reversed into the blood-sucking vampire feeding on its adult victim, so the nurturing mother or nurse could be the reverse of the "venomous" menstruating woman whose presence could dissolve the mortar of the Tower of Babel.[19] To return to Balmary's critique of Babel, Balmary points out that although it enumerates the names of more than seventy descendants of Noah (Gen. 10), only three women are named between chapters 4 and 11 of the book of Genesis, and women appear to be absent from the story of Babel.[20]

In the case of Paolino's text of 1328, the transition from Latin to a vehicular Romance language involves not exactly forgetting, but a form of resistance to the concept of a shared original language. At the same time, the *mantenedors* of Toulouse's nascent poetic school (its annual competition was officially founded in 1324) were engaged in the enterprise of "maintaining," safeguarding, and actively remembering a poetic language that they believed to be in decline. As the Toulouse Consistory sought to empty its poetic language of "foreign," corrupt, or heretical elements, it projected this process onto feminine personifications of Philosophy, and of the Virgin Mary, who are both described in implicitly maternal terms as fountains of (liquid) learning. While Avignon Occitan manuscripts such as that produced by Peyre de Paternas address female patrons, the Toulouse Consistory was for men only.

Luce Irigaray, whose work, like that of Balmary, reflects a critical engagement with the work of Lacan, has written on the energetic suppression of the feminine that characterizes much didactic and philosophical writing, to the extent that omissions may denote the site of the suppressed feminine.[21] The suppressed or forgotten feminine may by extension be the (m)other tongue. Certainly, in the work of Irigaray, women's language is grounded both in women's corporeality and in their cultural position as other. Irigaray's theory has been criticized by some scholars on the grounds of biological determinism, but (as she herself has implicitly acknowledged in her writings about medieval representations of the lineage of the Virgin) it is very pertinent to the broad association that was made in medieval culture between femininity and the corporeal. The Toulousain poets' Marian verses drew on sources such as Richard de Saint-Laurent's *Mariale* (c. 1239), which plays extensive variations on what Jill Ross has described as "the corporeal imagery of metaphor and allegory as modes of enfleshing." Maternal body and (m)other tongue are closely connected through the association of body and its enclosure in words or space. Ross cites the association that is implicitly made in vernacular Marian poetry (Castilian and Galician-Portuguese) between *mater* and *materia,* both earthly "matter" and the *materia* necessary for the composition of a text.[22] However, the maternal aspects of the mother tongue are singularly absent from the Toulouse Consistory's writings on language and poetics.

Pueritia and the (m)other tongue are directly connected to the tensions between Latin, Occitan, and French in fourteenth-century Toulouse. The Toulouse Consistory emerged from a sociopolitical situation that differed from the conditions in which Paolino's manuscript was translated in papal Avignon. Avignon in the 1320s had been the focus of intensive patronage by popes who were born and educated (at least in childhood) in Occitan-speaking lands. Two such instances have already been touched upon. There were links between Avignonese textual production and that of Toulouse, but Avignon was a multilingual, highly hierarchized environment. It is the site of a fertile meeting between Italian, Provençal, Languedocian, northern French, and many other (mostly clerical) communities through the vehicular language of Latin. Toulouse, however, was a city with a strong linguistic identity. The relationships that obtained in Toulouse between Latin, French, and the local vernacular were scored through with political and historical tensions. The work of the Toulousain Consistory was only one facet of a strong civic identification with the Occitan language, one that continued well into the early modern era. The Consistory aimed to develop a poetic idiom modeled on the troubadour koine, but Latin was used for official proclamations in alternation with Occitan (both spoken and written), and while French influence is very strong in both everyday and literary usage, it was not an imposed or official language until the decree of Villers-Cotterêts in 1539.

In the fourteenth century, Occitan was still the dominant language for the city's politicians, and the Occitan tradition of vernacular charters predated those that were written in French; this should have appealed to a royal administration that was increasingly using French in documents and decrees. Serge Lusignan has noted that although the royal chanceries under Philip IV and Philip VI employed staff who were native to Occitan-speaking regions, documents destined for the Midi were issued not in French but in Latin, on the understanding that they would be translated "in romancio," probably orally, on their arrival. Those Occitan documents that were sent to Paris were not translated (unlike those written in Flemish), which implies that there was little sense of a linguistic barrier. French was not imposed in the Occitan-speaking regions for quite some time, but vernacular expression was still presented as something that was subordinate to Latin both politically and in religious usage.[23]

The sociopolitical context of the Toulouse Consistory and its nascent Occitan linguistic identity has dominated much subsequent criticism, as the city and its leaders had experienced a century of repressive policing on the part of religious authorities, as well as its annexation by the French crown by force and ultimately by succession.[24] There has been much debate over the past two centuries over the perceived status of troubadour poetry in fourteenth-century Toulouse.[25] While it is now generally accepted that no attempts were made to repress either troubadour poetry or Occitan linguistic expression, it remains that the Consistory has been regarded as a public display of religious and civic conformity scored through, in its choice of language and genre, with cultural resistance. The Consistory produced a vernacular *ars poetria* it called the *Leys d'Amors,* which survives in two drafts that are usually attributed to the *mantenedor* commissioned to write the *Leys,* Guilhem Molinier. Both redactions present an unusual example of the relationships between three forms of poetic expression in French, Latin, and Occitan.[26]

The seven laymen poets of Toulouse who founded the *Consistori de la sobregaia companhia del gay saber* in 1323, with a view to holding an annual poetry competition marking Marian devotion and the feast of Holy Cross (from May 1 to 3), were engaged in a tripartite process of cultural resistance and assimilation.[27] They selected a Marian festival and civic ceremonies in emulation of northern French Puy poetry, a vernacular lyric genre that was at that time thriving in northwestern France and Paris, but attempted to use it as a vehicle for preserving the troubadour lyric tradition.[28] Their inaugural letter for the festival was sent out to "diversas partidas de la lenga d'Oc" (diverse parts of the region that speaks the language of Oc) (Anglade, I.i. 9), on the grounds that only poets using languages where the word *Oc* or *O* was used for "yes" could compete (II.ii.179).

According to Joseph Anglade, part of the institutional aspirations of the *Leys d'Amors* within Toulouse lay in the university's repudiation of the vernacular, an "Azotica lingua" (Philistine language) that had been forbidden within its schools by papal letter in 1245. Such policies were standard in a *studium generale.*[29] Elementary grammar classes, however, used the vernacular as a teaching medium, thus ensuring that boys acquired the rudiments of grammar and rhetoric with explanations, glosses, and examples in this allegedly rejected tongue.[30] The Consistory poet had to tread a fine line between his "native" use of the language of Oc, the acquired formal medium that he chose to use for poetic contests (and accessorily for Marian devotion), and the Latin basis for that acquisition. Here, his *pueritia* is made explicit, as he learns a specific poetic language in order to enter a masculine society of fellow practitioners of *trobar.* Education involves a twofold process: he acquires the refined poetic (vehicular) form of Occitan just as he rids himself of its less acceptable aspects. This process appears in the first draft of the *Leys d'Amors* as a strange rhetorical vice called *allebolus* (transcription mine):[31]

> Lo ters vicis es allebolus. Et es allebolus estranha sentensa so es improprietatz de sentensa. laquals improprietatz de sentensa se fay en motas manieras. segon qu'om pot vezer en jos en las figuras de tropus.

E dizem estranha sentensa. so es improprietatz de sentensa. a significar e demostrar que per so non es dicha estranha perque sia dautru ni destranh lengatge quom no entenda comunalmen. Ans es be dun meteysh lengatge. mas que impropriamen es dicha. Quar una cauza ditz e pauza. et hom ne enten autra.[32]

[The third vice is *allebolus,* and *allebolus* is an *estranh* (strange/foreign) sentence, that is, an impropriety of sentence. That impropriety of sentence is made in various ways, as one can see below in the figures of *tropus*. And we say *estranha sentensa,* that is, "impropriety of sentence," in signifying and designating [it], because it is not called *estranh* because it comes from another [language], or a strange language that is not commonly understood. Instead, it comes from the same language, but it is spoken improperly, for it enunciates and posits one thing, but you understand another.]

There follows a short mnemonic poem:

    Allebolus vol dir estranha
    Sentensa, perque s'acompanha.
    Tropus de luy. Que li desfassa.
    Lo vici ques am luy s'enlassa.
    Alleos grec es qu'estranh sona.
    E bole sentensa nos dona.
    Mas per estranh deu cascus prendre.
    Improprietat. Quar entendre.
    Fay comunalmen autra cauza.
    Qu'om ni pronuncia ni pauza.

[Allebolus means an *estranha* sentence because Tropus takes it as its companion, for it [Tropus] undoes the vice that winds itself about it. *Alleos* is Greek, it [designates that which] sounds *estranh,* and *bole* gives us "sentence." But by *estranh* everyone must understand "impropriety," for it commonly makes you understand something that differs from the thing it pronounces or states.]

By *sentensa* the *Leys* most probably designates a grammatical *sententia,* the precursor to our modern "sentence." However, *sententia* might also have meant "a sententious or moral proposition," and in this context an impropriety may have had either a moral or theological dimension. In the second draft of 1356, it is noted that a prize poem dealing with theology should be censured "if its *sententia* is not clear and manifest, or [not] approved by the inquisitor" (si donx la sentensa no era clara e manifesta, o aproada per l'Enquiridor) (Anglade, II.23).[33] Meanwhile, in grammatical treatises, *improprietas* concerns unclear expression and difficulties of communication.[34] There is something provocative about the use of a pseudo-Greek neologism to describe the disruptive and "improper" impact of an unfamiliar word on an enunciation. *Allebolus* is a puzzling intrusion, as he is described in an allegorical narrative as the father of many rhetorical tropes such as metaphor and allegory, both of which are defined by their ability to create several meanings in a single utterance.[35]

The term *estranh* is particularly tricky for the definition of *allebolus*. *Estranh* is glossed as a word or expression from the language shared by both speaker and audience ("un meteysh lengatge"), and it is defined neither by its foreignness nor by its rarity, but purely by its *improprietas,* its ability to garble the sense of an enunciation. Indeed, the text's insistence on correcting the reader's assumption that *estranh* signals foreignness or alterity is striking. *Allebolus* may be read, it seems, as either a disrupting insertion of a term in spoken expression, or simply an instance of clumsy or unusual expression, or (as its last feature) a device that creates double meanings beyond the literal sense of the words on the page. This clumsy definition points to innovation of a sort, for *allebolus* is in fact no more than a development of *soloecismus,* a mistake made in multiple words (as opposed to *barbarismus,* a mistake occurring in a single word). The *Leys* goes on to specify that the difference rests in the fact that *soloecismus* affects only *oratio* (speech), whereas *allebolus* affects *sentensa,* the sense arising from the discourse. *Barbarismus* affects *dictio,* and *allebolus,* again, affects only the *sentensa* (Gatien-Arnoult, III.18). However, as without *dictio* or *oratio* there can be no *sentensa* (as all expressions are products of speech), this definition would make the three vices more interdependent than the *Leys* claims.

Allebolus is an example of the pseudo-Greek learning that was in vogue in university grammars of the thirteenth century, and it specifically echoes etymologies provided in Uguccione da Pisa's *Derivationes* (c. 1200), Everard of Béthune's *Graecismus* (c. 1212), and John of Genoa's *Catholicon* (a simplified version of Uguccione's dictionary, dated 1286), all of which earn references in the second draft of the *Leys d'Amors* as, respectively, the "Derivayre"; the "Grecisme"; and, in the second redaction, the "Catholicon."[36] More specifically, *allebolus* reads like a calque of *allotheta,* a figure of construction that appears in the *Catholicon* between the categories of *schema* and *tropus:* "Allotheta est improprietas constructionis ex eo quod dictiones in ea posite construuntur in diversitate accidentum, ut ego Sortes, lego." *Allotheta* (taken by John of Genoa from Uguccione, as *allon,* "other" and *thesis,* "position") is an impropriety of construction, placing words together in confusing juxtapositions, such as "ego, Socrates, lego" (I, Socrates, read).[37] Unglossed copies of the *Catholicon* include a variation on the famous tale of the origins of *soloecismus,* and it provides a hint of what *allebolus,* a dissimilar twin of *soloecismus,* may represent in the *Leys d'Amors.*[38]

The citizens of the city of Soloi spent some time living in Athenian homes in the hope of learning Greek, but all they did was corrupt both their own and the Athenian language. In disgust, the Greeks coined the phrase *soloecismus,* that is, "the custom and habits of the people of Soloi." John of Genoa explains that they had a confused language ("linguam habebant confusam") because of the geographical location of their city between two linguistic regions ("in confinio grece et barbare") and because they sought to claim both the Greek and the Barbarian languages as their own. Undeterred, these intrepid if inept linguists traveled west to Rome and corrupted the Latin language to the extent that any mistake found in a sequence of words came to be named after them. They were incapable of stringing together a coherent sentence in Latin, and they infected Roman speech. John cites Donatus to emphasize that *soloecismus* is not *barbarismus. Barbarismus* is a mistake occurring within a single word, but *soloecismus,* far more damagingly, affects the order of all the components of a sentence and compromises communication.

John's story may have had a variety of meanings for readers in the schoolrooms of western Europe, but for the authors of the Toulousain *Leys d'Amors* there was much promise in the idea of converting incoherent and uneducated prose into poetry not by banishing but by embracing *soloecismus.* A vernacular poet who chooses to formulate his extracurricular learning in the language and structures of Latin grammatical treatises is at risk of acting like the inhabitant of Soloi, forsaking his barbarian territory to seek fluency in the learning of both Greece and Rome, only to produce a horrible and unintelligible compromise.

Such confusions might well have occurred in the schoolroom, as grammatical treatises were taught through the vernacular rather than Latin, a technique recommended by Alexander de Villa Dei, who advises the student to learn the *Doctrinale* by heart, but tells the *grammaticus* to use the students' vernacular as his teaching medium.[39] This implies that students learned the rudiments of poetic rhetoric in Latin through the vernacular from tutors who emphasized the importance of versified expression. Movement between Latin and Romance vernaculars may consequently be envisaged as a pragmatic and relatively transparent process. There are signs, however, of a more complex picture. As opposed to the direct translation expressed as "romanssar lati," the transferal of meaning and hermeneutical process of *translatio* appears as a key issue at other points of the text, especially in the allegorical treatise of the rhetorical vices that introduced *allebolus*, in book 4 of the first redaction (Gatien-Arnoult, III.112–321). John Marshall summarized this self-contained treatise as follows:[40]

> He [Guilhem Molinier] wished to show how the "vices" (of language or style) which may mar a literary work can also be seen to be connected with—even give rise to—a whole series of tricks of style which are acceptable and even laudable when used in their proper context and with a proper literary motive (when Rhetoric has "made peace," in fact). He also wished to show connexions between these tricks of style and the traditional flowers of rhetoric (*flores rhetorici*). (III.40)

The narrative frame for this subsection is initially clear and tripartite. First comes a psychomachia, next a genealogy, and finally a depiction of a garden in which harmony is restored through the gift of flowers. The structure peters out as the treatise moves into examples and subcategories among the granddaughters of *allebolus*.[41] There is a great war between three kings and three queens. King Barbarisme shoots ten arrows at Queen Dictio (the *vitia annexa*), and King Soloecisme shoots his ten arrows at Queen Oratio (further *vitia annexa*). Finally King Allebolus shoots only one arrow (Improprietat) at Queen Sentensa. "Madona Rethorica" makes peace by marrying each king to the sister of each queen, so that Barbarisme marries Dictio's sister Methaplasmus and begets fourteen *metaplasmi;* Soloecisme marries Oratio's sister Scema (also known as "Alleotheca," *allotheta*) and begets twenty-two *schemata*; and King Allebolus marries Tropus and begets thirteen *tropi*, who in turn produce fifteen daughters of their own.[42] *Allebolus* gamely joins *barbarismus* and *soloecismus* in attacking clear speech, expression, and oratory, but he does not have ten arrows at his disposal. He is credited instead with only one function, that of disrupting the sense of a sentence with improper expression. However, once he is allied with *tropus,* he may in turn be fruitful and produce thirteen equally fertile forms of oratorial display. Allebolus's daughter Allegoria marries "Alexis, que vol dir estranh parlar" ("A-lexis," which means *estranh,* "speech"), and produces seven daughters, including irony and sarcasm, which are all ways of saying something different from the literal sense of the words (Gatien-Arnoult, III.22–24).

Fruitful marriages are not necessarily happy, and Soloecisme and his wife, Scema, are continually at odds because she rails against her husband's outrageous treatment of her sister Oratio (III.20–22). Peacemaking Madona Rethorica picks flowers from her garden to console the offspring of the unhappy marriage of Soloecisme and the harmonious union of Allebolus. For example, the flower of rhetoric Translatio is allotted the role of soothing and cheering Allebolus's daughter Metaphora. As the verse summary of the text neatly says: "Metaphora s'alegra trop, / Quan ve Translacio de prop" (Metaphor cheers up enormously when she sees Translatio close by) (*Flors del Gay Saber,* lines 4333–34). Metaphor even seems to be subordinate to her, as Translatio has an enhancing function, "Qar es flors plazens agradiva, / Aquesta forma transsumptiva" (for this "transsumptive" form of speech is a pleasing, agreeable flower) (*Flors del Gay Saber,* lines 5937–39). *Transumptio* is yet another term for metaphor.

Translatio is lifted from the *Rhetorica ad Herennium,* book 4, § 21, and *metaphora* from the same source (§ 45) noting that they are synonyms: "Methafora es transumptios o translatios duna dictio que reprezenta autre significat" (Metaphor is the *transsumptio* or transposition of an enunciation so that it represents another meaning) (Gatien-Arnoult, III.194), and that both are to be constructed identically, "e fay se Translatios per aquela meteyssha maniera que Metafora" (III.200).[43] Marshall claimed that taking the Greek and Latin synonyms and treating them as different but complementary objects was innovatory. In fact, it is simply lifted from glosses on the *Graecismus,* which established connections between words, such as *transumptio* and *metaphora:* "Concordat autem metaphora cum quodam colore rethorico qui dicitur transumptio." Crucially, one commentator on the *Graecismus* also mistakenly identified *translatio* with the transferal of meaning from one language to another (the term used for this was *interpretatio*) and established yet another connection between two separate terms (*Graecismus,* bk. 10, line 72).[44]

Metaphora's impropriety is glossed in terms of linguistic diversity. To speak poetically of birds singing in their diverse languages is deemed inappropriate, for languages are spoken only by men and women, but it may be appropriate because languages are diverse (Gatien-Arnoult, III.198–200). However, *Translatio* rests on apparently "improper" connections that may be made between human and animal sounds. A young woman, Berta, is so frail that she barely meows, "Ta freols es, qu'apenas miula" and only cats are able to use that particular language (III.202). Metaphor draws attention to the diversity of tongues, and *translatio* may transpose the languages of animals into the human realm. Metaphor and *translatio* in the first redaction of the *Leys d'Amors* appear to be complementary, for *translatio*'s ability to transfer and to gloss its object from one idiom or context to another is helpful to Metaphor's transpositions of meaning. The *Flors del Gay Saber* add that *translatio* breathes new life into dead words (*Flors del Gay Saber*, lines 5953–54), a sentiment that hints at a less than flattering view of Latin. *Translatio* in other texts preserved its other sense of a transfer of power or a usurpation, and it follows that the vision in the *Leys* of transferal of meaning among the offspring of *allebolus* is surprisingly peaceful.[45]

In this allegory of rhetoric (within which Allegoria is married to *Alexis*, representative of *estranh* speech), metaphor appears to depend not on rhetorical effects alone, but on a heightened awareness of the relationships between styles of expression and languages. *Translatio* may be *transsumptiva* because it also stands for the hermeneutical activity of both performer and audience, as they transpose words into their own subjective and linguistic contexts. Elsewhere, the *Leys d'Amors* also attempt to reconcile vernacular usage with Latin proscriptions, for example, saying that tautology may not be well regarded, but that it is commonly used in the vernacular.[46] In these sections, it is evident that there is a more flexible interlinguistic policy at work, aiming not to bend vernacular usage to Latin models, but rather to create a rhetoric in which several registers and several languages may work together to produce new poetry.

There is no *allebolus* in the second redaction of 1356, for book 4 was cut. Yet *allebolus* is implicitly identified and banished in several parts of the revised work. The *Leys* appears to apply a dynamic perception of the relation between Latin and vernacular, as well as between vernaculars. It rules on the irregular orthography and grammar of troubadours of the previous two centuries, declaring that the usage of the past can be supplemented by regional or colloquial variations in the present (Anglade, III.iii.113). There remains one problem, however, and that concerns the vulnerable status of the Occitan koine itself (III.iii.113–14). If the poet turns to local usage, he may be unpleasantly surprised:

> E si per aquel maniera hom no s'en pot enformar, deu recorre a la maniera de parlar acostumat cominalmen per una dyocesi; et aysso es

la cauza mas greus cant a dictar en romans que deguna autre que puscam trobar, quar .I. mot que yeu entendray tu no entendras; et aysso es per la diversitat d'u meteys lengatge quar tu que seras d'una vila, laquals es en Tolza, hauras acostumat .I. mot et yeu que seray d'autra vila laquals sera yshamens en Tolza n'auray acostumat .I. autre et enayssi serem divers.

[And if one cannot find it out that way, one should turn to the speech commonly used in a diocese. And that is the hardest thing of any that may be found, concerning reciting poetry in *romans,* because I might understand one word, and you won't understand it. That is because of the diversity of a single language, because you, being from one district [*vila*] in Toulouse, will be used to using one word and I, being from another district, also in Toulouse, will use another, and so we will differ.]

In the first redaction, *allebolus* only arose within *meteysh lengatge*. Here, *meteysh lengatge* is indeed deeply *estranh*. If the Toulousain audience can understand only part of a Toulousain poet's words, it means that even a poem composed in the koine, adhering to the rules of rhetoric and versification, must be infected by *allebolus*. According to the second redaction, *estranh* refers strictly to vernacular words (Anglade, III.iii.106–8), which means that *allebolus* may be found in action in troubadour poetry. However, the concept of *estranh* has altered slightly, for the revised *Leys* declares those languages *estranhs* that are not allowed to compete in the poetry contests and do not contain the word *Oc* or *O* for "yes," such as French, Norman, Picard, Breton, Flemish, English, Lombard, Navarrese, Castilian, or German. The competition admits all the dialects of "la lenga d'Oc" with a single exception: "Pero de nostra leys s'aluenha / La parladura de Gascuenha" (But the speech of Gascony is distant from our laws) (Anglade, II.ii.178–79). The inhabitants of Toulouse include many who have picked up strange linguistic habits from neighboring Gascony (Anglade, III.iii.163–64). Toulouse is like Athens or Rome after the arrival of the inhabitants of Soloi, those students whose intent pursuit of second-language acquisition can only lead to the corruption of local speech. Despite its resonant borrowings of university learning, the second redaction hints at a fallen city similar in its confusion to the aftermath of the Tower of Babel, and the *Leys d'Amors* starts to look like a pointless monument to the aspirations of its inhabitants.

The *Leys* of 1356 mentions in passing that *nostre lengatje* suffers from a limited vocabulary, so the aspiring poet should turn to Latin for such useful words as, they suggest, *soloecisme, scema,* and *allotheta* (Anglade, III.iii.108). Lying unacknowledged behind more well-established technical terms, *allebolus* is built from fragments of an unfamiliar language to refer to the confusing effects of linguistic obscurity. In that process, language that is *estranh* is allowed into literary expression via the marriage of metaphor and translation. *Allebolus* highlights the tensions between rhetorical rules and vernacular expression. It also allows the aspiring poet to consider the extent to which he may or may not own the language that he may consider naively to be his mother tongue. Modern writers on diglossia have noted such moments of tension and inconsistency as evidence that literary composition may be placed in between the concepts of mother tongue and other tongue, in a realm of learned and authoritative expression that is always seeking official approval.[47] In "making strange" (or "making foreign") both Latin and the vernaculars, the *Leys* also allows them to exist side by side, to fertilize each other and to produce new and rich flowers of rhetoric.

In conclusion, the *Leys d'Amors* may be viewed as an enterprise that sought to explore and to develop a sense of the fertile multiplicity of languages, but that was marked by moral anxiety over the confusion of tongues. It is a text that transplants the (m)other tongue into the masculine preserve of the schoolroom and finds it wanting, full of impropriety. In nearby Avignon, language acquisition was celebrated as the liberation of the *puer* from the confines of a (m)other tongue that was represented as neither maternal nor *nutrix,* but as a masculine tyranny. Gary Cestaro glosses the linguistic pessimism of John of Salisbury, who concluded, he suggests, that "in a postlapsarian world, the arts are our only hope."[48] Both Avignon and Toulouse found different ways of imagining the hope that the arts curriculum could bring when the local vernacular seemed to be losing its literary prestige.

Part 2

LANGUAGE POLITICS

4

TRANSLATION SCANDALS

IN MEDIEVAL RHETORIC, *translatio* refers to interpretation and glossing, the transfer of meaning from one word to another. It also has the sense of the usurpation of either meaning or power, and by this gloss, the translator may be seen trying to seize control of a place or of a text.[1] As Catalan literary prose developed in the royal chancery and households during the last quarter of the fourteenth century, translation became the means of forging a new literary idiom. Latin treatises and chronicles, Ovid's *Metamorphoses*, Dante's *Divine Comedy*, and Boccaccio's *Decameron* and *Corbaccio* were all translated into Catalan by members of the royal households of Pere IV (1319–87), Joan I (1387–96), and Martí I l'Humá (1397–1410).[2]

Translation has an ambiguous relationship with multilingualism. It requires the intervention of at least one person in possession of several languages, but it invokes an intended reader who is, by definition, monolingual. The translator's complex task is to render a text in a credible and legible form for a reader who may not know about the original text's cultural or literary context. Lawrence Venuti has commented at length on the phenomenon of "domestication," by which he means those choices that are made to select a particular foreign work from many others, then to either omit or maintain cultural markers within that text, and finally to render the base text in a particular dialect or register. Canon formation and cultural stereotyping are both involved in the process of literary translation. Venuti emphasizes also that domestication is not coterminous with assimilation; a text may be appropriated by the varied domestic audience in ways that are subversive of the dominant ideologies: "Translation is scandalous because it can create different values and practices, whatever the domestic setting."[3] Venuti proposes an "ethics of translation" that would work across borders to create an "intercultural" identity, "not merely in the sense of straddling two cultures, domestic and foreign, but crossing the cultural borders among domestic audiences."[4] Venuti is concerned with translation from one language into another (usually English). Much translation in the later Middle Ages either worked through more than two languages at a time or used a combination of oral and written work.

There are instances of direct, solitary translation. In 1389 and 1390, King Joan I and Violant sent out letters urgently requesting copies of Guillem Nicolau's rumored translation of Ovid's *Heroides*.[5] Nicolau produced his own translation and gloss; others worked in teams for pragmatic reasons. According to Carlos Alvar, Alonso de Cartagena recounts the method he used with Juan Alfonso de Zamora in 1422 for translating the ninth and tenth books of Boccaccio's *De casibus virorum illustrium* into Castilian: one man translated orally from the Latin text into Castilian, as the other wrote it down.[6] This was because Juan Alfonso de Zamora knew very little Latin. He also had a weak command of Catalan, so his translation into Castilian of Antoni Canals's Catalan version of Valerius Maximus's *Facta et dicta memorabilia* (1418–19) was produced with a collaborator who checked a copy of the Latin text.[7] Such indirect networks of translation are not uncommon, especially with works that had been glossed and translated by many others. Alfonso Gómez de Zamora produced a Castilian Orosius (c. 1439) from Pedro de Parmerola's Aragonese version of an Italian translation by Bono Giamboni (1291).[8] Nor was the movement solely from Latin into the vernacular, as Antoni Ginebreda's Catalan version of Boethius's *De Consolatione Philosophiae* (c. 1390) was translated back into Latin in 1476.[9]

A further issue in translation is the context into which the translator placed the work. Alain Chartier's *Belle Dame sans mercy* (1424) was translated into Catalan by Francesc Oliver (before 1457). One marginal note shows that either this translator or a scribe identified one particular passage as a translation of Boccaccio's *Elegia di Madonna Fiammetta* and furnished the relevant section of that text in Catalan.[10] This is a very seductive example of a particular aspect of "domestication." We might assume that the translator worked from Chartier to the Catalan text without consulting other works, but in fact, he was actively reading the French poem in terms of a Tuscan prose narrative that would not appear to be directly relevant. The Catalan audience for Chartier read the poem in terms of an established literary canon predicated on Boccaccio; similarly, Ferran Valentí refers to Boccaccio's *Fiammetta* and *Corbaccio* on a par with classical works in his preface to his translation of Cicero's *Paradoxa stoicorum*.[11]

Translations may be "scandalous" in other ways as well. While other parts of Europe in the same period began to police the translation of the Bible into the vernacular on suspicion of heresy, Castilian and Catalan translators came under pressure to translate from Latin, rather than from Hebrew, scripture. Violant; her husband, Joan I; and his brother Martí commissioned and owned translated Bibles between the years 1400 and 1427. By the mid- to late fifteenth century, however, translated Bibles that included the Old Testament were destroyed by inquisitors, on suspicion that they were translated from Hebrew.[12] Similarly, Carlos Alvar has commented on the implausibly small number of Muslim names (only two out of fifty) that he collated as authors of fifteenth-century translations.[13]

In this chapter I will address three texts that make explicit the tensions of translation. First, Bernat Metge's *Lo Somni* shows how gender and borders are used to figure the complex work of rendering multiple sources from Latin and Tuscan in Catalan prose. In the second part, I examine a trilingual text, the anonymous *Història de l'amat Frondino e de Brisona*, with a view to asking how a culture that privileges monolingualism as an ideological goal can produce such a work. I close my enquiry with a short consideration of a later French manuscript that has no text, only images.

Lo Somni

Bernat Metge (c. 1340/46–1413) is a key figure in the development of Catalan prose literature. He inserts translated fragments of Alain de Lille's *Anticlaudianus* and Boethius's *Consolation of Philosophy* in his verse *Libre de Fortuna e Prudència* (internally dated to 1381). He also translated the Pseudo-Ovidian *De vetula* (*Ovidi enamorat*, before 1388) and Petrarch's tale of Griselda (dated 1388). In the turmoil surrounding the catastrophic end to the reign of Joan I (and probably when he was indicted as a prominent member of the late king's corrupt circle of advisers), Bernat Metge composed an intriguing and complex text, the *Somni* (The Dream).[14] The *Somni* (completed by April 1399) directs a dazzling display of Metge's erudition at his new king, Martí, in the hope of gaining readmission to the royal court.[15] As Stefano Cingolani has demonstrated at length, Metge's work inserts lengthy extracts of a Catalan version of Boccaccio's *Corbaccio* into a work that borrows its consolation narrative from Boethius and places the most extensive Boccaccian passages in the mouth of the mythological figure of Tiresias.

Synopsis

Book 1: Metge falls asleep in prison and dreams that he is visited by the ghost of King Joan I and his two companions, the blind seer Tiresias and the musician Orpheus. The king and his erstwhile servant discuss the immortality of the soul. Metge presents a skeptical, epicurean point of view and the king disproves it, citing classical and biblical authorities. Book 2: Metge asks the king how he died, but receives no exact reply. Joan narrates the debate staged between Satan and the Virgin Mary over his sins and says that he has been condemned to dwell in Purgatory until the end of the papal schism, despite his well-received endorsement of the Immaculate Conception. Book 3: Orpheus tells his story (taken from Ovid). Tiresias berates Metge for finding such stories pleasurable and rails against the frailty of love and women. Orpheus then describes the torments of Hell, and Tiresias tells his own story in an attempt to cure Metge's delusions, but their dialogue slips once more into a misogynistic tirade on his part. Tiresias urges Metge to believe that his mistress is unfaithful. Book 4: A downcast Metge defends women by citing exemplary women (including the new queen, Maria de Luna) and criticizing men, but Tiresias believes that he has won the debate. As dawn breaks, the three visitors fade away and the prisoner is left in gloomy isolation.

All four protagonists are liminal figures, placed in the borderland between sleep and awakening that is traditional in dream visions. The protagonist wishes to be freed from the spiritual burden of his involvement in his former king's sudden death, but he is not as yet freed from its political aftermath. He wants to love his mistress as a lover should, but he cannot resist feeling the negative impact of Tiresias's scornful comments. The king's soul inhabits a borderland between the damned and the blessed both because of his sudden death and his support for the Schism during his lifetime. He devotes most of book 1 to defending the very idea that his soul could have survived his death, and book 2 to describing the trial it has endured in the other world. He is further tormented by the constant presence of an irritable old man and an irritating minstrel. Orpheus has visited the underworld while he was still alive and acts as the mouthpiece for a description of Hell and its torments. He describes a loving devotion to his wife that leads him to reject the love of all women and to die at their hands. Tiresias is placed in between masculine and feminine identities. He draws on his personal experience of living as a woman to urge his listeners to avoid any relationship with women at all. The text is equally divided, replete with quotations from existing translations, translations from Latin and Tuscan, and allusions to other texts.

The *Somni* is uneven in part because it falls into two very different halves. The first two books are concerned with immediate spiritual and political matters relating to the king's death, and the second two are catalogs of commonplaces in the *querelle des femmes,* framed by mythical narratives. Book 1 contains translations of extracts from Cicero, Aristotelian treatises, and Patristic writings. Book 2 cites Petrarch, as do books 3 and 4, which also draw heavily on Boccaccio. Metge's dialogue with Tiresias in books 3 and 4 clearly parodies that between Boethius's protagonist and his Philosophy, and it dominates the second half of the *Somni.* There is surely a new layer of irony in the misogynistic seer's adoption of a role allotted to this most famous of feminine allegorical personifications. Given the abrupt contrast between the two halves, it is tempting to argue that Metge uses traditional material concerning men's attitudes toward women to develop ideas that were already present in books 1 and 2. This is all the more likely because of the sudden introduction in book 3 of the married protagonist's doubts concerning his mistress, which appear to bear no relation to the theological musings of the political prisoner in books 1 and 2. I would argue that Metge uses gender as an accessible medium in which he can explore more complex ideas concerning authority and control in translation.

In book 4, Tiresias delivers an attack on women based on his personal experience of being a woman. He underlines their patronage of both languages and literature:

> De venitat han axí plen lo cap, que inpossible és que t ho pogués tot dir; emperò diré't ço que me'n recorde. Elles entenen ésser en gran felicitat haver molt delicament e loçania, e saber parlar diverses lengatges, recorda moltes cançons e novas rimades, al.legar dits de trobadors e las *Epistolas* de Ovidi, recitar les ystòrias de Lançelot, de Tristany, del rey Artús e de quants amorosos són stats a lur temps; argumentar, offender, deffendre e rahonar un fet, saber bé respondre a aquells qui de amor les enqueren, haver les galtes ben plenas e vermellas, e grossas anques e grossos pits.

> [Their heads are so full of vanity that it is impossible to tell you all of it, but I will tell you what I remember. They are very happy when they get a great deal of flirting and praise, speak several languages, recall many *cançons* and *noves rimades,* know the tales of troubadours and Ovid's *Heroides,* recite the stories of Lancelot, of Tristan, of King Arthur, and of all lovers who have existed since their time; when they are arguing, proffering, defending, and reasoning a fact, when they can reply well to whoever asks them for their love, [and] when they have cheeks that are round and red, big buttocks, and big breasts.]

Tiresias's speech is already evidence of this patronage, because it is adapted from the antifeminist rants of Boccaccio's notoriously unreliable narrator in the *Corbaccio*.[16] The pleasure to be found in knowing several languages is embedded in this translated citation of a Tuscan text, placed in the mouth of a figure borrowed from classical literature. Tiresias's words allude to the literary passions of the court of Joan I and his second wife, Violant de Bar.[17]

The *Somni*'s defense of women is an extended display of Metge's already well-known skills as a translator. Tiresias cites Boccaccio to attack women, and much of the protagonist's defense of women is translated from Petrarch's *Familiares*. This includes praise of those women who invented writing, wrote poetry, and knew languages, such as "Proba, the wife of Adelphus, who was expert in Latin and Greek and other languages" (328). Metge adds a reference to his own translation of Petrarch's tale (itself a translation) of Griselda, "la istòria de la qual fou per mi de latí en vulgar transportada" (the tale of whom was translated by me from Latin into the vernacular). He claims that it is now so famous that women recite the tale by night and when they are spinning by the fire. It seems that women may provide an audience for the works of Petrarch if a translator is willing to accommodate their wishes. Of course, this is ironic. Petrarch's Latin text was a translation of Boccaccio's tale, and Metge's contribution seems to have been to restore a moralizing, slightly allegorical Latin rendering back to the vernacular to the point that it appeals to oral storytellers.[18] Metge's paradoxical praise of "his" Griselda echoes Tiresias's words, in that he dismisses the intellectual and social value of his women patrons at the same time as he acknowledges their role in making him a famous author. This is especially intriguing with respect to the complex treatment of women readers in the Griselda tradition. The ideal reader and transmitter of the tale might well be an uneducated peasant woman, in line with its humble heroine, but Metge's dedicatee, Isabel de Guimerà, was a prominent female member of the bibliophile royal court and it is debatable if she would have found such an association attractive, unless it was intended to amuse her. After all, Metge had framed his *Valter e Griselda* with his version of Petrarch's prefatory words, urging his women readers not to seek to emulate the peasant martyr, but to view the tale figuratively as a spur to greater virtue in themselves (118). Were a noblewoman to transmit the tale while spinning at her hearth, her actions would reveal the superficiality of her reading of it, as she would have resorted to masquerading as Valter's humble wife.

Tiresias is also a turbulent figure for the sexual and literary politics of the *Somni*. He appears in several myths as a figure of interruption and unwelcome knowledge.[19] Tiresias interrupts two snakes as they are mating and is punished by being turned into a woman. Seven years later, she is restored to her original male form when she witnesses yet another pair of snakes mating. Tiresias is invited to arbitrate in a debate between Juno and Jupiter (who are in bed, making love) over whether women enjoy sexual intercourse more than men. He reveals Juno's secret knowledge that women take more pleasure than men, and she blinds him. The blind seer of the *Somni* interrupts Metge's theological conversation with the shade of the king to forbid any insight into future events (specifically the deeds of royal women) and later breaks into Orpheus's account of his mythical adventures to sneer at the musician's naive faith in heterosexual love. Metge protests Tiresias's interruptions of his pleasure both in a debate and as an audience. This stresses that Tiresias's main function is not, as he believes, to disenchant his listener (Tiresias repeatedly confuses his role with that of Boethius's Philosophy), but to interrupt pleasurable encounters between male and female, narrator and listener, or two interlocutors. Metge in turn identifies the seer's crude behavior as masculine. He sets women's good taste in troubadour poetry against men's dubious affection for the lower uses of rhetoric:

> Dançes e cançons dius que escolten les donas ab gran plaer. No m'en meravell, car natural cosa és prendre delit en músicha, e especialment que sia mesclada ab retòrica e poesia, que concorren sovén en les dançes e cansons dictates per bons trobadors. Poch se adeliten los hòmens en oyr semblants cosas, les qual deurien saber per fer fugir ociositat e per poder dir bé lo concebiment de lur pensa. Mas deliten-se molt en oyr truffadors, scarnidors, raylladors, mals parlers, cridadors, avolotadors, jutyadors e migensers de bacallarias e de viltats. (368)

> [You say women listen to *dansas* and *cançons* with great pleasure. I'm not surprised, for it is a natural thing to take delight in music, especially if it is mixed with rhetoric and poetry, which come together often in the *dansas* and *cançons* recited by good troubadours. Men do not take much pleasure in hearing such things, [things] that they should know about to dispel idleness and to express their thoughts well in words. Instead, they delight in listening to tricksters, mockers, jeerers, slanderers, shouters, liars, gamblers, and the fomenters of quarrels and ruin.]

The troubadour Orpheus, armed with his rote and devoted to his lady, has described himself as a man devoted to music and rhetoric. It is Tiresias who finds pleasure in discordant aggression. Interestingly, this passage echoes Bernat Metge's letter on behalf of Joan I, published in 1393 to order the citizens of Barcelona to host a poetry competition modeled on the Toulouse *Consistori de la Gaia Sciencia*.[20] Metge says on that occasion that men should cultivate poetry in the vernacular to avoid idleness, as well as to find entertainment.

Book 2 of the *Somni* describes Orpheus's successful performance before an all-female consistory of Furies, Fates, and goddesses. It seems that somehow the Toulouse school, as it was translated into Bernat Metge's multilayered text, hit a curious translation problem. What Metge seems to be doing is redefining the all-male Toulouse poetic school and competition by aligning himself with "feminine" tastes. Through Tiresias's paradoxical claims and Orpheus's troubadour activity, it emerges that women are the multilingual and educated patrons of good music, poetry, and narrative. They form the ideal audience for multilingual, educated authors such as Metge, but they are also the weak link in a system of secular patronage that was attacked (most famously by Eiximenis) for its sinful frivolity.[21] Femininity is problematic in the *Somni* because what is feminized is literary patronage itself. Metge, the protagonist, is the translator of a tale that has found success among women, he enjoys female patronage, and he hopes that his return to favor will be marked by further success among noblewomen such as the new queen, María de Luna.

The development of Catalan literary culture could be envisaged as a strikingly explicit agonistic process, in which language, genre, and authors are set up in lively new dialogues. Metge's Tiresias struggles to master some form of language that may enable him/her to narrate the experience of having been a woman. Paradoxically, the only cultural register that is available to the blind seer is the tradition of comic misogyny. Metge furnishes him with an example of that discourse that is both decontextualized and misinterpreted, as Tiresias ventriloquizes not the words of a learned sage, but those of a grossly unreliable narrator. Regina Psaki has underlined the recent critical consensus that the *Corbaccio* is an ironic work that plays on male fears of women's "secret knowledge."[22] Tiresias's mythical role is to provide unwanted insight for men into that secret experience, and it is for that reason that Juno strikes him blind. Metge's Tiresias can do no more than repeat ancient commonplaces concerning women's frivolity and cosmetics, but his words overlap with those of serious misogynists such as Eiximenis. Psaki makes the important point that "when an author carefully contextualizes certain utterances to rob them of all validity, but an audience persists in reading them straight, we have the literalist habit of misreading which makes of *Huckleberry Finn,* for example, a racist book."[23] Metge's selective quotations from the *Corbaccio* turn the *Corbaccio* into the misogynous sermon that (according to Psaki) it may be undermining. In so doing, he makes the process of cultural "domestication" in translation explicit. Despite the multiple layers of Tiresias's utterances, he remains stubbornly (and deludedly) "monolingual," insisting that his stereotypes about femininity are empirically based rather than part of a literary tradition.

Metge's knowing translations in the *Somni* are eclectic, displaying the author's learning and what Rosi Braidotti terms "nomadism." Braidotti rests her theory of nomadic reading on the critical distance from patriarchal language that is afforded by the simultaneous experience of several idioms: "The polyglot is a variation of the theme of critical nomadic consciousness; being in between languages constitutes a vantage point in deconstructing identity."[24] It is this concept of the "being in between" that seems to emerge with Metge's Tiresias. His words, traversed as they are by a multiplicity of texts and languages, establish an essential critical distance from their content. Semantically, Tiresias's misogyny becomes the words of an identity so complex that it cannot be fully invested with authority, an illustration of Braidotti's key idea of "a difference within the same culture." Cultures of translation are acutely aware that, in Braidotti's words, "the polyglot has no vernacular, but many lines of transit, of transgression." In the *Somni*, women as both readers and linguists are constructed through several clashing discourses as objects of a mixture of fascination and horror, viewed as the containers for multiple voices, or as empty vessels that may be filled with a tale such as that of Griselda without being capable of doing more than passing it on. However, their discernment in matters of language and expression is praised, to the point that even the Furies are invested with emotional responses to Orpheus's music. Metge uses gender conflict to highlight the cultural conflicts that are usually concealed in a translation and, in so doing, points out the intercultural polyphony that constructs his text. Venuti proposes that if translators maintain awareness of the foreignness of their texts, "culture is not viewed as monolithic or unchanging, but as a shifting sphere of multiple and heterogeneous borders where different histories, languages, experiences, and voices intermingle amid diverse relations of power and privilege."[25]

História de l'amat Frondino e de Brisona

Where fragments remain of a multilingual context for literary production, it is sometimes tempting to prescribe a single language as the dominant one and to ignore the possibility that language choice may carry an ideological or didactic element. Homi Bhabha's writings on colonial oppression point to the development of a "third space" within national cultures, a "cultural space . . . where the negotiation of incommensurable differences creates a tension peculiar to borderline existences."[26] This borderline existence is, I would argue, where such multilingual texts can find voice. If Metge's Tiresias deconstructs the illusory nature of monolingualism at its most triumphant, in the form of a unified prose work, other texts may point out explicitly that they are the products of a multilingual environment.

The trilingual *História de l'amat Frondino e de Brisona* (c. 1400) uses a simple narrative to frame its sophisticated play on language and genre.[27] It offers no narratorial comment on the use of several languages in this text. Each language is confined to its generic frame. The tale's narrative sections are composed in *noves rimades* (octosyllabic rhyming couplets) in a hybrid Occitan-Catalan.[28] Its rondeaux and *virelais* are in French, and its letters are in Catalan prose. In the following summary of the text, I have labeled the Occitan-Catalan narrative verse N, the French lyric element L, and the Catalan prose P:

> (N) Frondino, a squire (line 35), loves the noble lady Brisona (lines 43–45). He asks her permission to go on crusade, and she asks him to swear to wear black and green for her sake (she will do this too): "Ayço faras, / amics: tu portaras / le neyr e.l vert per mi, / ez eu per tu axi" (lines 193–96).
>
> (L) They exchange two poems in writing (hers is on black paper, written in "refined" blue ink. "scrit sus neyr papier / ab color de blau fi." (lines 244–45).
>
> (N) Two years later, he returns and finds out from gossips that she has been unfaithful. The gossips' allegations come in a letter that is not cited.
>
> (P) He writes her, accusing her of forgetting him, and appends a mournful rondeau (L).
>
> (N) Narrative link.
>
> (P) She replies that she is innocent, thinks about him often, and appends a poem too (L).
>
> (N) Narrative link.
>
> (P) Brisona says his letters enable her to imagine his presence when she is alone.
>
> (L) She appends a rondeau.
>
> (N) Narrative link.

(P) Frondino replies with a letter in which he develops a dual theme of speech and food and claims that he is simultaneously "eaten up inside" and starving.

(L) He appends a rondeau.

(N) Narrative link.

(P) She replies in kind and says she is "choked," so that her mouth can only emit sighs. She needs to see him in person because (a) she can no longer write rhetorically because of her intense emotion and (b) she's ruined the paper and ink with her tears and is so blinded that she can no longer write.

(N) Frondino meets up with Brisona. Reunion.

The N sections depict a conventional tale of decorous lovers who exchange vows, poems, and tokens, but Frondino confronts the possibility that Brisona might be less courtly than she seems. Brisona sends to Frondino her first rondeau, written in blue ink on black paper. This medium (not reproduced on the page) hints at her inadequate authority, for she has composed a French song that expresses her emotions, but she needs to add a visual emblem of her loyalty. Moreover, blue ink on black paper might well be illegible, but Brisona's letter might not be designed to be read by Frondino, as it supports a song. The black paper functions as a visual token of the emotion that is represented in turn by the poem, especially given Brisona's later claims that writing and reading involve visual hallucination (*meditatio*) (111–13).

When he reads the gossips' allegations, Frondino writes to her claiming that his anguish has caused him to unbind the tongue of the lover, who should always be tongue-tied before his lady. This letter claims to bring an end to silence, but it highlights a problem: if Frondino has been "tongue-tied" beforehand, were his written and spoken words false? The prose letter, then, appears to represent Frondino's direct communication with Brisona, addressing her as *tu* and presenting his complaints one by one. He explains his decision to write by saying that he is incapable of weeping out his emotions, because he is a *ferm amador* who should not weep. So Frondino's letter aims to supplant the lover's previously inarticulate and emotionally repressed behavior.

In the narrative section, Brisona's reaction to his letter is to weep, before she replies to him by letter. Is she then not a "ferm amadora"? If she has put her reaction into tears, words should be unnecessary. What she does is to complain that Frondino's letter, not his rondeau, seeks to rename her by claiming that she is "falsa e desconexent amadora," when she would rather he persisted in naming her a "leyal e ferma amiga tua" (84). She demands that he writes her more pleasantly, to show deference to her fidelity, and to comfort her with his written presence (84–85). Brisona's next letter expands on the problematic role of the letter as a questionable substitute for an absent lover. She plays on the letter as a cell of memory, which gives her the opportunity to meditate alone on her love from afar, while insinuating that her solitary state was made more painful still, as she found herself "desolada e trista" (86–88).

The narrative says Frondino reads and rereads the "lletra plasent" sent by Brisona (lines 377–79). He sends her by messenger something he hopes is a "clearer" message. What follows is the most dense and strained metaphor of the text. He addresses her as his beloved "sister." He says that their separation has caused his heart to split into several parts within his body, to the extent that bystanders could hear his insides grinding ("cruixents") like sea rolling over ground. Not content with emitting loud crunching, his body is starved of the "vianda" provided by his gazing upon her beauty in his mind. His limbs can now no longer bear to lift food to his mouth, which is just as well because his mouth is emitting the sighs of his heart, "vianda amargosa qui passa per mes estretes dents ab algunes sordes e tristes veus planyents" (bitter food that passes through my clenched teeth with some downcast and miserable wailings) (89). He is simultaneously starving himself of Brisona's "food" and vomiting his own internal (emotional) "food." So, he adds, she should take pity on his aching, sleep-deprived head and let him see her. The French poem makes its point far more simply:

> Le gran desir que jay puyse veoyr
> Ma douce dame
> Si duramant mon doulant cuer aflame,
> Que nuyt et jour me fayt playndre et gemir.
>
> (lines 390–93)

[The great desire I have to see my sweet lady so harshly kindles my suffering heart that it makes me lament and wail both by day and by night.]

Both lovers' letters include ever more sophisticated metaphors for their unhappy love. It is as if Frondino's attempt to be clear were sucked into an ever more symbolic epistolary frame. Brisona asks him to read her letters several times, as she does his. They are engaged in *ruminatio*, and their purpose is to incorporate the letters into their minds and hearts. She has, she says, taken to her bed: "Penssament disseca mon cors e gasta mos membres, així com la forts llima d'acer gasta lo ferre moll" (Sad thoughts desiccate my heart and whittle my limbs, like the strong steel file thins down soft iron) (92). She cannot dispel idleness by doing handiwork, because her limbs are tied by her emotional state. In her case, food cannot enter her body; her throat is tight and her stomach is tired. Her mouth will not ingest food either for it will only emit sighs from her heart. If Brisona cannot work with her hands, she cannot write. Unlike Frondino, she draws attention to the fact that limbs are needed to write letters. Her thinking in bed is also connected to *meditatio*, the process of written composition. She puts an end to the correspondence in her last letter. In this, she orders him to stop the letters and to speak to her in person: he must come to see her, in daylight, so she can see his face. Brisona seems to call attention at this point to the deceptiveness of any written language. She adds:

> Frondino, si lo dictat d'aquesta lletra no et sembla meu, per tal cum no he gardada en dictar alguna manera de retòrica, segons que he acostumat, creure pots que sí és, mas la gran cuita ab què e volia escriure mos treballs m'ha feita venir en plor qui m'ha torbat lo cap, tant que no he gardada ciència a fer ma lletra. E si la trobes tort escrita o pus mal que no solia escriure, no t'en maravelles, car la multitud de l'aiga qui m'eixia plorant dels ulls me torbava la vista e anul.lava lo paper, perquè la tinta s'hi estenia massa, mas bons me seran aitals plors, ab que et veia. (128)

> [Frondino, if the style of this letter does not look like mine, it is because I did not take care as I wrote with any kind of rhetoric, as I would usually do, you can believe it is mine, but the great suffering with which I wanted to write down my sufferings has made me weep; this has disturbed my head so much that I have not considered learning in writing my letter. And if you find it to be written badly, or worse than I used to write, do not be surprised, for the many tears that streamed from my eyes disturbed my sight and ruined the paper, for the ink spread out, but these tears will be good for me, with which I will see you.]

Her letter does not include a rondeau. Brisona's last letter seems to stage a physical language that melts down the possibility of writing altogether.

She says the letter is illegible, so how is the reader to understand the communication between them at this stage? Her sodden paper, with its blurred inks, is in any case highly rhetorical, even as it disclaims any rhetoric, as she develops a metaphor that was initially fed to her by Frondino, so her parting shot that she will see him through her own tears of distress offers an interesting final rejoinder.

Catalan scholars have claimed *Frondino e Brisona* as a key stage in the development of an autonomous literary language, as well as, according to António Cortijo Ocaña, an important early incorporation of the epistolary style in the inception of the *novela sentimental*. The text seems to stage the emergence of a genre from the interaction in Catalan royal circles of several genres: Catalan-Occitan *noves rimades,* French lyric poetry, *prosimetrum* devices borrowed from Machaut's *Livre du Voir Dit* (c. 1363), and the *ars dictaminis*.[29] However, I am tempted to avoid concluding that this text is offering three facets to a single tale, providing us with verse narrative, lyric emotion, and epistolary analysis. The text also seems to present the underlying issue that the protagonists and their audience do not regard any of the three languages as their mother tongue. Indeed, Brisona complains to Frondino that when he resorts to Catalan prose, he is giving her a name she finds foreign or strange. She draws attention to the physical work that is involved in letter writing, as well as to the need to compose in a rhetorical, controlled style, even when she claims to be overwhelmed by the language of the body. She has in any case initially commented on the opacity of written language by sending him a poem written in blue ink on black paper.

Frondino believes that he can communicate more clearly through the use of epistolary prose informed by the *ars dictaminis*. Brisona, echoing Bernat Metge's suggestions about women readers, seems to be more receptive to lyric expression than to the alleged clarity of prose. At no moment does any section of the text mention which language is the more immediately accessible to the protagonists. The tale ends with Frondino's body usurping his letter writing by emitting all kinds of indiscreet signs. Her body destroys the letter that she is, in any case, unable to write.

The *novel.la* queries communication on several levels. A reader who is not familiar with one of its three languages would find him- or herself at differing levels of hermeneutic disadvantage, depending on which language proved incomprehensible. The French sections are simple lyric poems, which minimizes their reliance on the reader's semantic understanding, so they may function primarily as shorthand for an erotic message. The Occitan-Catalan narrative verse is grammatically straightforward and may have been comprehensible also thanks to its simplicity. The Catalan prose, which should have been most accessible to a native speaker of Catalan, is dense, filled with complex imagery. It depends on the reader's recognition of rhetorical features learned from the *ars dictaminis*. Ironically, therefore, in *Frondino* the apparently straightforward medium of vernacular prose is the language that is made most strange, and the most artificial medium of vernacular courtly lyric becomes the most transparent. In between these two extremes, the hybrid verse narrative in a blend of Occitan and Catalan verse acts as a mediator, the go-between that relays the characters' actions while they write and display their self-absorbed construction of emotional worlds. Occitan-Catalan verse here acts as the vehicular language, deterritorialized and free of associations (at least in principle) with either the royal authority of the Catalan court or the competing literary prestige of French courtiers. It exists in between the two competing idioms and genres, and it appears to do so discreetly, without drawing attention to its function as the prime (indeed, the only) source of information about what actually happens between the two protagonists. The mediating idiom is in fact crucial to the intelligibility of this apparently simple text. If the passages in *noves rimades* were cut, the tale would quite literally fall apart.

The narrative of *Frondino e Brisona* appears to conclude that visual communication is the only reliable form of language between the two confused lovers. This in turn depends on the reader's ability to imagine several images, those of blue writing on black paper, a sheet of writing that has been made illegible by tears, or the bodily symptoms of anguish exhibited by both protagonists: their disheveled hair, belching guts, or pallor. All three imaginings are highly coded, for a letter may be just as easily blackened by smoke, written signs may equally be dissolved by rainwater or a spillage, and a body may become ill or unkempt for all kinds of reasons. All the reader has to rely on is the pattern of written signs constructed by the three-voiced narrative and (once again) the narrative thread provided mostly by the Occitan-Catalan *noves rimades*.

A Text Without Words

A multilingual context may produce the fantasy that individuals can find voice beyond the diversity of tongues. Ramon Llull's *Llibre de Amic e d'Amat* (c. 1274) expresses the aspirations of an author who sought to use several languages (Catalan, Latin, and Arabic) in order to express ideas that lay beyond speech:[30]

Cantava lauçell en lo verger de lamat vench lamich qui dix a laucell si nons entenam per lenguatge entenam nos per amor cor en lot eu cant se representa a mos hulls mon amat.

[A bird was singing in the garden of the Beloved. The Lover came and said to the bird: "Even if we cannot understand each other in words, let us understand each other through love, because in your song, the image of my Beloved appears before my eyes."]

An early sixteenth-century manuscript produced in France presents a tale as apparently simple as that of *Frondino e Brisona* entirely through images. Patricia Stirnemann has given the book the title *Histoire d'amour sans paroles*. It consists of a series of fifteen narrative illuminations, divided into sections by three blank folios, as well as thirteen folios that show either abstract or heraldic designs, some on a black background.[31] Like the tale of *Frondino*, seems to be a conventional courtly narrative. A young man who wears a brooch on his hat marked "I"/"J," appears to pursue a troubled love affair with a woman who is occasionally associated with the motif of a gold wing: "ele"/"L." The tale of J and L, perhaps Jehan and Louise, or possibly Je and Elle, has not been identified. The book draws attention to the fascinating relationship between narrative images and the viewer's cultural preconceptions. Mieke Bal has pointed out the radical omissions and oversights (what Venuti would term "the choices") that result when a viewer reads an image in terms of one canonical narrative. Stirnemann writes that she has presented the book to more than fifty individuals and produced no consensus about its narrative.[32] She published the book with the suggestion that the most apposite interpretation for this early sixteenth-century narrative came from Jacqueline Cerquiglini-Toulet, who noted that an image of a green bird on a black background (perhaps an attempt at a parakeet) may signify "J's" infidelity (14v).[33] It would be a visual allusion to the works of Guillaume de Machaut, and this suits both the cultural and the linguistic context of the book reasonably well. The facing folio depicts "L" weeping in her chamber as two women argue with her (15r). Stirnemann's hypothesis has the advantage of endowing the nonfigurative folios with narrative content as evocative depictions of the characters' emotions through color and heraldic signs. This would make them the pictorial equivalent of lyric insertions. She does not expand on what these narratives were, but it is intriguing that only one reader (in this instance, a noted Machaut scholar) should have been able to decode this text as an allusion to Machaut.

Green is a color that has many cultural and literary associations. *Frondino i Brisona*'s French rondeaux betray the Aragonese fashion for Machaut around 1400, but black-and-green clothes in that text are treated as tokens of fidelity. In Occitan troubadour poetry green refers to spring, youth, or immaturity. Indeed, French also interpreted green as the color of spring (in lyric genres such as the *reverdie*) or of lechery. Given the possible dating of the manuscript, and the weeping woman on the facing folio, would it not be more likely to allude to the dead parrot of Jean Lemaire de Belges' *Épîtres de l'amant vert* (1505)?[34] Despite its very persuasive literary and cultural credentials, there is no firm foundation for interpreting the *Histoire d'amour sans paroles* as a tale of infidelity. Moreover, its illuminations are replete with gray black, gold, red, and blue; and blue, especially, may signify fidelity or even virginity. Furthermore, a non-Francophone reader would find different significations in the lady's apparent association with the emblem of a golden wing, no longer as *aile* signifying *Elle* (Her, She) or perhaps the initial *L* (pronounced like *aile*) for a name such as Louise. In Castilian, *ala* might yield new names or nouns, but would the color gold (*oro*) play a more significant role? An Anglophone reader may resort to heraldry to decode the golden wing. This reader might also have interpreted the bush of red and white roses depicted on one folio (8v) as a heraldic motif alluding to the Tudor rose emblem that was used by King Henry VII after he seized the throne of England in 1485. The date would certainly chime with the possible dating of the manuscript, but it would affect its location, purpose, and (inevitably) narrative, as the most likely candidate for a patron in France would become Henry VII's daughter Mary Tudor in her short marriage to the French king Louis XII in 1514. Stirnemann suggests, in keeping with the dominant hypothesis that this is the emanation of a courtly French milieu, that the varicolored rose bush is an erotic motif derived from the *Roman de la rose*. Both these readings leave other aspects of that particular image unexplored, as the young man is wearing spurs and might be returning from battle, heading to a chivalric *emprise*, or setting off on crusade, as in *Frondino*.

In folio 11r, an allegorical tower is besieged by "J" and his men (fig. 4). They are scaling the tower on siege ladders, but the heroine's maid is standing next to "J," holding a set of keys. The gold frame contains a statement in French that runs clockwise from the lower left side of the frame: "QVANT. LA.TOUR.NOERRE.SAFOEY.GARDERA.ET.CEUX.QVI.ONT.LES.CLES.LEVR.SERMENT. GARDERONT.EN.MOEY.NEST.SOUSY.ET.IAMES.NE.CERA." (Provided the black tower will keep its faith and those who have the keys will keep their sworn promise, I have no concern, and never will.)

Fig. 4 The Lover besieges the Beloved's tower, *Histoire d'amour sans paroles*, Chantilly, Musée Condé MS 338, fol. 11v. © RMN/René-Gabriel Ojéda.

Does this scene depict the lover's attempt to breach the heroine's enclosure by a jealous husband or father, as the literary context of many courtly romances would imply? The first-person statement seems to support this interpretation: the black tower and the keeper of the keys are required to keep their word. Do they, however, keep their word by freeing the woman, or by keeping her enclosed? Worse, my assumption that she is enclosed in the tower derives from the cultural baggage of medieval romance and lyric allegory. Perhaps the tower represents the young man's enclosure; perhaps the words are not his, but those of "L," or even of another, absent, character. Also, French mottoes, *devises,* and phrases were often deployed for purely decorative reasons in court culture of this period. Catalan and Occitan texts play on French *devises* much as the text of *Frondino* inserts French poems without glossing their words.[35] The content of the French writing is far less important than its function as a representation of courtly refinement.

Little else can be concluded from exploring this later and difficult example, but it points to the fragility of narratives when they are robbed of their linguistic key. Even a text that looks like a succession of clichés may prove frustrating or disorientating to the most specialized of readers. *L'Histoire d'amour sans paroles* also draws attention back to the black letter inscribed with blue ink in *Frondino and Brisona*. The *Histoire* includes several folios with a black oblong in a frame (4v; fig. 5). It may be that Brisona's illegible letter denotes the lack of communication between the lovers, perhaps their inability to use three languages and three forms of rhetoric to establish transparent communication with each other. The *novel.la* makes demands on the reader's linguistic and interpretative skills, but it also underlines that these are essentially *learned* discourses and that even the language of the body is in some way acquired and certainly dependent on subjective interpretation. A trilingual text and a text without narrating words can reveal the extent to which reading and viewing are predicated on our "domestication," sometimes unconscious, of a foreign or alien text. They make explicit that fact that the reader (whether monolingual or multilingual) is "not so much the subject of a language as the subject of language."[36]

The poet and critic Alfredo Arteaga has suggested that "interlingual" poetry should be read carefully for the ways in which it constructs a "confluence of cultures." He moves away from rigid notions of code-switching and code-mixing to note how languages are placed vis-à-vis one another, in discrete blocks or blended into a single poetic shape. *Frondino* separates its three languages into three separate genres, in a move that acknowledges the text's confluence of (literary) cultures while appearing to prevent it,

Fig. 5 Histoire d'amour sans paroles, Chantilly, Musée Condé MS 338, fol. 4v. © RMN/ René-Gabriel Ojéda.

for it requires that the reader should at least have some grasp of the *razo* of its lyric French inserts and certainly should comprehend its other two idioms. It also undoes the hierarchies that may be derived from medieval writings about language, as there is no dominant language in this *novel.la*. The narrative creates a unifying thread for the three sections, making it properly intercultural, as *ars dictaminis* meets lyric rondeau and *noves rimades* in a conceptual borderland, with each element staying autonomous, yet engaged in an energetic multilingual dialogue.

Monolingualism emerges in late medieval Catalonia as the expression of the expansionist ideological agenda of the royal court. Paradoxically, it does so through the medium of translation. Where Metge's *Somni* explores the difficulties of a culture built on translations, *Frondino e Brisona* depicts the multiple dialogues that existed within the same courtly environment. Both texts are discontinuous, frustrating, and elusive. Both depict explicitly the illusory nature of literary languages and genres as they emerge from a "confluence of cultures" and of languages. In opposition to this, a narrative constructed from unglossed images highlights the extent to which all readers "domesticate" a text as they encounter it.

5

LANGUAGES AND BORDERS IN THREE *Novas*

Sitot Francess a bel lengatge
No-m pac en re de son linatge,
Car son erguylos ses merce,
E-z erguyll ab me no-s cove,
Car entre-ls francs humils ay apres;
Per qu'eu no vull parlar frances.
Car una dona ab cors gen
M'a fayt de prets un mandamen,
Qu'una faula tot prim li rim,
Sens cara rima e mot prim,
Car pus leus, se dits, n'es apresa
Per mans plasenters ab franquesa,
Per mans ensenyats e cortes.

(lines 1–13)

[Although the French have a beautiful language, I do not like their lineage at all, for they are mercilessly proud, and pride does not sit well with me, for I learned among honest, humble people. Which is why I do not wish to speak French. For a lady with a lovely body has given me a command of great worth, that I should rhyme her a neat fable, without "rich rhymes" or subtle words—for it is said it will be more easily learned by many pleasant and sincere people, [and] by many knowledgeable and courtly ones.][1]

ONE OF THE EARLIEST SURVIVING VERSIONS of the tales of "Sleeping Beauty" is an anonymous fourteenth-century *nova* titled *Frayre de Joy e Sor de Plaser*. The prologue posits an opposition between, on the one hand, the *linatge* (lineage) and *lengatge* (language) of the French and, on the other, the unnamed language the narrator claims he or she has acquired among people who are "*francs* humils": sincere and humble. The narrator announces that he or she has been commissioned to compose a tale by a lady who is defined only by her physical beauty and by her request for a short narrative or fable composed in *prim* verse, without *cara rima* or *mot prim*. The lady's request is double edged, and she may be read as having asked for either an "easy" poem without "easy" words, or a "subtle poem" without "subtle" words. The narrator responds by criticizing the choice of French in this context, as a sign of both linguistic and political subordination to an undefined French lineage. The lady has asked for a *faula* couched in a particular style of poetry, but not in a specific language. It is the narrator who has decided that the simplicity, humility, and precision that she requires are best expressed in a language that is not French, for the benefit of a designated audience that shares the virtues of "franquesa" (sincerity) and humility.

The prologue sets up an opposition between the ethically dubious language of "the French," characterized as a mixture of arrogance, powerful lineage, and insincerity, and the desirable qualities (especially for a woman reader) possessed by the language of the poem: subtlety, sincerity, and simplicity. This is not a statement concerning the mother tongue of the narrator, for she or he says that the language was acquired in a particular social and ethical context ("for I have learned it among honest, humble people"). It is rather a statement about the political associations of genre and language choice in a particular political and cultural context. Moreover, the poem is composed in an artificial literary idiom, a hybrid mixture of Occitan and Catalan in *noves rimades*, octosyllabic rhyming couplets. This hybrid language was used by Catalan poets of the fourteenth century in what appears to have been a transitional period between the decline of Occitan lyric poetry and the rise of Catalan prose and verse.

What the prologue depicts as a dramatized political tension between a humble language and an oppressive rival is in fact a cultural tension between Occitan lyric poetry, its Catalan derivatives, and the perceived ascendancy of written French, and I would argue that this tension is also a gendered one. Between the lady whose mother tongue is not defined and the narrator, there is a gap. The prologue does not say that she has commissioned the content of the narrative (what troubadours termed the *razo*), merely that she sought to dictate the style of a *faula*. As readers, we are obliged to read and to understand the Catalan-Occitan poem, so do we assume that the lady would have done so too? Is she a Frenchwoman whose request is met only halfway, in a second (literary) language that she is also able to comprehend? The narrator's refusal to use a particular language imperils the lady's comprehension of "her" work, should she prove unable to read it. Or is she someone whose courtly upbringing ensures that she has learned both French and Catalan-Occitan without either being her first language? The *Francess* (both "Frenchman" and "the French language") who is proud of his lineage is a silent, masculine presence in the prologue, vehemently rejected by the narrator. Neither the lady nor the narrator is ascribed a particular mother tongue. Such tensions appear elsewhere, for example, in Francesch de la Via's *La Senyora de Valor* (1406) the narrator observes some birds teaching their chicks their first words, "piu piu." The little birds amaze him by eventually producing a *baixa dansa* complete with French lyrics, "e suy meravelhat / de l'auzel qui ffrancès / Havion gent après" (and I was amazed by the birds that had beautifully learned French).[2] Chicks in the nest acquire courtly French lyric as their "mother tongue," but the emphasis is on the fact that it is acquired with effort from their parents.

The narrator does not make his or her gender explicit in the prologue. Narrator and lady are connected by a shared comprehension of two literary languages, but they are not complicit. I would argue that their relationship is constructed as an encounter between two autonomous subjects. The poet does not merely provide the *faula* that has been commissioned, and the lady's wishes are not fully fulfilled, but the poem is created nevertheless. Their contract (if it may be termed thus) is one of intersubjectivity, rather than a straightforward transaction between the patron and the poet.

In this chapter I will examine *Frayre de Joy e Sor de Plaser* as a poem that stages the complex political, linguistic, and sexual anxieties that surround linguistic conflict. Accordingly, I will examine first the problems that this poem poses as a work straddling two linguistic and disciplinary boundaries. In the second part of this chapter I look at what the poem has to say about language, boundaries, and consent. Finally, I will compare the work with two closely related texts, the Catalan *Blandin de Cornoalha* and the Franco-Italian *Roman de Belris*.

Frayre de Joy e Sor de Plaser survives in two manuscripts. One is a collection of fourteenth-century Catalan romances that was originally located in Carpentras and is now in Paris. The other is a miscellany of Catalan allegorical and lyric pieces that includes a fragment of the Occitan *nova Flamenca*.[3] Despite its evident formal and internal resemblances with such recognized "Occitan" narratives as *Blandin de Cornualha* or *Flamenca*, it has taken some time for *Frayre de Joy e Sor de Plaser* to be classified alongside these works. *Frayre de Joy* was published in 1884 as a Catalan-Occitan text and in 1983 included in an anthology by Arseni Pacheco of Catalan short texts. In 1996,

Suzanne Thiolier-Méjean reedited the text as an Occitan *nova* and subsequently included it in a coedited anthology of courtly *nouvelles* in Old French and Occitan. This courteous border dispute between genres and disciplines is a fruitful issue, in that it illustrates the potential for fresh readings of texts once their context is altered. In this instance, the distance stretches from the southeastern borders of the Pyrenees to Aquitaine. The poem's closing words, stating that the narrator has moved on to see the king and his *corts* (lines 823–24), places the text under Catalan aristocratic patronage, in common with the political as well as the literary situation for Occitan lyric poetry of the fourteenth century.

Synopsis

The unmarried daughter of the emperor of Gint-Senay dies suddenly. Her parents place her perfect body in a moated tower accessible only by a bridge of glass, surrounded by a garden, and the empire goes into mourning. The girl's tower has a magnetic attraction for visitors from other lands, including the son of the king of Florianda. This youth, Frayre de Joy, goes to Rome, to ask a magician named Virgil to teach him sufficient art to break into the tower and see the girl. He does so, finds her smiling face welcoming, and has sex repeatedly with the corpse. Despite being dead, she becomes pregnant. Nine months later, the corpse of Sor de Plaser gives birth to a baby son, much to the consternation of her parents, who find the infant feeding from her breast. In response to their prayers, she lifts her hand. At this moment, a jay appears with a curative herb. It brings the girl back to life once her parents have left. The jay is the gift of Virgil to Frayre de Joy (in exchange for Frayre's own birthright, the kingdom of Florianda). He is from the lands of Prester John and is a skilled linguist and diplomat. He tells the girl the child's father wishes to marry her. Sor de Plaser refuses to give her consent, on the grounds that he committed rape. The jay tries flattery, threats, and promises, but she relents once she hears that it is Frayre de Joy, a young man who has a great reputation. Their wedding is attended by the kings of every nation, the Holy Roman emperor, Virgil, Prester John, and the pope. Their son is named Joy de Plaser. Frayre de Joy becomes emperor of Gint-Senay.

The Perrault *conte de fées* now known in English as "Sleeping Beauty" (tale types 550 and 551 in Stith Thompson's *Motif-Index of Folk-Literature*) is believed to be drawn from Basile's Neapolitan tale collection, *Lo Conto de li cunti* (1634–36). In variants on the tale, a youth makes love to a sleeping woman in order to win an enchanted bird for his father.[4] Another Occitan-Catalan narrative composed in the fourteenth century, *Blandin de Cornoalha*, contains a condensed version of the tale that is closer to this variant narrative, in that Blandin obtains a falcon and saves a girl from an enchantment that keeps her asleep and imprisoned in a tower.[5] There is a distant echo of *Frayre de Joy* in sixteenth-century Castile, as the chivalric romance *Palmerín de Oliva* (1511) includes an episode in which Palmerín, helped by the Muslim magus Muça Belín, travels to obtain a bird that will cure princess Zerfira of her disfigurement after she has breathed the scent of some poisoned flowers (chaps. CXXI–CXXXV).[6] At the end of this chapter, I will examine the tale as it appears in a Franco-Italian text dating from about the same period as the two Catalan works.

From Perrault on, modern versions of the tale have tended to suppress the heroine's rape and pregnancy, most recently in reflection of Bruno Bettelheim's influential interpretation of the tale as an allegory of puberty.[7] Marc Soriano suggested that the tale was an irreverent exploration of the virgin birth; this seems quite credible for *Frayre de Joy*, as will be seen below. However, recent critical work on seventeenth-century French *contes de fées* (which were mostly female authored) has traced a pervasive concern with the perils of pregnancy and childbirth.[8] This emphasis on cultural sources overlooks literary predecessors such as the late antique Greek romances and their "false death" (*Scheintod*) motif (typically, the heroine is thought to be dead and placed in a tomb), which resurfaces in Chrétien de Troyes' *Cligés*.[9] Translations of and commentaries on Ovid's *Metamorphoses* also ensure that we may credit strong thematic relationships with the myth of Persephone and Demeter, but as there is as yet no single identifiable source for this particular tale beyond the similar story told in *Blandin*, we must suppose that the literary circles of Occitan and Catalan courts provided a fertile environment for its composition as a *nova*.

As with *Blandin*, there is no explicitly Arthurian setting for *Frayre de Joy e Sor de Plaser*. The texts most obviously share generic and formal features with some Breton *lais*. *Blandin de Cornualha* has been viewed as either an ironic pastiche of French Arthurian romance or a provocatively minimalist stylistic exercise, termed by Jean-Charles Huchet the "degré zéro du roman arthurien," or a precursor of the Catalan chivalric romance.[10] Cornelis Van der Horst offered a detailed refutation of *Blandin*'s reliance on any one French model and preferred to read it as evidence that Arthurian material was received in Occitan regions with some irony. His and Huchet's views appear to be based on a definition of Arthurian romance in terms of the works of Chrétien de Troyes and the Tristan tradition, both of which are well attested in Catalonia by the fourteenth century.

If Catalan patrons are so present in the *novas*, the *novas* start to look less closely tied to the sociopolitical context of Languedoc. Several romances exist that are sometimes included in the corpus of Occitan *novas*, such as *Jaufré*, which was composed for a king of Aragon, either Alfonso II or Jaume I (c. 1268–76) and was known to court circles in northern Spain for several centuries, as the romance eventually entered the popular literary canon of Spain, not of France. All the Catalan texts placed under the generic term *noves rimades* come from the fourteenth and fifteenth centuries and emerge from a sophisticated, international literary culture that had strong connections with Provence, the Balearic Islands, Sardinia, and the kingdom of Naples. Catalan-speaking courts offered patronage to poets writing in the troubadour tradition consistently between 1175 and 1450. Several manuscripts show that the royal court also produced compilations of poetry that seem more inclusive than the collections produced in Italy at the same time. Pere, count of Ribagorça and Ampuries (1305–c. 1358), composed poems that were performed at coronation ceremonies and was the dedicatee of a treatise on *trobar*. Treatises on Occitan language and versification were composed for Jaume II of Aragon (1291–1327) while he was ruling Sicily.[11] Nor is this purely a question of influence, as between the thirteenth and the fourteenth century the Angevin court of Provence and Naples produced manuscripts of French and Occitan verse that were subsequently owned and added to by Catalan poets, no doubt in the Neapolitan context, in the fourteenth and fifteenth centuries.[12]

Do we then have a corpus of courtly narratives composed by often Catalan poets for Catalan patrons, which happens to have been divided into two distinct groups on the grounds of date and transmission? Or should it be read as a corpus of Occitan poetry, most of which happens to have been written by and for Catalan speakers? The *novas* corpus is the starting point for Catalan literary history and of tragic decline for the Occitan lyric tradition. To deny the borderline dividing the two is tantamount to denying two important and complementary modern constructions of literary history. When confronted with confusion, contradiction, and compromise, it is desirable to question generic classifications.

If language is political in *Frayre de Joy*, geography is deterritorialized, in that it is overtly fantastical. The fictional empire of Gint-Senay and the kingdom of Florianda are surrounded by the empire of Prester John and a Rome that is inhabited by the magician Virgil.[13] This contrasts with the geographical and temporal precision of Raimon Vidal's *novas*. In *Frayre de Joy*, the possession of many languages is the greatest asset of the jay, a bird from the lands of Prester John, one who is a diplomat as well as a messenger. He is said to carry letters, *salutz* and *novas*, but in this context, he acts as the essential gift from Virgil to Frayre, in his capacity as someone who can fly across the world to find medicine as well as a diplomat, a bird that combines the marvelous traits of travel literature with the lyric function of the bird as go-between. His name may be based on etymological play: he is *jais*, destined to serve the *joi* of Frayre de Joy, as he would have done "en aquel temps c'om era jais." The jay's function as go-between is essential, because the denouement depends on obtaining Sor's consent. By extension, this problem rests in language. The jay can communicate directly with the revived girl in a way Frayre was unable to when she was dead. Furthermore, the text makes the problem of communication explicit.

When Frayre enters the tower, he contemplates and interprets the girl's beauty in terms that suit his own desires. She is immobile and expressionless, but he attempts to read her features for a sign:

> Que ja- m mostr'ab sos uylls abdos
> Per semblant c'ab me vuyla parlar.
>
> (lines 156–57)

[For now she shows me with both her eyes, and her appearance, that she wants to speak to me.]

Frayre makes a speech to Sor (lines 164–209), in which he emphasizes the emotions to which he wishes to see her respond:

> Ay! gentil, plasent creatura,
> La plus bela re que anc vis,
> Axi con me mostrats al ris
> Amor e-m fayts als ulls semblant,
> Amessets me, e no ges tant
> Con eu a vos.
>
> (lines 164–69)

[Alas! Noble, pleasing creature, loveliest thing I have ever seen, how you show me your smile, and show me the semblance of love with your eyes, you could love me, and not as much as I love you.]

He decides that he will ascertain if she loves him by kissing her, because her face will show an emotional reaction to his action (lines 204–9). He kisses her a hundred times until he forces her lips to move in apparent response:

> E fo li semblant c'un dolç ris
> Li fass,' e qu'en fos paguada;
>
> (lines 212–13)

[And it seemed to him that she was smiling gently at him, and that she was satisfied.]

Frayre reads consent in Sor's eyes and in her smile. Can a smile be taken to indicate consent? It seems that it can as far as this character is concerned. Frayre's next move is to remove the coverlet that is concealing Sor's body. The narrator points out that it is "gent cosit d'estranya guisa" (nobly embroidered in a strange manner) (line 219). The signs on the coverlet are unreadable. He interprets her tunic, however, as a clear message: embroidered in silver and gold, it is beautiful because, he decides, she put it on for him. However, Frayre's subjective reading of the inert body before him needs to find some confirmation. This comes through explicit linguistic signs. He discovers that she wears a ring on her finger, which is "escrit ab letres que desien / Aycells que llegir-les sabien" (inscribed with letters that say, for anyone who can read them) (lines 231–32),

> Anell suy de Sor de Plaser
> Qui m'aura leys pora aver,
> Per amor, ab Plaser viven,
> Can ach de joy pres complimen.
>
> (lines 233–36)

[I am the ring of Sor de Plaser; whoever will have me, can have her as well, through love, with living pleasure, when he has taken his full measure of joy.]

Since Frayre also wears a ring inscribed with his name, all he needs to do is swap her ring for his, and their mutual consent will have been given. His ring also exonerates his rape, as it promises that Frayre de Joy will love a woman not like a peasant, but as the son of a king (lines 240–43). He swaps the rings and has sexual intercourse with her. The text endorses his forceful reinterpretation of her dead body as a consenting partner with a proverbial expression:

> Plaser ama, plaser desira,
> Pesar fai regard, plaser guia.
>
> (lines 253–54)
>
> [Pleasure loves, pleasure desires; thinking brings worry, pleasure guides.]

Since the pleasure invested with such autonomous desire is part of Sor's name, the fact that Frayre has taken pleasure from a dead woman is erased by the pretence that Pleasure is an active participant. Frayre has read the signs disposed on Sor's body in a certain way, has swapped one name for another, one sign for another, and thereby assumed that she has given her consent. In terms of canon law, Frayre's actions have effectively placed the words of exchanged consent on Sor's lips. The words on the ring bestow *verba de futuro*: future consent. According to formulations of marital law from the late thirteenth century onward, the presumption of marriage was sealed by the sexual consummation that follows this apparent exchange of consent by the two parties. Sor de Plaser is, after all, not related by blood to Frayre de Joy, and she has made no prior betrothal. She is neither underage nor insane. The fact that she is dead should, of course, preclude the use of force on her body. According to Pope Alexander III, proven force in coerced marriage had to be sufficient to "move a constant man," and in this instance, no force is needed.[14] Needless to say, canon law made little comment on marrying corpses.

Sor becomes pregnant. Her mother notices her rounded belly, and she cries out that this is "against nature and against reason," since only a bird or the Holy Spirit could have entered Sor's tower-tomb (lines 283–85). The mother views Sor's dead maternity as a paradox, for the dead do not give life, whereas living women fear for their lives during childbirth (lines 289–93). Sor's mother prays for her daughter to revive. Sor's body promptly makes a gesture that the narrator interprets as one of reassurance:

> La donzella la ma levet,
> Quays que dixes—mas no parlet—
> "Viva son, no plorets huymay";
> E torneron lur dol en guay.
>
> (lines 312–15)

[The damsel lifted a hand as if to say (but she didn't speak): "I am well, do not cry anymore." And they turned their grief into joy.]

Here, Sor's body presents an ambiguous sign that is interpreted as if it were a coherent speech. Her paradoxical body, lying in between life, death, and gestation, makes bodily gestures such as raising a hand and suckling an infant, but her mind plays no role in these movements. For her aggressor, Sor's smile was a sign that Frayre chose to interpret as consent, not calm repose. Theoretically, Sor's consent to sexual intercourse (which would have implied her consent to marriage, according to some canonists) should have been given verbally and before witnesses, while Frayre has acted unseen. In practice, a woman's consent was often an irrelevance and there were instances where a girl's smile (for example, if she was an infant who had not yet learned to talk) could be taken as sufficient consent not to her suitor but to her father's choice of husband. However, the public bestowal of consent depends on language, whether verbal or physical, as much as on the exchange of rings. Frayre's interpretative gestures are an illustration of the fragility of consent when it rests on such signs, a point made by Irwen Resnick:[15] "Consent theory . . . introduced enormous difficulty by its reliance on some more or less explicit sign of consent expressed either at betrothal or in the exchange of marriage vows. Because it was clearly understood that consent could be forced by threat of physical violence, expressed in secret, or attested by unreliable witnesses, a theory that relied upon consent alone as the sign of a marriage appeared to place in jeopardy the stability of that marriage." The words inscribed on the rings are more important in this text than their function as material signs of betrothal, for they interpret Frayre's gesture as his obedience to an external command that states that Sor already "belongs" to him. In an intriguing piece of narrative sleight of hand, the rings already destine Sor to Frayre, and the fusion of their names and bodies is cemented in the name given to their child (Joy de Plaser) at the story's close. Canon law on abduction and rape made it possible to ratify a clandestine marriage that had been made without witnesses or public declaration and without parental consent. In this context, the fact that Sor raises her hand before her parents, "as if to say" that she is unharmed, would appear to make her complicit with Frayre's actions. Furthermore, it was argued by some authors that procreation indicated that a woman had experienced some form of carnal pleasure (*delectatio*) even if she was raped, and the very name of Sor de Plaser associates her with this.[16] However, once Sor is returned to life and regains her status as a rational being, the narrative focuses on making her give her consent retrospectively.

From the moment the jay opens a dialogue with Sor, the issue of consent becomes a matter of explicit debate within the text as well as outside it.

The importance of Sor's consent is emphasized once it is compared to the treatment of a similar scene in *Blandin*. In this text, Blandin is encouraged to revive a sleeping girl by her brother. He enters the tower in which she is sleeping, but only looks at her. He then goes to a second tower where he kills a dragon, a serpent, and a Saracen giant, in order to free a white falcon that he must place on her hand, in order to free her from her sleep. In this text, the girl's body is kept safely enclosed within her tower, and Blandin's aggressive assault is redirected toward a second tower, where the falcon (her cure) and the supernatural creatures (her guardians) are located. Once she is awake, Brianda offers him marriage and her lands as his reward, but Blandin insists that he wants to marry her for love. Brianda's chastity is preserved to the point that Blandin must ensure that even her own offer of marriage is based on love, not coercion. The narrator subsequently states that this is a conquest, but seems to be uncertain of who has conquered whom:

> Ar vos hai dic de Blandinet
> consi Brianda lo conquistet.
>
> [Now I have told you about Blandinet, and how Brianda conquered him.]
>
> Blandinet anet recontar
> al bon Guillot de Miramar
> l'aventura que atrobet
> quan Brianda conquistet.
>
> [Blandinet went and told good Guillot de Miramar about the adventure he had when he conquered Brianda.]

Brianda later reveals that she orchestrated the chain of events that led to her release, thus suggesting that she has indeed conquered him by posing as an enchanted prisoner. By comparison, Sor has no doubts about the nature of Frayre's conquest. She refuses the jay's offer of Frayre's love on the grounds that he has violated both her body and her mind:

> –Ja no diray que Deus vos sal
> Vos ni lui, N'auzell, per ma fe,

Per so car anc gauset de me
Reprendre ses lo meu voler;
Mas si-l mal sofris ab plaser
Que-l joy d'amors li dones
E mon causiment atendes,
Axi-l tengra eu per gentil.
Que-l mon no ha dompne tan vil
C'om dege pendra ni tocar
Re del seu sens luy demandar;
C'aytal fait forsat no so bo,
Ne tant no saubrets de rayso,
En gay, qu'eu dret no-us gazany
D'amor qu'un anelet d'estany
Dat per amor no vayla mays
Que d'aur emblats ab fis balaxs.

(lines 397–413)

[I won't ask God to save either you or him, Sir Bird, by my faith, because he has dared to take something from me against my will; but if he had endured with pleasure the suffering that joy of love was giving him, and if he had waited for my consent, I would then regard him as a noble man. For there is no lady in the world so vile that anything of hers could be touched or taken without asking her first; such forced deeds are not good. And you will not have enough reasons, Sir Jay, to oppose to my proving to you that, according to love, a little ring of tin given with love is worth more than a stolen ring made of gold and set with rubies.]

Sor says she has not given Frayre her love, and that he has stolen her "car puncelatge" (line 429), her prized virginity. Sor's argument may be logical, but it is legally weak, for, according to Peter Lombard, her uncomplaining cohabitation with Frayre after his first rape constituted "subsequent consent (*consensus ille consequens*)," although admittedly Sor has no possibility of escape during the time she is visited by Frayre.[17] The jay changes his strategy and abandons his initial protestations concerning Frayre's courtly valor and love. Instead he turns to political arguments and obtains her consent by reinterpreting Frayre's actions as his purchase of the empire of Gint Senay. The jay tells both Sor and her parents that Sor's body was part of the price paid by Frayre, along with his ring and his kingdom of Florianda ("a kingdom more powerful than France") (line 502), to revive her:

> E com per haver son cors bell
> Li det apres lo seu anell
> E com per haver sa amor granda
> Donet lo regne de Florianda.
>
> (lines 678–81)

[And how, in order to have her lovely body, he gave her his ring, and how, to have her great love, he gave away the kingdom of Florianda.]

In fact, Frayre subsequently gives Florianda to Virgil in exchange for the jay (lines 345–52), which does not sound quite as altruistic. The jay also points out to Sor de Plaser that she is now owned by Frayre, as she bears a ring that announces, "De Fray de Joy suy" (I belong to Brother of Joy) (line 517). The ring's inscription has shifted from a statement that it (the ring) belongs to Frayre, into the proclamation that Sor's body is now his possession.

Sor surrenders to the dominant interpretation of her predicament. She comments that that "when she was alive," she knew Frayre de Joy by his great reputation (lines 521–22). She reconsiders the marriage in terms of their exchanged rings and their compatible names (lines 539–44), although strictly speaking a brother and sister could not have been awarded official consent to marry, and courtly Joy and unthinking physical Pleasure are incompatible in terms of *fin'amors*. Sor is forced to concede after the event that Frayre's purported sacrifice of his father's lands makes sufficient repayment for her own body, honor, and reason, as well as for her own parents' lands. The jay seals the enforced match by building and populating a magnificent castle for the couple (lines 716–21). At the close of the text, the empire of Gint-Senay passes into the hands of the son of the king of Florianda, and of an heir he has obtained through rape, deceit, and diplomacy, with the public approval of the Holy Roman emperor, the pope, Virgil, and Prester John (lines 793–822). Lands are granted in exchange for bodies, and Virgil the magician is the new king of Florianda.

It is tempting to read *Frayre de Joy e Sor de Plaser* as an allegorical narrative of an aggressive conquest, followed by diplomatic activity and an official alliance. The child's birth has already sealed Frayre's appropriation of Sor's body, but Sor has to be seen to give her enthusiastic consent to the match, and this has to be followed by the negotiations of the go-between and her parents. The linguistic conflict signaled in the prologue as the narrator's refusal to speak French because she or he protests the arrogance of the French lineage is expressed in the narrative in terms of the triumph over reason and chastity of the ambitious foreign prince's manipulation of his lineage and power. Virgil is a figure symbolizing the importance of both learning and trickery for ambitious princes.

María Rosa Menocal has suggested that the Iberian Peninsula in the Middle Ages offers an exceptionally clear picture of the "agonistic process" through which official languages emerge. Languages are seen literally fighting for supremacy in territories to which they might be linked indirectly, as the vehicles of an ideology, or an ambitious power group. I would add to this a comment made by Kathleen Biddick, that the position of linguistic go-between, when it is combined with that of a culturally transitional position, requires a certain distance vis-à-vis the language that is presented as the mother tongue.[18] In *Frayre de Joy e Sor de Plaser*, there are numerous ways of reading written and visible signs, but only one language seems to be the preferred idiom. Yet this language is not a language associated with either religious authority (Latin), a monarchy (French or Catalan), or a poetic corpus (Occitan). It is a hybrid blend of Occitan and Catalan, lyric and narrative. It cannot be the mother tongue of either the narrator, or the lady, or even their audience. *Frayre de Joy e Sor de Plaser* explores the flexibility of verbal signs and the skill with which any language may be used to present rape as consent, death as life, and the conquest of an empire as a fair transaction. The language used in the text is an artificial mode of artistic communication that may be learned by those who intend to twist the words to make them suit the desired facts.

In this context it is telling that, unlike the other versions of the tale, this text affirms repeatedly that the girl is neither asleep nor enchanted, but dead. It hinges on several impossibilities: a corpse that does not decompose and one that may conceive, give birth to a child, and breastfeed it. The reader, like Sor's mother, may begin to doubt the value of the term *mors*. The dead body is passive but fertile and nurturing. Whether alive or dead, and despite an initial attempt on her awakening to contradict Frayre's version of events, Sor de Plaser cannot act autonomously. Sor de Plaser's body becomes more than a victim of others' enchantment or potions, as it appears to be at odds with itself. She cannot decompose or become invisible, and she cannot, even in death, avoid pregnancy. In this tale, only a nonhuman creature can bring her back to life. Her story is suggestive of Hélène Cixous' explorations of the complex workings of the (m)other tongue and of language, especially her concept of the *entredeux*: "The word *entredeux*: it is a word I used recently in *Déluge* to designate a true in-between— Between a life that is ending and a life which is beginning. For me an *entredeux* is: nothing. It *is*, because there is *entredeux*. But it is . . . a moment in a life where you are not entirely living, where you are almost dead. Where you are not dead. Where you are not yet in the process of reliving."[19] It is also a moment of interruption, "everything that makes the course of life be interrupted" (9). When the interruption happens, "strange material" is uncovered that may be fruitful if it is then written out in the "passage" (10) from "l'une à l'autre," not from the one to the other, but from an other to an other. Only through a process of radically "other" writing, of distancing oneself completely from the language being used, can the *entredeux* be written about. This concept may encompass the "strange material" uncovered by such problems as a corpse giving birth, or a woman complaining that she was not asked to give her consent when she was dead.

This "strange material" is only to be expressed in a language that passes "de l'une à l'autre," from the narrator to the lady in the prologue. For Cixous, what defines the *entredeux* is internal conflict and estrangement within the self: "This being abroad at home is what I call an *entredeux*." The *nova* corpus straddles a sensitive cultural and linguistic boundary. By highlighting the slipperiness of official or authoritative language, it also points out the extent to which apparently simple transactions may be the product of force. In this text, the hybrid Catalan-Occitan language is "abroad at home": used to pass an awareness of "strange material" and to point out the existence of the *entredeux*.

Is this conflict pertinent only to this particular text and context? It is useful to turn to a near analogue in Franco-Italian. Like the Tuscan *cantari* of *Il Bel Gherardino* and *Carduino*, the Franco-Italian *cantare* of *Belris* (c. 1350–80) derives in part from the French *Bel Inconnu* tradition, but it also provides a parallel to both *Frayre de Joy* and *Blandin*.[20] The poem is written in the Italianized (or rather Venetian) version of French that developed as a literary language in northern Italy, most probably in the workshops where many French and Occitan literary manuscripts were copied.[21] While Günter Holtus prefers to view Franco-Italian as a written language, Carla Cremonesi suggested that it was developed as a performance tool for *cantastorie* who would have rendered Old French text into a culturally domesticated idiom closer to that of their audience. A few autonomous texts (neither translations nor adaptations of French works) appeared in Franco-Italian during the fourteenth century, but it never became a major literary idiom.

Monfrin edited and reconstructed the lost sections of the *Belris*, surmising that the missing folio at the middle of the poem narrated Belris's rape of a sleeping woman in her enchanted tower. Belris says as much later, when he recounts his actions to her (lines 811–33). The summary below follows Monfrin's reconstruction:

[Lost opening: King Galafre of Livaris sends off his two sons for his capital, Varia, to capture an enchanted falcon. The successful son will become his sole heir.] Belris follows a hind into a forest and meets Machabia, who reveals that she knows he is looking for a marvelous falcon. She promises him her help in exchange for his promise that he will return to her; he takes her ring and makes love to her. The hind guides Belris to a revolving castle, in front of which a lion and a serpent are fighting. Belris kills the lion and the serpent kisses him. Belris rushes into the castle and sees four chained lions. A lady appears and tells him she was the serpent and that she and her two sisters have now been saved by his kiss from a magician's enchantment. She sends him on his way by boat with four maidens who inform Belris that all the events to date have been engineered by their lady Machabia. On their seventh day at sea the enchanter attacks them astride a dragon. Belris kills both and finds a golden box inside the dragon's body. Four days later, they reach the deserted city of Salubrea/Salubera. Belris climbs the thirty floors of a tower that is guarded by a lion and defeats two swords wielded by a golden and a silver arm, affirming his loyalty to Machabia as he goes.

[Lacuna. *Belris later says he reached the top of the tower and found a woman lying asleep on a bed, next to the falcon. He made love to her and took away the falcon, but left a note with his name and the name he wished her to give to the son she had conceived.*] Belris travels on with his falcon, avoiding further assistance, but one of the four maidens appears flanked by a lion, predicts a combat, and gives him a box containing curative "flowers of Paradise" that were brought back by Alexander the Great from the Dry Tree. Belris defeats three knights and cures himself by ingesting the flowers. However, his older brother Malçaris claims victory for himself before Galafre. Galafre besieges Belris in the fortress of Montclier/Cliermont (lines 557, 561). Meanwhile, Queen Anfelis wakes up when she gives birth to Clairavis, and the city's enchantment is broken. She is delighted to find she has a "bel rité" (heir), reads the letter Belris left behind him, and gathers her army to find him. She reaches Varia, challenges Galafre by letter and embassy to surrender Belris to her, and sets a test of courage that allows Anfelis to unmask Malçaris's false claims. She threatens to destroy Varia if Galafre does not surrender Belris to her. He complies and makes peace with his son. During his coronation and wedding at Salubrea, Belris sends a letter written in letters of gold to Machabia in which he invites her to visit his city and to meet his wife. Machabia sends Belris the ambiguous reply that she will soon come to Salubrea, with her son, Manador. She stabs herself and writes him a letter in her own blood. The four ladies sail with her body and the baby to Salubrea. Belris holds a grand funeral for Machabia, and he and Anfelis raise Manador as joint heir with their nine children. Machabia's four servants marry, respectively, the kings of Armenia, Spain, Montpellier, and England.

The tale is a dense intertextual mix of *Bel Inconnu* and other romance traditions.[22] *Belris* shares its motifs of the enchanted sleep and the falcon with *Blandin de Cornualha*, although it overlays it with the rape of *Frayre de Joy e Sor de Plaser*. It splits the heroine into two rival figures. Anfelis is restored to life and made a wife, and Machabia dies and leaves an orphan son.

Because of the emphasis on the rival claims of the two boys fathered by Belris during his adventures, it seems that Machabia's intervention in the dynastic crisis of Livaris is predicated on the settling of inheritance on Belris, and ultimately on their son. The tale opens with Galafre's decision to forego primogeniture and to decide inheritance through a competition he creates between his two sons. Belris complains to his father that he is no longer his heir: "Ça non son vostra rité, / Char m'avés desarité" (I am no longer your heir, for you have disinherited me) (lines 726–27). Machabia pushes her son's claims even in death, by constructing a tableau that proves successful, as Belris raises Manador with Anfelis's son. The poem appears to resolve a crisis of succession by privileging opportunism and adoption over aristocratic concerns for the maintenance of primogeniture. In the *Belris*, the language of consent is less important than the power of written words in matters of inheritance.

Belris's sons are both born illegitimate. Manador is conceived a fortnight before Clairavis, but Belris's written note to Anfelis means that he has recognized Clairavis at the moment of the child's conception (lines 589–90), whereas Machabia makes Belris aware of the existence of only Manador, first verbally and then in writing, after she reads his letter announcing that he has an heir (lines 968–76, 1119–59). Machabia as the text's substitute narrator hopes that Manador will be recognized as Belris's heir, but she fails to tell Belris enough about the narrative she has "written" in advance. His lovemaking to Anfelis's unconscious body disrupts Machabia's narrative in that he dedicates his victory to her in words, but he places his written signature and seed at the point of his (and therefore Machabia's) success. Machabia continues to give Belris assistance after this episode, as if she were unaware of the subplot he has created in Anfelis's tower. Indeed, when Belris announces his victory to his brother Malçaris, he says he has won the falcon through the love of God and of his "dama çentil, / Machabia la signoril" (lines 499–500).

Anfelis does not object to Belris's behavior, as she credits his theft of the falcon as her liberation from the enchantment and identifies herself as "la dama d'onor / Char trova se al pavion" (the woman of honor [or lands] who was in the pavilion) (lines 849–50). However, the test of courage and largesse that she imposes appears to symbolize a more dubious aspect of Belris's actions. She has cloth of gold laid on the road that leads from the *bourg* to the *cité* and invites "the man who took the falcon" to ride upon it (lines 648–52). Belris tramples on the cloth, demonstrating not so much his courage or largesse as his willingness to inflict physical damage on a precious object in pursuit of his aims. This is another instance of Belris's writing on a surface, this time imprinting hoof marks on gold cloth. Galafre sees his own dynastic plan undermined by events, as Belris is taken away to become the king of Salubrea, and he is compelled to make the cowardly Malçaris his heir (lines 871–904).

Belris writes to Machabia in a *brief* (letter) that he composes in letters of gold (lines 935–36), the reverse of the dirt he has flung onto the cloth. The letter tells Machabia that she should not hold him guilty of *vilania* and should visit Salubrea, to see his city, his heir, and his wife (lines 938–53). On reading this, Machabia faints several times and is laid on a bed. She sighs to her ladies, "Le civalier ben m'aunoré" (The knight has honored me indeed) (line 962). The verbal message she sends to Varia echoes Belris's letter and points out that he now has two male heirs:

> E lo re Belris me salué
> e Anfelis ch'é soa muier
> e Cleravis ch'é soa rité.
> da la mia part si li conté
> avanti che sia tre mes pasé,
> io si sero in soa cité
> cun Manador le fiol me,
> car de son cors son gnenere.

(lines 968–76)

[Send my greetings to King Belris, and Anfelis, who is his wife, and Cleravis, who is his heir. Tell him from me that before three months have elapsed I shall be in his city with Manador, my son, for he was conceived from his body.]

Machabia sends out her four attendants into the garden and stabs herself in the chest. She gathers her blood in a basin of gold and uses it as ink to write a letter to Belris (lines 1011–17). Her bloody riposte to Belris's gilded words is also an assertion of her connection by blood to his son (lines 1019–59). She identifies the blood as the expression of her physical suffering, her death for love, and the surrender of her body to his (lines 1120–24). Body, letter, and child are sent by ship to Belris, so he can view both Machabia's words and the tableau she has constructed to prove their son's claim: "Vit Machabia al vis clier / E Manador ch'é soa rité" (He saw Machabia of the bright face and Manador, who is her/his heir) (lines 1114–15). She is a woman "al vis clier," a challenge to Anfelis and Belris's chosen name of Clairavis for their son. The exchange of letters operates on two levels, through close reading of the words and a manipulation of both letters and inks as objects (gold and blood) that are distinct from the finer points of language. The letters have both a linguistic and a supralinguistic aspect.

Machabia's elaborate suicide puzzled Monfrin, as it seemed to jar with her similarity to fairy mistresses in French and Italian texts.[23] Ovid's *Heroides* are most probably an influence on this poem, as Dido associates her suicide with her living son, Iulus (as well as with her destruction of Aeneas's unborn child), and with the creation of a bloodstained self-portrait through her letter (*Her.*, bk. 7, lines 181–90). Machabia sends both her letter and her corpse to Belris, with her infant son, Manador, laid out beside them. Machabia's letter is written with the blood she sheds after she stabs herself, making literal Dido's promise to Aeneas that once he has read her words, he will not be free of the mental image of his wife's bloodied face ("coniugis ante oculos deceptae stabit imago / tristis et effuses sanguinolenta comis" [*Her.*, bk. 7, lines 69–70]). Machabia's blood also makes literal the blood connection that will be perpetuated by their son, Manador. Letter and action are closely associated through the creation of an ironic gap between the literal and the figurative sense of words.

Belris appears to blend disparate material such as Ovid's *Heroides*, the travels of Alexander the Great, and the Christian legend of the Dry Tree, as if it were engaged in a process of intercultural dialogue. This permeability and flexibility also affects the protagonists' names, as Na Belris (Lady Beautiful

Smile) is a *senhal* used by Lanfranc Cigala (PC 282, 12, Branciforti, song XIV, line 19).[24] Anfelis's name may be derived from the Saracen wife of Foucon de Candie, who reappears as Anfilizia in the Tuscan *Narbonesi*, or it may echo that of a *chanson de geste* character mentioned by a troubadour.[25] The Veneto is the location for the compilation of a significant number of troubadour *chansonniers*, as well as *chansons de geste* such as *Macaire*, which subsists only in the Franco-Italian *Geste Francor*.[26] Machabia's name is probably not a reference to Macaire, but rather an echo of the Macchabees, who were a biblical model of altruistic suicide and were also heroes of a *chanson de geste*.[27] These allusions confirm the cultural breadth of *Belris*'s intended readers.[28]

Belris raises a number of questions, as it displays many similarities in form and style to the two Occitan-Catalan *novas* studied above. This undeniable family resemblance may reflect the presence of minstrels and scribes who had experience of many courts and language areas.[29] It is tempting to place the Franco-Italian *Belris* opposite the two Catalan-Occitan poems and to suggest that although all three works are concerned with the delicate processes of negotiating language and lineage, the *Belris* positions its *entredeux* in a confident literary and epistolary culture that is completely multilingual: Latin texts cohabit with French and Italian poems. Machabia wields both spoken and written language to leave Belris in no doubt about her consent and her resistance to the events of the narrative.

The "Sleeping Beauty" motif appears to be fruitful for reading texts in which languages are brought into dialogue. In the following chapter I will examine texts in Old and Middle French that appear to explore an ambiguous perception of monolingualism in another border zone, that between French and Flemish. Here, I will explore the possibility that monolingualism is associated with the negative effect not of conquest, but of its opposite, endogamy.

6

MONOLINGUALISM AND ENDOGAMY:
FRENCH EXAMPLES

RAIMON VIDAL DE BESALÚ SUGGESTED THAT "la parladura francesa" was more suited to narrative than to lyric expression, and it should come as no surprise to find French versions of the "Sleeping Beauty" tale of *Frayre de Joy e Sor de Plaser*. The near identical tale of Troÿlus and Zellandine in *Perceforest* has often been compared to the Occitan-Catalan tale and will be discussed in the second part of this chapter. In the first part I will examine the opening of the thirteenth-century Old French romance *Richars li Biaus*, which begins with an episode that has striking similarities to that of *Frayre de Joy e Sor de Plaser*. In examining an Old French text that predates the Catalan and Franco-Italian texts by more than a century, I am not making any claims for its status as their source. Quite on the contrary, *Richars li Biaus* demonstrates that when a fairly common narrative motif appears in a monolingual romance, as opposed to a text composed in a hybrid language, it appears to allude not to the politics of maintaining and breaching borders, but to the opposite problem, that of incestuous sameness (represented by the threat of endogamy) that has to be wrested by an intruder from another realm or family into fertile exogamy. In this chapter, the sexual-political matrix of *Frayre de Joy e Sor de Plaser, Blandin,* and *Belris* remains the same, predicated on the idea that medieval sociopolitical ideologies relied heavily on exogamy (the obligation to marry someone to whom one is not related, by blood, affinity, or spiritual affinity) as a justification of territorial expansion through both marital alliances and warfare.

The Old French *Richars li Biaus* (after c. 1250), by a certain *mestre* Requis, has been identified as a text from the northern Picard or Walloon regions, a linguistic border area between Dutch and French where French was cultivated as a literary language from the mid-twelfth century, but coexisted with Dutch and Latin in administrative documents from the early thirteenth century onward.[1] A significant part of the romance is reproduced or echoed in the mid-fourteenth-century prose epic *Lion de Bourges,* which also implies some degree of diffusion in the regions bordering the French and Flemish regions (its editors agree that it was composed in the region of Tournai). The vast prose romance *Perceforest* (c. 1337–44) is from the same region and appears to be the work of a Flemish author who worked in French for Count Guillaume I of Hainaut.[2] Manuscript C of the *Perceforest* (Burgundian, c. 1459–60) gives the fullest and most coherent version of the tale of Troÿlus and Zellandine.

Richars li Biaus is most noted for its "grateful dead" narrative, where Richars is assisted by the ghost of a knight whom he has buried. This striking story of gratitude, debt, and reward opens with Richars' birth as a result of rape, but it has also been identified, most recently by Elizabeth Archibald, as a "near-miss" incest narrative.[3] A widowed king believes that his beloved daughter, Clarisse, will be seduced should he ever leave her unattended (lines 183–88). He builds a walled orchard encircled by *entes entées* (grafted trees), fills it with fruit trees, and plants a shady sycamore at its centre. He encloses Clarisse inside it with her governess and advises her that she is safe to eat as much of the orchard's fruit as she likes before his return (lines 189–240). Clarisse stays in the orchard for a few days. The narrator does not say if she eats the fruit as she is told to do, but she develops a fever that makes her teeth chatter as she shivers with cold (lines 252–62). Her governess makes her drink seven cups of claret laced with "pieument et . . . mouré" (honeyed spices and hydromel) to heat her blood and—strangely—to make her forget her sickness:[4]

> Buvez, fille! ch'est bon clarés,
> par bon boire plus caut arés;
> dont buverez ce bon pieument,
> s'engignerez plus soutilment
> le mal qui si trembler vous fait,
> tout oublïerés entresait.
>
> (lines 281–86)

[Drink, daughter! It's good claret; by drinking it you will feel hotter. By drinking this good spiced wine, you will deceive the sickness more subtly that is making you tremble; you will forget everything.]

Clarisse staggers drunkenly under the shade of the spreading sycamore tree, where she collapses; lies *souvinne* (prone); and falls into a deep sleep, having taken the precaution of covering her face from the sun's rays with a piece of silken cloth (lines 296–304). A young knight errant, Loÿs le Preus, makes his way to the king's orchard desiring to catch a glimpse of both the good herbal garden and the princess that it contains (lines 333–41). He climbs up an apple tree; leaps over the wall; and enters the orchard, where he finds Clarisse lying in her drunken stupor, "sans garde" (unguarded) (line 352). He removes the cloth, gazes on her sleeping face, and rapes her. She conceives a son, Richars, who is abandoned and brought up by a count and countess. Richars' adventures are a quest to identify, reunite, and marry his parents.

This opening part of *Richars li Biaus* is most striking for its treatment of the unconscious incestuous desire in the relationship between the king and his daughter, whom he has named after his dead wife (lines 108–28), a desire that is consciously acknowledged when the adult Richars meets Clarisse and nearly falls in love with her. This incestuous subtext determines the romance's treatment of sexual desire. *Richars li Biaus* is also striking for the narrative's near obsession with the hero's violent conception. The rape of the sleeping Clarisse by a trespassing stranger is told five times in all, once by the narrator, three times by Clarisse, and once by Loÿs. The first account underlines Loÿs' determination to trespass in the girl's enclosed orchard and presents some similarities to Frayre's behavior toward Sor. Loÿs notes that she is unprotected (lines 351–52). He crosses himself, then lifts up the cloth protecting Clarisse's face from the sunlight: "s'a descouviert / le vis Clarisse tout a plain" (He uncovered Clarisse's face completely) (lines 362–63). As she does not move when he kisses her three times on the lips, he reaches the same conclusion as that of Frayre de Joy, that her lack of violent response gives him consent to have sex with her, and he acts on his sexual impulse (lines 384–86).

The scene is charged with erotic signs emphasizing exogamy, as the encounter is in a fruit orchard surrounded by *entes entées,* trees that have been grafted to increase their fertility. There is no need to expand here on the commonplace associations that were made between genealogy, degrees of parentage, and the branches of a tree. Suffice it to say that the grafted branch, often added via the female line, introduces new seed to the lineage. Clarisse's beauty in her father's eyes includes her similarity to a fruit tree: "ains arbres ne porta telz branchez; . . . et la mamelle que ot dure . . . reonde aussi con une pomme" (No tree had ever borne such a branch; and her hard breasts . . . were as round as apples) (lines 164, 167–69). A grafted branch also served as a metaphor for illegitimacy, and Richars' conception is both illegitimate and surreptitious. Loÿs enters the orchard, where her sickness has made Clarisse tremble like a leaf (line 254), by climbing an apple tree. Enclosed fruit trees in related texts are inevitably bound up with fertility, as well as beliefs regarding the effects of fruit on both conception and gestation.[5] In the anonymous Breton *lai* of *Tydorel,* for example, a barren queen is abducted and impregnated by a *chevalier faé* after she and her ladies eat a great deal of fruit and fall asleep in an orchard (lines 23–68). The line "li plusor ont mangé du fruit" appears again in the lady's subsequent account to her son, who can never sleep (lines 28, 372), as if eating fruit and sleeping were important contributory factors in his conception.[6]

Clarisse wakes up and only when Loÿs trips over his own spurs on the wet grass that surrounds the tree does she realize that he has impregnated her (lines 359–60, 387–96). Loÿs' access to Clarisse is ensured by a fruit tree associated with the Fall and with the acquisition of knowledge, but the garden's wet fertility ensures that he cannot escape unseen. In this marshy Eden, Loÿs flounders to stay upright, and the woman of this garden is purely a passive, even initially faceless, object. Clarisse's sycamore may shield her from the rays of the sun, as does her silken cloth, but the sun is not her worst enemy in her father's apparent haven. Worse, it turns out that Clarisse has been abandoned, although she is sick, drunk, and unconscious, because her governess has gone to hear Mass (lines 425–26).

In her distress on awakening, Clarisse tells her governess that she has been killed: "Uns chevaliers fu or cheens, / . . . qui m'a morte" (There was a knight in here, . . . that has killed me) (lines 432–33). She may have lost her name ("tost en avrai perdu mon nom") because she does not know the lineage of the man who has impregnated her (lines 437–38), but the governess replies that Clarisse has merely had a dream and that dreams are always deceptive (lines 445–48). If the governess attributes Clarisse's lies and her "dream" to her consumption of the medicinal wine, Clarisse's interpretation of events of which she has little conscious knowledge draws attention to the ambiguous circumstances of her father's protective enclosure of her, for her "name" is not her own: it is that of her dead mother. By losing both her life and her name through a deathlike sleep and a sexual assault, she has symbolically reenacted her dead mother's transference of both life and name to herself in childbirth. It follows that Richars' conception is placed within a lineage of dead mothers, one dead through childbirth, the other "dead" at the moment of conception. Before his encounter with his own double, the anonymous dead knight, the line between the living and the dead has been narrowed for Richars.

Clarisse's violent illness prior to her rape is not developed after she awakens, as if her sickness contributed to the conception of her son, and was dispelled by it. When Clarisse's tells her own version of his conception to the adult Richars, she says that she was asleep, but she does not say why (lines 2957–67). Like Loÿs, who has never spoken to her and did not know why she had lost consciousness, she omits to mention that she had fallen ill. In Loÿs' boastful account of his youthful adventure (lines 3696, 3711–32), he merely says that he raped the princess while she slept. However, he says that he read the shudders she made on waking up as a sign that he has taken her virginity and made her pregnant:

> Ens en entray et vi la bielle
> Endormie en une praiielle,
> Et tant li fis je de damage
> Que li toli son puchelage;
> Je m'en revinch mout tost arrier,
> Car grant paour och d'encombrier.
> Dont s'esveilla la damoisielle
> Et tressali si comme chelle
> Qui dist que de moy ert enchainte,
> Ne sai se fu parole fainte,
> Mais grant paour, ains qu'en ississe,
> Oy que la tieste ne pierdisse.
>
> (lines 3721–32)

[I went in and saw the beautiful girl asleep in a meadow, and I harmed her so that I took her virginity. I drew away very quickly because I was afraid I would meet some opposition. Then the girl woke up and shuddered, like someone who was saying that she was pregnant by me. I do not know if her words were false, but I was most afraid that I would lose my head before I got out of the place.]

Loÿs suggests that even her body language may be a lie, "Ne sai se fu parole fainte," and blames her shuddering rather than his own fear of discovery for his flight from the orchard. Richars is delighted to hear Loÿs' version of events, as it correlates exactly with the description he was given by his mother. Neither he nor the narrator condemns Loÿs' actions or beliefs. However, Loÿs' account does set up a troublesome question, as he was correct in surmising that her shiver signaled pregnancy, but did not know that she was lying in a drunken stupor after her governess had administered a remedy for this very shivering. He muses that her *parole* may have been *fainte,* in that the shivering itself, as the continuing symptom of her sickness, may not have signaled the moment of conception. The governess presented the medicinal wine to Clarisse as a means of deceiving her sickness through forgetting about it. It seems necessary to return to the opening scenes of the text and to reassess Clarisse's conception of Richars as it is told by the narrator, rather than its protagonists.

Prior to her rape, Clarisse's consumption of food and drink is placed in an incestuous continuum, in that Clarisse's father has displayed his young daughter in the public hall throughout her *norreture,* her upbringing, and enjoyed the sight of her (line 129). He has made her eat every day at his royal table "sans dangier" (without threat) at the marriageable age of fifteen (lines 180–81). As she reaches puberty, the king realizes that his daughter's public consumption as a substitute wife may make her vulnerable, or at least he fears that *someone* will eventually ravish her. He replaces his banqueting table with the enclosed garden traditionally used by the jealous husband to imprison his wife (lines 189–212). Clarisse becomes a *puella custodita,* familiar from other texts. In Gautier d'Arras' *Eracle* (a text preserved in the same manuscript as the sole copy of *Richars*), Athanaïs' adultery is excused on the grounds that by imprisoning her, her husband made her adultery inevitable.[7] The imprisoned wife or marriageable daughter is the target for many seducers in literature, but unlike Athanaïs or Flamenca, or indeed the mythological figure of Danaë, all Clarisse experiences is a diet of fruit, indigestion, and assault.

If a bodily tremor is taken by her and by Loÿs as a sure sign of pregnancy, her symptoms on awakening may well be misinterpreted by both of them, as she has merely returned to the state she was in before she drank the spiced wine. In medieval and early modern gynecology, shivering was a known sign of quickening, the first movements of the fetus that are felt by the mother some three months after conception. Clarisse has already displayed the sure sign of either conception or established pregnancy before Loÿs enters the garden. As her father has imprisoned her in an orchard and encouraged her to eat her fill of its fruit on the grounds that she is safe to do so (in the same way that she could eat at his public table "without danger"), there is a strong hint that he, not Loÿs, has planted the seed that will make Clarisse bear fruit. This possibility may in turn be silently recognized by the governess, for abortions were traditionally induced through the administration of a heavy dose of alcohol mixed with medicinal herbs, and this orchard doubles as a herb garden.

Clarisse's father returns and notices immediately that his daughter's face has altered in color (another sure sign of pregnancy). Both Clarisse and the governess suggest that she is merely suffering from a sickness of three days' standing that will pass within a week, but the girl spends eight months in her father's castle, and in the ninth, she becomes a mother (lines 471–76). Her father has a violent reaction to the infant's birth (lines 481–92). Richars is exposed, wrapped in a silk cloth given by Clarisse (not the cloth that covered her face in the orchard), and a luxurious belt and buckle (lines 521–26). He is unbaptized and has a pinch of salt (in a ritual observed for newborns prior to baptism) tucked into his clothes (lines 562–63).[8] He is found by a huntsman, who undresses the child and observes that he is a "belle proie" (line 646). Richars is viewed as a good prey, just as Clarisse regretted losing her son's soft flesh ("tendre chars") (line 531). The huntsman takes Richars to his wife, who also unwraps the infant and scrutinizes his face (lines 647–62). Both agree that their find is a good piece of game and observe that "il est dignes de haute table" (he is worthy of a noble table) (line 667). Richars is literally presented as the fruit of Clarisse's imprisonment in the orchard, albeit turned into hunted game, "chars" (line 531), by his exposure. He, like his mother, is worthy of consumption at a nobleman's table, and he, like Clarisse, is stripped of a covering of silk cloth by someone who perceives his unveiled face as good prey for a predator. These images continue the subtle hints of exploitation that surround Clarisse's fate in her father's court. The two crosses on the baby's shoulder should identify his noble lineage, but they are noted by the countess only after she has identified him as a fine object of consumption (line 669).

Joan Brumlik has suggested that the medieval romance tradition known as the Flight from the Incestuous Father thrives on actively suppressing the father's rape of his daughter, because heroines such as Manekine and Emaré flee before their fathers can act on their desires.[9] However, Elizabeth Archibald has pointed out that although father-daughter incest was silenced in both legal and literary texts, medieval adaptations of incest narratives find common ways of symbolizing without naming the consummated incest of their source, mostly through riddles and through food metaphors. One example cited by Archibald from the Prose *Tristan* combines a verse riddle and a food metaphor that is particularly apposite for *Richars li Biaus:*[10]

> Un arbre, fait il, oi jadis,
> Que j'amai plus que paradis.
> Tant le gardai que fruit porta;

La biauté del fruit m'enorta
A ce que je la flor en pris.
Après le fruit tant en mespris
Que le fruit manjai sanz refu.
Vassal, devine que ce fu!

[He said, "I once had a tree that I loved more than Paradise. I watched over it so long that it bore fruit; the beauty of the fruit excited me so much that I took its flower. Afterward, I despised the fruit so much that I ate it without any refusal. Vassal, guess what happened!"]

Here the father, a cannibalistic giant, boasts that he deflowered his daughter, the "fruit" of his beloved wife, and later ate her. It is striking that a fourteenth-century adaptation of *Richars li Biaus, Lion de Bourges,* should contain an explicit father-daughter incest narrative.[11] Such texts are also strongly concerned with the tensions between a marital system that was predicated on exogamy but that sought to keep lands within kinship and alliance groupings, something that would be guaranteed by marrying a blood relative or affine (endogamy). As Yin Liu has pointed out, in medieval romances, "to be strictly accurate, the threat is not only incest but also the violation of exogamy."[12] The majority of the French and Middle English incest-themed romances play on the threat that is posed to exogamy by possessive parents and by courtiers who privilege the maintenance of patrilinear succession. In this context, *Richars li Biaus,* composed in a linguistic borderland region but in a single language, appears to question the reliability of grafting a family tree. Clarisse is emphatically associated with both father-daughter incest and with an ambiguous conception scene, one that is narrated repeatedly in order to display its inherent unreliability. Loÿs is a passing stranger who makes an opportunistic assault on a desirable, enclosed noblewoman, but he may well be accidentally led into membership of an incestuous lineage that has already been established.

Food and consumption mark Richars' reunion with this problematic maternal lineage. When the adult Richars meets his grandfather and mother, they are eating together at a table that is illumined by Clarisse's beauty (lines 1951–58). Richars' sexual desire for Clarisse is stalled only by the prompt warnings of Nature, who tells him not to touch her, and he sits down at the same table to join in their meal (lines 1981–82). Clarisse scrutinizes this handsome stranger and calls on God, the "father of all" to witness that he looks like the man who lay with her when she was sleeping alone in the orchard (lines 1991–93). Later, as Richars fights their assailants, she prays to God, her father, "who made your daughter into your own mother" to save this man but cannot fathom why she feels a loving and protective urge toward him (lines 2055–60). It is the silken cloth, not his birthmark of two crosses, that enables Clarisse to recognize her son, as if the ostensible sign of noble birth were a red herring throughout the text, and her recollection of her rape were the true marker of their connection by blood (lines 2328–46, 2363–68). A silk cloth, initially placed over her face to protect it, stripped away by Loÿs, and another cloth used to wrap and identify the infant as a noblewoman's child, act as the sign that *almost* allows exogamy to happen: the king is both pleased and aggrieved to see the arrival of his grandson Richars (lines 2369–70). The narrator adds that this piece of silk was originally sent to Clarisse from Carsidone (line 2366), which is the city ruled by the sultan who is currently, many years later, besieging the court in the hope of abducting Clarisse and marrying her (lines 2813–15). This cloth represents yet another vain attempt to move the daughter out of her father's clutches and into an exogamous marriage. Clarisse may be an adult who has long ago experienced childbirth (and therefore betrothed by *unitas carnis* to the child's father),[13] but she is still imprisoned within her endogamic fortress and is besieged by a foreign suitor who is fought off by both her father and her son. Richars, in turn, is tormented by the need to find his biological father in a location as far removed as possible from this incestuous court, but he forbids Clarisse to marry anyone else until he has found him (lines 2400–2409).

Richars li Biaus provides striking contrasts with the Catalan and Franco-Italian tales studied in the previous chapter, because they relate their sleeping, enchanted, or dead heroines with exogamy as the consequence of violent invasion and deceptive diplomacy. Clarisse, like Sor de Plaser, Brianda, and Anfelis, is her father's sole heir. However, the French text is concerned with the deadly impact not of a stranger's invasion, but of imprisonment within the family unit. According to Catherine Jones, the silken cloth Clarisse uses both to drape her face and, later, to wrap her newborn son, is a term used often in other texts for a shroud.[14] Clarisse's reaction to her rape, on awakening, is to say that she has been killed. After her son is exposed, she resumes an incestuous cohabitation with her father. Clarisse only perpetuates this stifling family unit by marrying her rapist, because the initial ambiguous conception comes full circle to ensure that Loÿs can be made king of Frisia by Richars' claiming the right to act not as Clarisse's son but as "li niés le roy" (the grandson of the king) (line 5433). Richars' quest to find his father may be viewed as an attempt to make himself legitimate, but it also ensures that Clarisse is definitively enclosed within the violent manipulation of her body that was inaugurated by her father, and that ties her irrevocably to his decision to imprison her within his orchard.

This text that predates *Frayre de Joy e Sor de Plaser* and *Blandin* draws attention to the threat of endogamy that can be traced in the Catalan tales. Sor is visited in her tower only by her parents, whose distress at seeing her pregnant encompasses only two possibilities: a bird, or the Holy Spirit. As Sor was not deemed to be marriageable even before her death, her mother does not assume that a lover could be involved. Frayre's invasion of this enclosed space, like Loÿs', is presented as *raptus*. He has already prepared remedies and made arrangements to reward Virgil with lands, as if he already knows he will marry the emperor's daughter. Yet the protagonists are designated as siblings by their names and hold corresponding rings, not as a sign of pre-destined love between social equals, but rather as a gesture that highlights the suppression of marriage outside the kinship group and the fear of invasion by a "foreign" lineage and language that marks the prologue. In *Blandin*, Brianda's rescue is made possible by her brother's request and orders to Blandin, as if he were explicitly welcoming the opportunity to allow her to marry a knight errant from a distant land.

It is tempting to ascribe a direct connection between the orchard rape of *Richars li Biaus* and the tale of Troÿlus and Zellandine, which is woven into the adventures in the third part of the romance *Perceforest*.[15] Gilles Roussineau emphasizes one key divergence from the early modern Sleeping Beauty tradition as well as from *Frayre,* which is that the two protagonists are already in love and have exchanged rings before Zellandine falls into her enchanted sleep.[16] However, this detail is important to the interlaced structure of the romance, rather than to the tale itself. Zellandine's sleep is set among a number of other episodes in which sleep, both natural and enchanted, offers opportunities for trickery or influence. Such episodes are especially important when they are slotted between episodes of the story of Troÿlus and Zellandine (L, LI, LII, LIX, LX). In chapter LIII, Estonné has an enchanted dream that assists him in consummating his marriage to Troÿlus' sister Priande at the most propitious moment for conceiving an heir. In chapter LIV, the villainous Bruiant sans Foi puts Maronès to sleep to do him harm, and in chapter LVI, King Perceforest wanders through the enchanted forest, alternating between sleeping and waking. The sequences continues after the tale of Zellandine has moved on. In chapter LVII, Bruiant sans Foi and his men kill two knights in their sleep. It is thematically important to this vast and complex work that Zellandine's unconscious state should be identified as sleep rather than either death or sickness.

When the episode is read in the light of *Richars li Biaus,* the emphasis on endogamy resurfaces. Zellandine has returned home to the island of Zellande, which is ruled by her father, Zelland, and, it seems, by his unnamed sister, who sleeps in a room near to his own (LII.90, lines 449–50). Zellande is a realm marked by doubles and deceptively incestuous sibling relationships, but Zellandine's own brother Zellandin is absent on a quest to find his lady, so any hint of excessive sameness between this sibling pair is neatly averted (L.58). The only place where people live together on this barren, flat, depopulated island is the Chastel Jumel, but the castle is deceptively placed next to another unnamed castle, and it is not clear to observers such as Troÿlus which one of the twin castles is King Zelland's seat.[17] Zellandine is already destined to marry Nervin, the son of a neighboring lady of the Nervinois lineage, and Nervin tries to act as Troÿlus's substitute in order to win Zellandine (L). Meanwhile, Troÿlus is adopted as a curative fool with the patronage of a "natural fool" at Zelland's court (L.293–96).

The island's divine rulers are the three goddesses of love, childbirth, and destiny: Venus, Lucina, and Themis (or Sarra). It is Venus who ensures Troÿlus's successful conquest of the endogamic fortress. Zellandine falls into a stupor after pricking her finger while spinning flax, but her elderly aunt has forgotten Themis's curse to this effect, one she overheard soon after Zellandine's birth during the feast of thanks she organized for the divine trio of midwives. As the aunt forgot the curse, she also forgot that Venus promised to rescue Zellandine from her enchantment by ensuring that the offending shard of flax would be sucked out of her finger (L.70, lines 464–85; LIX. 211–12). The aunt knows both the cause and the cure for the girl's coma, but her forgetfulness ensures that events pursue their course in making Zellandine bear Troÿlus's son. Forgetfulness is a feature of the island of Zellande, as Nervin's mother makes Troÿlus both amnesiac and insane in the hope of leading him away from his quest to find Zellandine, and this enchantment is broken only by Venus.

Nor is Troÿlus's intellect much valued in this realm. Once he is released from the enchantment that turns him into a court fool, Venus gives an oracular order to Troÿlus to enter the tower where a beautiful girl is lying "like a stone" and to "pluck the curative fruit in the furrow" (LII.80, lines 46–53). He cannot interpret her words. Venus's feminine voice ("la voix femenine") explains curtly that the only gloss her riddle requires of him is his physical action as a man:

> Les vers n'ont point mestier de glose.
> Non pourtant je dys une chose:
> Amours trouvera la raiere
> Et Venus, qui scet la maniere
> Du fruit trouver, le queillera.
> Nature le composera.
> Se tu es homs, tantost va t'ent.
> Ne nous fay cy long parlement.
>
> (LII.80, lines 67–72)

[The verses need no gloss, but I'll say one thing anyway: Love will find the furrow and Venus, who knows how to find the fruit, will pluck it. Nature will construct it. If you are a man, go your way now. Do not keep us talking here.]

As the maternal goddesses covertly weave events, King Zelland takes the advice of his physicians and places Zellandine at the top of a walled tower in the hope that she may be cured by the intervention of the sun god. Zelland and his forgetful sister are Zellandine's only visitors. Like Clarisse, Zellandine is enclosed within an endogamic fortress marked by the faulty mental processes of her protectors. This cognitive malfunction affects the king and his sister's interpretation of the events that follow.

Zellandine's tower is walled up except for an east-facing window, which has been left open as "la voie des dieux" (the way of the gods) to welcome the divine visitor whom Zelland hopes will come to cure his daughter (66, lines 331–33; 82, lines 123–24). He believes that a god has indeed come to visit when he sees a bright light shining at the window (91, lines 433–59), but it is in fact a torch that has been lit by Troÿlus to enable him to see in Zellandine's room. This ironic detail has been interpreted in various ways,[18] but it points most strongly to an intertextual connection with Jupiter's visit to the bed of Danaë in the form of a shower of gold.[19] Danaë, a paradigmatic *puella custodita,* is particularly relevant, as she is enclosed in a bronze chamber by her father to prevent her conceiving a child:

> In thalamum Danaë ferro saxoque perennem
> Quae fuerat uirgo tradita, mater erat.
>
> (*Amores* 3.4, lines 20–22)[20]

[Iron and stone, indestructible materials, composed the bedchamber Danaë entered a virgin; she left it a mother.]

Danaë's chamber is located at the top of a tower in Ovid, and underground in other versions.[21] In the *Perceforest*, Zellandine's chamber is accessible first via an underground tunnel, then by climbing to the top of the impregnable tower (91, lines 452–57).

Zelland and his sister glimpse the intruder as he escapes through the window, clad in full armor, on the back of a giant bird. Zelland concludes that this must be Mars, the god of battles, because he is their lineage ancestor (92, lines 471–74). Zellandine's aunt interprets her crumpled bed linen as a sign that the ancestor's cure may have been more than medicinal, and the narrator exploits the double meaning of *niepce* to hint once again at an incestuous continuum: "la dame se doubta que Mars, dieu des batailles, n'eust trop acointé sa niepce" (The lady suspected that Mars, god of battles, had been too familiar with her niece/his granddaughter) (93, lines 506–9). In *Amores* 3.4, Ovid comments that placing women under armed guard is futile, as Rome's founding fathers were engendered by the god Mars "non . . . sine crimen" (not without crime) (lines 39–40), alluding to the conception of Romulus and Remus (see also *Amores* 2.19, line 27). Intriguingly, the tale of Danaë was interpreted in divergent ways in the Middle Ages, both as a narrative concerning a prostitute and as an allegory of virginity.[22] Zellandine's predicament is certainly ambiguous, but the interpretation of it by her paternal relatives seems perverse. They prefer to ascribe her "cure" to someone within their kinship group, despite having been repeatedly told that Troÿlus is the predicted agent of her awakening. Zellandine's family maintains an endogamic ethos, certain that fertilization by its own patrilinear ancestor can only add to its prestige (211, lines 58–63). The rulers of this island that worships the three goddesses of sexual reproduction appear to suffer from a distorted vision of what constitutes aristocratic fertility.

When Zellandine awakes and her aunt remembers both Themis's curse and Venus's promise (§ LIX.209–10),[23] this does not affect how the family interprets the pregnancy. The aunt still believes that Mars has fathered the child, especially when a bird-siren (in fact an emissary from Morgane la Faee) takes him away (212–13, lines 119–26). It is only a fortnight later, when Zellandine recalls her love for Troÿlus (and, in redaction C, plans to conceal her rape and childbirth from him [318]), that she notices that she is no longer wearing the ring she exchanged with him, and she puzzles over how he could have visited her to exchange their rings (213–14). Even as she realizes that Troÿlus visited her as she slept, Zellandine retains the illusion of divine conception. In version C, she concludes with a powerful, absurd logic that Mars must have stolen the ring.[24] She seems to have absorbed her family's belief that only a paternal ancestor can be at the root of her mysterious adventure. She is soon disabused and reunited with Troÿlus, and the tale ends with an ironic acknowledgment by Zellandine of the family's distorted interpretation of events. As she elopes with Troÿlus, she sends a maid to tell her father and aunt that she has been taken away by Mars to his lands, to escape the forced marriage to Nervin that they had planned (LX.236, lines 780–84). Throughout the tale, Mars acts as the Zelland lineage's encoded sign for the maintenance of a hermetic, self-perpetuating kinship group against the pressures of exogamous suitors.

If Zellandine's situation dramatizes her family's psychological entrapment in sameness and lineage, Troÿlus breaks into this endogamic stronghold in several ways. He reaches the island of Zellande thanks to two chance meetings with the mariners seeking out Zellandine's brother Zellandin, whose ship refuses to take them to England (§ L; § LX, 225–26). If her brother cannot make good his escape from the patrilinear fortress, Troÿlus finds it equally difficult to obtain access. Once he reaches the island, he is saved from a rising tide by Nervin's mother. She casts a spell on Troÿlus in his sleep that makes him both forgetful and mad, so that her son can don his armor and win Zellandine for himself. Troÿlus gains access to Zellandine's tower only thanks to the intervention of Venus, who cures his madness while he sleeps (again) in her temple and sends him the spirit Zephir as his helper (L.85, lines 226–28). Two periods of sleep allow Troÿlus to obtain the right kind of assistance in his quest, but they also illustrate the connection between sleep and forgetfulness, especially the kind of forgetting that may (as in *Richars li Biaus*) mask an uncomfortable truth about the causes and motives of the protagonists' actions.

Troÿlus's actions are consistently more passive than those of Frayre de Joy, in keeping with the former's role as the enactor of the three goddesses' plan, and with his hope that he may cure, not seduce, Zellandine. He is carried to the window by Zephir in bird form and finds himself in a room that is lit by a single lamp (§ LII.86–87). He finds Zellandine lying naked on a bed hung with white drapes and hears her gentle breathing. He lights a torch to look at her more closely and it seems to him that she is of a healthy color (87, lines 300–310). Troÿlus whispers to her to wake up, and then prods her repeatedly with his finger, "il la bouta de son doy par plusieurs foys" (87, line 318). He despairs that his lady, as beautiful as a goddess ("belle comme une deesse"), should be so insensible to his efforts (87, line 322). The gods continue to intervene in his actions. Prompted not by his own thoughts but by Venus's son Amours, Troÿlus asks Zellandine to give her consent to his kissing her: "Pucelle, plaise vous que je vous baise?" (88, line 343). At this point the personifications Discretion and Reason appear to caution him against intruding further into a sleeping woman's private space (88, lines 345–48). Personified Desire then makes an appearance and pleases Troÿlus by contending that his kisses may well cure Zellandine: "car baisier porte medecine en pluseurs manieres, et par especial il resuscite les personnes tressaillies et sy appaise les troublez" (For kissing is curative in many ways, and especially in that it resuscitates people who have lost their senses, and it appeases those who are troubled) (88, lines 353–55). He kisses her lips more than twenty times over, but he loses confidence as she does not revive. Troÿlus then prays to Venus for help, as she promised that Amours would assist him in finding "la raiere ou gist le fruit dont la pucelle doit estre garie, et vous mesmes le me devez aprendre a coeillier, car je ne sçay ou celle herbe croit!" (the furrow where the fruit lies that will cure the girl, and you [Venus] in person must teach me to pluck it, because I do not know where this herb grows!) (89, lines 374–77).[25] Venus stands invisibly beside Troÿlus and urges him to make love to Zellandine, despite the protestations of Loyalty (89–90). Thanks to these allusions to the closing passages of the *Roman de la rose,* the lover obeys the orders of Venus and breaches the imprisoning tower of this lady, once again via a window, to pluck not a flower, but a curative piece of fruit: "le fruit est coeilliet dont la belle sera garie" (The fruit is plucked through which the girl will be cured) (90, lines 422–23). Unlike Frayre de Joy's and Loÿs' solitary decisions to overlook their victims' lifeless state, the small room is crowded with literary allusions, personifications, and invisible deities, who urge Troÿlus to act on his erotic "heat."

However, these elaborate discussions of Troÿlus's wish to "cure" Zellandine of sleep are undermined by his reaction to the "bref soupir" (short sigh) she lets out after he has finished taking her virginity (90, line 415). He leaps away from her, ready to deny his actions should she accuse him of rape, and leaves at Zephir's prompting (lines 416–19). Troÿlus's guilty reaction at this point is very reminiscent of Loÿs' flight in *Richars li Biaus*. No matter how much his supernatural helpers present metanarratorial justifications, Troÿlus remains conscious of the fact that he is a man who has abused a sleeping woman in her bedchamber. The most obvious distinctions of the *Perceforest* episode at this point are that Zellandine is immobile but far from either physically sick or dead, and that Troÿlus is not motivated by opportunism. On the contrary, the narrative emphasis is on his preordained role in freeing her from her imprisonment.

The tale in the *Perceforest* cannot be separated from its place in a much more complex genealogical romance. The goddesses and Morgane la Faee place great emphasis on Benoÿc, the "fruit" of this transgressive cure, who is destined to be the ancestor of Lancelot du Lac. Troÿlus's sufferings in the cause of his love match with Zellandine seem to be overlaid with intertextual allusions to Lancelot's troubled love for Guinevere. However, what seems evident is that it is also a description of the efforts made by both Troÿlus and Venus to undo Zellandine's entrapment within a stiflingly close patrilinear structure and an intended marriage to a nobleman of the island of Zellande whom she does not love. Intriguingly, Zelland persists in his determination to marry the reawakened Zellandine to Nervin (LX.226–27). This is despite the fact that Nervin has confessed to his mother's dishonorable manipulation of Troÿlus (LI.77, lines 35–44). In manuscript C, Zellandine remembers her love for Troÿlus a fortnight after her reawakening, but her love has, says the narrator, been asleep a full year, not nine months. Its "sleep" dates from the sickness that struck her on her departure from England.[26] It seems that it was her return to her father's castle, not the enchanted sleep caused by the pricked finger, that made her forget her love for Troÿlus.

This is only a short tale set within the imposing spread of the *Perceforest,* and it forms part of a lengthy exploration of perception and interpretation, focused closely on the nature of signs and writing. This broader thematic element returns us to the fruit metaphors that were explored earlier in *Richars li Biaus*. Troÿlus has an adventure before he is reunited with Zellandine in which he defeats Bruiant sans Foi, the paradigmatic traitor-knight villain in book 3 of the *Perceforest,* thanks to an apple that is handed to him from the Fairy Queen's mysterious chariot (LX). This apple, I will argue, shed significant light on the tale of Zellandine. Troÿlus encounters the Fairy Queen's horseless and driverless chariot as it travels silently through various scenes in this part of the romance. He hears the voices of two women keening behind its thick cloth-of-gold drapery, and he fears that it may contain someone on his or her deathbed:

> Or advint que au passer du charriot le bacheler perceut une main qui se boutoit hors parmy la couverture, tenant une pomme vermeille, et oÿ que dedens le charriot une demoiselle disoit: "Chevalier, tenez cette pomme et la donnez a vostre hoste." Le chevalier, qui entendy ses moz, print la pomme, et lors il perdy soudainement la veue du charriot, dont il fut moult esbahi. (LX.215, lines 33–39)

[Now it happened that when the cart went by, the youth glimpsed a hand that stretched out of the drapes, holding a red apple, and he heard a young woman inside the cart saying, "Knight, take this apple and give it to your host." The knight who heard these words took the apple and suddenly lost sight of the chariot, which amazed him.]

Troÿlus looks at the red apple and sees that it is marvelous ("moult merveilleuse"),

> car l'en avoit escript dessus aucuns signes dont il ne sceut cognoistre la substance. Sy s'appensa qu'il la mettroit appart et que elle ne lui estoit point donnee sans grant mistere. (215, lines 39–44)

> [for on it were inscribed some signs that he could not decipher. So he thought that he would set it aside and that it could not have been given to him without some great mystery.]

Troylus seeks hospitality overnight in a sinister castle and falls through a trapdoor into a pit. He eventually remembers that this "pomme a plenté de figures par dehors escriptes" (apple inscribed with many figures on the surface) (219, lines 164–65) may be destined for his captor and may help to free him and his fellow prisoners. The Chevalier au Dauphin exclaims that such an apple cannot be mere fruit and must possess special powers, "il ne peut estre que ceste pomme ne ait aucune vertu" (line 169). Accordingly, the prisoners use the nobly worked apple ("pomme noblement ouvree") (line 188) to bribe their jailer. The jailer covets the bribe as an object that is richly worked ("ouvree"), but its immediate action on his heart stems from it being a mere apple (lines 193–96). He helps the men to escape by replacing them with statues and poses as a madman before his master. Bruiant sans Foi kills the jailer for his absurd corruption by the gift of an apple when a gold coin would have sufficed (222, lines 271–78). The *mistere* and *vertu* of the apple appear to be promised by its unreadable inscription, but once it has been handed over to Troÿlus's jailer, its unreadable signs seem to be invisible both to him and to Bruiant, and its impact comes from the fact that it remains simply a piece of fruit. At the moment of its transfer from the dark cell to the jailer's space outside it, the coveted object begins to act within those who hold it, rather than from the outside. The "figures par dehors escriptes" of the apple determine the jailer's actions; unreadable signs have been absorbed, despite the material worthlessness of the bribe. The double action and opaque interpretative status of the inscribed apple secures the knights' release from their unlit, underground dungeon. This reminds the reader of Troÿlus's incitement to rape by an assemblage of opaque fruit and medicinal metaphors, invisible deities and personifications that make him read the wordless, opaque signs of Zellandine's unconscious body (her slight blush, her short sigh) in the light of a sexual invitation.

Through this apple, which is interpreted as either an enchanted object covered in unreadable signs, or plain food, Troÿlus is reunited with the "fruit de la medicine" that he was told he would find in Zellandine. He is led to Morgane la Faee's castle and introduced to her charge, their son Benoÿc. Benoÿc bears a mysterious image on his shoulder, designed, explains Morgane, to protect him from the jealous cunning of bad mothers, "car quant elles se voient delivrer de mauvais fruit, souventesfois par leur malice elles le changent a ung bon" (for when they discover they have given birth to bad fruit, they often exchange it maliciously for a good one) (LX.230, lines 565–67). Benoÿc is the closely protected fruit that he and Zellandine produce to cure her of her entrapment in endogamy, in the double prison of an impregnable tower and of sleep. He is destined to grow up in the care of Morgane, because he is the ancestor of a great lineage. As was seen earlier, Zellandine's family systematically misinterpret Benoÿc's conception and disappearance. Troÿlus, however, achieves knowledge through encounters with unreadable signs, the engraved apple and his son's protective mark, as well as his own willingness to accept their power without demanding a gloss of their symbolism.

It is not the beauty, still less the significance, of the apple's signs, that impress the jailer enough to free the men. Somehow, his emotions are altered when he realizes that all they have given him is the object itself. The apple, a simple object without other meanings ascribed to it, prompts him to assist the men. Similarly, Zellandine's family consistently fail to comprehend that their daughter's impregnation at the hands (so they believe) of the god Mars is in fact exogamy, the grafting of a new branch onto their etiolating family tree. When Troÿlus achieves an understanding of the role that he and Zellandine have played in creating a new lineage through the conception of Benoÿc, he also accepts that their own narrative has been no more than an element in the service of a metanarrative (the Arthurian cycle) that he is closed to him. Venus tells Troÿlus invisibly in the temple of the three goddesses, "De toy . . . est issue la semence dont la fleur de proesse naistera. Sy n'en demande plus, car nous l'avons en garde" (From you came the seed from which the flower of Prowess will be born. Now do not ask any more about it, for we are looking after him) (LX.230–31, lines 587–89).

For all its complexity, Troÿlus's encounter with Zellandine was, it seems, no more than an act of fertilization.

In two monolingual narratives, it would seem that women who consume fruit and who fall asleep are exposed to invasion by lovers and that these tales are subtended by a silenced narrative, that of incest. In her essay *Vivre l'orange*, Hélène Cixous redefines the patriarchal commonplace associating women with the giving of apples (Eve, the Hesperides, the apple of Discord) by playing through languages, to enable a feminine writing that would have access to concepts not otherwise allowed in patriarchy.[27] These intensely autobiographical, physical modes of association and signification are termed, in Cixous' blended authorial and personal voice, the orange. Cixous' essay deploys different ways not of consuming the orange (a pun on her multilingual birthplace, Oran), but of living it: of entering a dream state, beyond conscious reality and within languages, that allows the unconscious to be experienced rather than mediated:

> Dans la traduction de la pomme (en orange), j'essaie de me dénoncer. Façon de prendre ma part. Du fruit. De la jouissance. De me risquer à dire ce que je ne suis pas encore en mesure d'assurer par mes propres soins. De me pousser au-delà de mes limites, de m'obliger à m'avancer où je n'ai pas pied, au risque de m'abîmer.[28]

> [In the translation of the apple into an orange, I try to betray/denounce myself. It's a way of taking my part. Of the piece of fruit. Of *jouissance*. Of trying to say something that I am not yet able to ensure I can say by my own means. Of pushing myself beyond my own boundaries, forcing myself to move forward into a place where I cannot touch the floor, where I run the risk of sinking/damaging myself.]

Cixous' words draw attention to the multiple connotations of languages. Will she sink into the depths of the unconscious (*s'abîmer*) or be bruised, like a dropped fruit (*s'abîmer*)? The writer's task, she suggests, is to peel off the layers of social obligation and to ripen autonomously. In this state, the feminine author can write for no audience or patron: "Et elle écrit pour personne, elle donne des noms, des fruits, la main, dans le noir" (And she writes for no one, she gives names, fruit, her hand, in the dark) (43). Just as the disembodied hand emerges from a curtained cart to give Troÿlus an apple inscribed with signs that neither he nor anyone else can read, so he has to read Zellandine's body and both consume it and fertilize it, without a gloss.

The *entredeux* emerges as a highly permeable, multilingual, and atemporal state that may be both vulnerable and fruitful and may potentially allow hidden narratives to be put into corporeal form. In this way, the statement "Elle n'écrit pour personne" has two inferences: she writes for the eyes of no one, and she writes in the voice of no one but her own. Yet a writing that has no Other at all can hardly avoid falling into self-referential traps, "s'abîmer" into its own *mise-en-abyme* of the creative process, or (worse) it risks committing what may appear to be incest but without an aggressor. Incest with the self, without a desired Other, may resemble the underlying concerns of the monolingual narratives produced in linguistic borderlands that have been examined in this chapter.

The narration of love in the *entredeux* may be reinscribed as a mode of writing, one that also may be read "in the light of an apple," overturning traditional constructions of gender, eroticism, and narrative. It could be argued that the fruitful sleep of these heroines is less vulnerable than it seems, in that such scenes interrupt the workings of the marital traffic in women, the basis of exogamy in terms of a social system controlled by the spouses' parents, and allow them to conceive in secret, in ways that are represented as incest, but that are hidden narratives, only represented through unreadable signs. The unreadable apple refers to the unspoken incest narratives that subtend both the tales in *Richars li Biaus* and the *Perceforest*. It also points to the perils of assuming that a monolingual text is to be viewed as a simple expression of a collective mother tongue.

Part 3

THE *Monolangue*

7

THE MULTILINGUAL *Paris and Vienne*

JACQUES DERRIDA'S FAMOUS ESSAY *Le Monolinguisme de l'autre* constructs a series of imagined dialogues to explore the proposition "Je n'ai qu'une langue, ce n'est pas la mienne" (I have only one language/tongue, it is not mine). Derrida's essay unpacks the complex modern associations that are made between the French language as a sign of culture, nation, and race, in order to expose them as illusions, just as the "mother tongue" itself is a deeply embedded fantasy.[1] Derrida's *monolangue* reflects the fact that language, while it shapes and determines our every perception, is also multiple, unreliable, and alienating. Every language, even the "mother tongue," comes from the other, and it may be lost, forgotten, or taken away.[2] In this final section I examine fifteenth-century works that are marked by the developing association of French and Catalan with national languages. If the *monolangue* is characterized by an uneasy awareness that the mother tongue is an illusion, neither mother nor a single tongue, these texts may be viewed as three very different explorations of that tension.

Seeing is not necessarily believing; so says the opening *auctoritas* of the romance of *Paris et Vienne* by Pierre de La Cépède:

> Alain, qui moult fu saige, a escript au livre de ses doctrines une auctorite que dit en latin: *hoc crede quod tibi verum esse videtur*. Et veult autant dire ceste auctorite, extraicte du latin en francois: tu croyras des chouses que te resembleront estre veritables. (Kaltenbacher, 391)[3]

> [Alanus, who was very wise, wrote an *auctoritas* in the book of his doctrines that says in Latin: *hoc crede quod tibi verum esse videtur*. This *auctoritas* means, once it is taken from Latin and put into French, "You will believe in the things that appear to be true to your eyes."]

Pierre warns his reader twice, once in Latin and once in French, to be wary of what they see. He comments that he has always taken pleasure in reading romances and ancient chronicles ("romans et croniques des ystoyres anciennes") that are impossible to credit with any truth value ("impossibles a croyre"), but he makes an exception for a work such as *Paris et Vienne* on the grounds that "la matiere me semble estre bien raisonnable et asses creable, et aussi que l'ystoyre est asses plaisant" (its matter seems to me to be quite reasonable and believable enough, also because the story is quite pleasing) (392). He draws attention in conventional terms to the perils of reading fiction while praising his choice of story on the grounds that it seems reasonable enough to him. Pierre's subjective assessment as a reader who is fond but critical of romances is that tales such as this are endowed with more verisimilitude than are others; this implies that his reader owes the text primarily to La Cépède's moral discernment and good taste in literary matters. The prologue also places *Paris et Vienne* at further remove from its audience, as he claims that his preferred tale is accessible only through two layers of translation: "j'ay tenu ung livre, escript en langaige prouvensal, qui fu extraist d'ung aultre livre, escript en langaige cathalain . . . cy ay entrepris a vous estrayre l'ystoire du langaige provincial en francoys" (I had a book that was written in the Provençal language and had been translated from another book written in Catalan. . . . I set out to translate the tale for you from the language of Provence into French) (392). Lest we should believe that we are dealing with a reliable translation, Pierre apologizes for his poor French, "que je ne suis pas Francois de nature, ainz fuz nes et nouris en la cite de Marcelle" (for I am not French by birth, but I was born and raised in the city of Marseille).

This is an ambiguous opening for a romance that draws its authority from its credibility. If entertaining texts are deceptive illusions, what can the reader make of Pierre's assertion that he has the impression ("me semble") that this tale has some credibility and that he has struggled to render his secondhand source into a language he does not master? He makes no assurances within the text that the story is true. It is never anything other than a fiction that relies more on psychological motivation than on the marvelous, unlike its Arthurian rivals. All we are given to rely upon is an *auctoritas* that spells out a simple warning against gullibility but that needs a translator to make its sense accessible to the reader.

Compared to the opening of *Le Livre de Boece de Consolacion* (c. 1350–60), which became in the fifteenth century one of the most widely read French translations from a Latin source, Pierre's prologue seems ever more tentative.[4] Here, we are told that too many people are led by the evidence of their senses into illusions and ill-humored disappointment about worldly and sensual things. They can learn to use their reason in an educated manner to move away from their entrapment in superficial impressions: "A telz gens doncques est proufitable la translacion de cest livre et mesmement a ceulx qui n'entendent pas le langage des Latins" (The translation of this book is useful for such people, as well as for those who do not understand Latin) (Cropp, 19–20). Here, vernacular translation is designed to primarily serve the original text, to clarify it, and to teach the intellectual skill of clear reasoning to a wider public. By contrast, Pierre's prologue is almost opaque, for vernaculars are piled on top of vernaculars and the text itself seems to derive its credibility only from the subjective impressions of its reader and scribe. However, Pierre depicts his heroine, Vienne, as someone who seeks to emulate "l'ystoire qui se nomme 'Boece, de Consolation,'" a tale she has heard often and that she assumes is as familiar to others as to herself, as if her sufferings were intended to be read both as a vernacular translation and as a *translatio* from masculine to feminine subjects, of the French text: "Et pourtant quant a moy, que ne suis que une simple fame, en qui a peu de scens et de vertu . . . je ne scay trover aultre remedde, fors seulement comme ledit Boesse trova, c'est avoir bonne pacience en tout et louer Dieu de tout ce qu'il luy plaira ordener" (Yet as for me, a mere woman bereft of good sense and virtue . . . I can find no other remedy save the one that Boethius found, that is to say, to be patient in all things, and to praise God for whatever he wishes to ordain) (Kaltenbacher, 531).[5] Listening to the translated story of Boethius has been *proufitable* to Vienne, who is, it seems, as discerning a reader (or listener) of vernacular texts as La Cépède.

The geographical origin of this romance is not in doubt, as three of the surviving manuscripts of Pierre de La Cépède's *Paris et Vienne* were copied in Provence in the first half of the fifteenth century. A copy dated internally December 1438 (n.s. 1439) attributes the text to two names: "escript par Pierre de la Cypede de Marseille, traslatie par Inart Beyssan."[6] By the midfifteenth century, *translater* had acquired its modern sense of "translation" as well as of "rendering or reworking"; Beyssan appears to relegate La Cépède to the role of a mere scribe.[7] Kaltenbacher noted that Beyssan's copy of La Cépède's romance was strongly marked by Occitanisms, and he certainly seems to be working from an Occitan or Catalan source, since he names the heroine Viana. This, along with the date of the manuscript, makes it possible that Beyssan, and not La Cépède, was responsible for rendering an Occitan or Catalan text into French. Another manuscript (Paris Bibl. de l'Arsenal 3000) was copied in the Provençal castle of Orgon, which also points to local diffusion through its connection with the house of Anjou-Provence.[8]

La Cépède's text is a long and evidently expanded version of the *Paris et Vienne* tale that circulated widely, mostly in print, in the last decades of the fifteenth century. Anna Maria Babbi has named La Cépède's text version α, and the anonymous shorter version β. Ironically, no Occitan text survives of a romance that was read from the late fifteenth century in Italian, English, Dutch, Swedish, Castilian, *aljamiado-morisco* (Castilian transliterated into Arabic script), Catalan, Yiddish, and Armenian.[9] Babbi's extensive published work on the multiple versions of *Paris et Vienne* demonstrates the remarkable popularity of the tale. This is also reflected in the speed with which multilingual book markets such as that of Antwerp responded to the demand for translations. Gherard Leeu printed a French text in Antwerp in 1487. In the ensuing year, Leeu published translations of this text into Flemish, German, and Dutch (Low German). He also reproduced Caxton's English version of 1485 in 1492. The Tuscan version of the romance (printed in Treviso as early as 1482 and also edited by Babbi), was later translated into Armenian (printed in Marseille in 1540 but probably composed in Venice), and an *ottava rima* poem in Yiddish attributed to the humanist Elia Levita (*Pariz un' Viene*, c. 1514, printed in Verona in 1594). Later, the Italian version was adapted into Greek verse by the Cretan poet Vitzentzos Kornaros (*Erotokritos*, 1640).[10] The tale was rendered into Latin for the instruction and amusement of children by the humanist bishop of Rieux, Jean Le Pins (printed in Venice, 1516, and Paris, 1517). It is true to say that *Paris et Vienne* version β was both a multilingual and a popular text.

Only one manuscript in French survives of version α, and this along with the manuscript evidence suggests that until it was printed, La Cépède's text had an aristocratic reading public.[11] Some two decades after La Cépède's work, Antoine de La Sale announced that he would write his own version of the tale as part of a series of tales dedicated to Jean de Calabre, the son of René d'Anjou.[12] This version does not appear to have been written, but it was intended by this Provençal-born author for an Angevin patron who was familiar with Provence, northern France, and the kingdom of Naples and whose court was keenly aware of the competing prestige of its political rival, the Aragonese court. La Cépède presents his romance as one he prefers to Arthurian and marvelous tales, and his choice is reflected in La Sale's projected compilation, which placed it alongside similar narratives: an extract from a chronicle; the chivalric romance *Jehan de Saintré*; and Rasse de Brunhamel's translation of a Latin *novella* by Nicolas de Clamanges, *Floridan et Elvide*. La Sale terms the couple "martirs d'amours," as does Fra Rocabertí's *Gloria d'Amor*, a fifteenth-century emulation of Petrarch's *Trionfi*, which extols

Vienne (Viana) as a singular example of martyrdom in the cause of love, placed as she is between the murdered troubadour Guilhem de Capestany and Tristan and Iseut.[13] I will return to Viana's martyrdom in the second part of this chapter; the following section concerns the importance of mother tongue and acquired languages in the text as well as in its transmission.

La Cépède's prologue was dismissed by earlier scholars as the clichéd attribution of an exotic source to a text that had been newly composed in French.[14] However, this is not an author's alleging that his source was either a Latin chronicle at Saint-Denis or a romance written in Arabic, as La Cépède states at the outset that his mother tongue is the Occitan of his purported source. He implies that his language choice defers to his patrons but reflects his personal taste in literature and his wish to share his favorite reading matter with a readership that could not understand his form of Provençal, and still less the Catalan original.[15] Alfred Coville viewed these claims as a political justification of language choice by a Provençal author aiming to please the Francophone Angevin court.[16] Moreover, the dates of 1432 to 1439 may be significant, as this was the period of René d'Anjou's failed attempt to win the kingdom of Naples from the claims of King Alfons el Magnànim of Aragon, who owned a copy of a Catalan romance of *París i Viana*, one of three Catalan manuscripts (all now lost) that have been traced prior to La Cépède's French text.[17]

It is not possible to know if this lost Catalan version was in prose or verse, as the verses inserted in Fra Rocabertí's *Gloria d'amor* (c. 1461) are probably not direct quotations. Certainly, Cortijo Ocaña has credited the romance with the inception of the distinctive generic markers of the Spanish *novela sentimental*.[18] In the absence of any stronger evidence, it seems wisest to accept Cátedra's conclusion that the story found its first appreciative audience in Catalan and entered French through the medium of Occitan. The only surviving Catalan text, however, is a printed text (Girona, 1495) that has been identified by Cátedra as a translation of the Tuscan version of β that was first printed in 1482.[19] Anna Maria Babbi's analysis of the Italian and French traditions leads her to conclude that as the sole French manuscript of version β (which is also the source for the printed French text) also seems to be strongly influenced by the Italian versions, this may indicate that the romance enjoyed an extensive period of transmission in Tuscany after its initial composition in Catalan.[20] There is, of course, no doubt that the Angevin court in Provence and Naples, the Aragonese court in Barcelona and Naples, and the papal court of Avignon all provided a supportive environment for the kind of cross-fertilizations that are suggested by the Tuscan, Catalan, and French texts. It would seem that the movements across the Mediterranean within the diegesis of *Paris et Vienne* is echoed in the transmission of the text.

It remains that La Cépède does not specify what his mother tongue is, but presents his Marseillais upbringing as an impoverishment, as it limits his fluency in French. Provençal Occitan is not flagged up as some kind of personal possession. Instead, he depicts it as a mediating language between French and Catalan that is accessible to him alone, not to his audience. He suggests that the Occitan text is less authoritative than the Catalan version, which he has not translated, but which he presents as his source. La Cépède places himself as writer-translator in the same mediating position as the "langaige provencial" that mediated between the Catalan and French versions. Both language and writer facilitate movement between two speech communities. The context for the writer and the language is the cultural environment of Marseille, a port that was the site of several languages, French, Provençal, Genoese, and Catalan. This appears to distinguish the text from those produced in other environments. For example, Gaston Phébus' preface to his *Livre de la chasse* makes a more conventional apology for his use of French as his second language, in that he cites no second, mediating vernacular and minimizes his use of Latin.[21]

It is clear that La Cépède is adopting a role familiar to postcolonial studies as that of go-between, or linguistic and cultural mediator. His treatment of French is similar to that of poets and novelists who have chosen to write creatively in a second language, usually one learned as an adult as a result of migration, and have termed their complex relationship as one with the "stepmother tongue," that is to say, either an adoptive parent or a hostile rival.[22] Assuming that La Cépède's version α represents an eccentric treatment of *Paris et Vienne*, version β, his authorial and translating action start to seem paradoxical. He takes a short romance and extends it, displaying his mastery of French, and in so doing creates a new text that erases the prior languages he cites as his source.

Despite the evidence in favor of a Catalan source for the romance, it would still be unwise to assume that *París i Viana* was identified by its readers as a Catalan work. In Francesc Alegre's *Somni recitant lo procés d'una qüestió enamorada* (c. 1470), París is identified as "lo francès París" and attacked by Macías for his shameless behavior as a Frenchman ignorant of the mores of "los nostres espanyols."[23] Alegre, who was a merchant in Barcelona who also spent some years in Sicily, underlines the tale's Frenchness, embodied in París' name, in order to identify his readership as part of "los notres espanyols" and to present what Cortijo Ocaña sees as an intriguing development of an opposition between "national" treatments of love literature. Whatever its origins might have been, the tale was received by the end of the fifteenth century as an example of a particularly French-influenced view of love, and this surely reflects the success it enjoyed in print. In the following discussion, all references to version β will cite the Catalan text edited by Cátedra, with references as necessary to the French text edited by Babbi.

Synopsis

París' talent as a musician and singer is the starting point of his love for the higher-born Viana, for he serenades her incognito. Viana's outraged parents suspect he is a minstrel. Both París and Viana use the bishop of San Lorenç as an unwitting go-between, by claiming religious concerns in order to meet at his house. París wins prizes at a tournament that has been arranged to identify the mystery lover. Viana and her mother visit París' father, who is ill, and Viana gains access into París' bedroom and private chapel. There, she sees his tournament prizes and takes them away. París returns, discovers the theft, and accuses his mother of letting intruders enter his bedroom. Viana pretends to the bishop that she wants to confess her theft to París. When Viana's parents refuse the match and arrange her marriage to someone else, the couple attempt to elope, but Viana is captured. Viana's parents imprison her and her companion Ysabel in an underground cell they have built specially for her within their house. París runs away to Genoa. Viana and Ysabel are on a diet of bread and water, but they are fed in secret by París' friend Aduardo, who also sends París letters with news of developments. Before her father's approved suitor is introduced, Viana's father attempts to fatten her up with a meal of roast chicken. She places bits of the chicken under her armpits, to put off her suitor by her smell. She claims to be sick. Three years pass. París travels to the eastern Mediterranean, grows a beard, learns to speak Arabic fluently, and earns himself high office at the court of the sultan of Babylon. Meanwhile, Viana's father is sent by the pope to spy on Babylon in preparation for a crusade. When the Dalfin is arrested and jailed in Alexandria, París asks to be allowed to question him, with a friar as interpreter. The Dalfin promises to give París his lands if he succeeds in freeing him. París frees the Dalfin, accompanies him back to Vienne, and asks for Viana's hand in marriage. He visits her in her prison, and has been forewarned by Aduardo's letters, so overlooks the sickening stench. The friar, who is faint at the smell, acts as interpreter between the imprisoned lady and the Moor. París then hands Viana the ring she gave him and speaks to her in their language. There follows a speedy disclosure of París' identity, reunion, and marriage. Ysabel weds Aduardo.

A poetic young man who feigns religious conversion in order to gain access to his beloved has echoes of the Occitan romance *Flamenca*, as does Viana's cunning manipulation of imprisonment to gain her own emotional freedom. However, Viana's role is ambiguous, in that she is a virginal noblewoman who makes false confessions to a bishop, steals objects from a young man's bedroom, and makes herself repulsive to unwanted suitors.

París' response to Viana's predicament is surprising, for he appears to turn to language acquisition as a means of ensuring their reunion. He travels to distant lands and learns to speak Arabic, "e apres de parlar morisch tam be com si fos nat alli" (and he learned to speak Moorish as well as if he were born there) (Cátedra, 157). He wears Moorish clothing; grows a beard; and travels through the lands of India and Prester John before returning to Babilonia, where he gains the sultan's favor. Three years later, when Viana's father is imprisoned in Alexandria for spying on behalf of the pope, París obtains permission from the sultan to travel to question him, with a friar as interpreter, for he pretends not to know the Dalfin's language. He gets the Dalfin's agreement to give him his lands in exchange for freeing him. He then offers to return the Dalfin's lands to him if he will marry Viana to him. At Vienne, París is careful to speak only Arabic (163), and uses both the friar and the bishop of Saint Lorenç to present his offer of marriage to her (163–64). Viana uses her hidden rotting meat, as a person "mig podrida" (half rotted) with sickness, to chase away this unwanted suitor (164), but París makes the friar tell her that he can overlook the illness (164). He gives her the ring she gave him as a token of their love (165) and speaks to her in their shared language:

> E Viana que estaue merauellada del diamant fon mes merauellada com hoi parlar aquell qui iames hauia parlat: entant que estech espantada. (165)

> [And Viana, who marveled at the diamond, was more amazed when she heard speak the one who had never spoken: so much so she was frightened.]

Viana is fearful at hearing a silent man speak and in seeing a ring she thinks belongs to a dead man. París tells her he has returned, and her reaction is so intense that she, in turn, nearly dies (166). When París reveals his identity to the Dalfin, he is stricken dumb for an hour (168). Both the father and daughter, who have been imprisoned, are unable to speak when the sultan's go-between reacquires their language.

París' manipulation of languages to gain access to Viana seems unusual, but it makes sense within the tale as a whole. Viana first identifies her nighttime musician as a noble knight when she visits his bedroom and private oratory, on the basis of visual signs such as his armor and the prizes he has won at a tournament (131–33). She steals his prizes. She manipulates the bishop of Saint Lorenç into enabling the pair to meet by claiming that she needs to confess her theft to París. In the first part of the tale, Viana uses language to give a respectable gloss to her pursuit of her own desires, whereas París uses disguise and concealment, posing as a *joglar*, a postulant, and a masked knight. París' flight abroad leaves Viana trapped in a pretense of illness and real starvation. París takes on a new linguistic and cultural identity as a Christian who speaks Arabic (a Mozarab). Viana uses olfactory and visual signs to indicate her refusal of marriage: she is "half rotted" in her prison, hostile to any suitor except the one she has selected for herself. París learns and uses an international language, and a shared courtly understanding of falconry, as means of winning wealth and lands both overseas and in the city of Vienne.

Readers of the Catalan version printed in Gerona and Barcelona (1495), as well as of the French version written by a secular man raised in the thriving mercantile port of Marseille, would have appreciated the linguistic turn taken by París in winning Viana. An ultimate sign that the text can be read as a recommendation of the advantages of languages and go-betweens is that in the Catalan version, the children of París and Viana marry into the royal houses of France and Aragon (Cátedra, 169).

In the French β version of *Paris et Vienne*, Paris uses translation in subtle ways. He approaches the imprisoned Dauphin with a friar whom he uses as his interpreter, introducing a go-between he does not need, as someone who speaks Arabic proficiently, in order to construct a convincing negotiation between the Dauphin and himself. The friar is at this point presented as a tool: "Paris commença a le consoler par la bouche du frere" (Paris began to console him through the mouth of the friar) (Babbi, XXXVIII.125).[24] Later the friar speaks to Vienne "en personne de Paris" (in the role of Paris), as his interpreter, but in fact enacts París' disguised identity as the unnamed Moor who has freed her father (XLII.132). In both instances, Paris uses the interpreter as a mask, not as a channel for clear communication. On París' second meeting with Vienne, he carries a magnificent "espee moresque," but hands her the diamond ring she gave him in pledge; one sign marks him as Moor, the other as Paris. Vienne is then surprised to hear the Moor speaking in "plain langage" (XLIII.135). Ysabel wakes up to see Vienne in the arms not of Paris but of a Moor:

> elle s'eveilla et, quant elle vit demourer Vienne entre les bras du maure, dist:—Ma dame, et qu'esse s'y? Avez vous perdu le sens que ainsy demourés entre les bras de ce maure? Vous a il enchantee que vous souffrés que si grant privance il ait desja avec vous? Et esse la foy que vous tenez a Paris, pour lequel avons tant de maux souffert? (XLIII.136)

> [She woke up and when she saw Vienne in the arms of the Moor, she said: "My lady, what is this? Have you lost your mind to be staying like this in the arms of this Moor? Has he cast a spell on you to make you accept him already having such intimate contact with you? Is this what has become of your loyalty towards Paris, for whose sake we have suffered so much?"]

Ysabel's appeal to Vienne's *foy* puns on her misreading of the scene as a cross-religious as much as an unfaithful love. Robert Muchembled has noted the frequency of assaults in late medieval Artois (a linguistic frontier for French and Flemish) against men who were overheard speaking a foreign language, whether English, Spanish, or even Latin.[25] Ysabel's aggression is aimed primarily at the Moor's appearance and religion, but the linguistic aspects of his persona, as a man who may have enchanted her mistress with his interpreted words, are important too. When Paris kneels before the Dauphin to say who he is, he hands him his "espee moresque" with which he invites him to punish him, as if his visual token of foreignness were to be turned against him (137).

Paris' *engin* sheds new light on Vienne's trick, for she is surprised to find that Paris does not react to her own subterfuge because he finds the smell of the rotting meat good: "estoit a Paris toute la puanteur bonne, car ne sentoit riens et disoit:—Je ne scay pas que vous sentez, car je ne sens nulle chose de mal!" (Paris found the stench good, because he smelled nothing, and said, "I don't know what you are smelling, because I can smell nothing wrong!") (XLIII.133). The friar cannot interpret the stench intellectually (he does not know its cause), so he is disgusted by it, whereas Paris is immune to its effects because he translates it as "nulle chose de mal." Paris inhales the same smell as the friar, but both of them apply a moral reading to the evidence of decomposition, as signs of wrongdoing or disgusting phenomena.[26]

Jean-Jacques Vincensini has studied Vienne's stratagem as an exercise in making abject both her body and the generic conventions he ascribes to the text as a *roman idyllique*.[27] While Vincensini's argument is convincing, it rests on Julia Kristeva's thoroughly modern definition of what constitutes abjection in physical and psychoanalytical terms. It is important to reassess what a reader, in any of the many cultures that translated the text in the late fifteenth century, may have considered abject about what William Cotton has called the "chicken incident."[28] In Christian ideology of the later Middle Ages, abjection is strongly associated with penitential activity and with martyrdom, something that may be reflected in the treatment of Vienne as a martyr to love. La Cépède's Vienne associates her imprisonment, starvation, and physical humiliation with the patient suffering of Boethius. Her stratagem for protecting her virginity is in fact drawn from the ambiguous preaching exemplum of two Lombard noblewomen who hide chicken meat in their bodices to avoid rape. In the version that circulated in fifteenth-century Castile, the young women are contrasted with their mother, who surrenders their castle to a besieging army because she is lusting after its king. Her daughters are rewarded for their chastity with a kingdom each, whereas the mother's *luxuria* proves fatal to her.[29] This makes Vienne's action emblematic of women's bodily struggle between chastity and lust. Her abjection is less connected to moral opprobrium, and to comedy, than it may seem to a modern reader.

Vienne's behavior breaches none of the codes of courtly behavior in terms of dress, language, and action, and there is a risk of anachronism in assuming that a smell of natural putrefaction, as opposed to one of evil, would have been offensive. As the text twice overlays a love narrative with connotations of interreligious conflict (a lack of faith) and of sexual misbehavior, it seems that the texts should be read closely for pointers to the scene's full significance. William Caxton's translation omitted only anticlerical words from his French source and did not alter Vienne's self-imposed stench.[30] Stench is a diffuse and subjective concept, but bodily smells were most frequently associated with diseases such as leprosy.[31] In *Jaufre*, a murderous leper is likened to a well-dressed man, like a painted wooden panel that has rotted internally. The stinking leper is viewed as a man whose sickness is caused, or expressed, through sexual appetite. Vienne's stratagem makes her symbolically a leper, as does her isolation within her family home and the contrast it presents to her beautiful appearance. However, Vienne's stratagem is strongly connected to her gender, as in addition to the exemplum mentioned above, it also alludes to a commonplace of misogynistic literature expressed in works such as Francesc Eiximenis's *Llibre de las Donas* (1396):[32]

> Qui pren muller que no sap què sera
> Ell mateix se pos' a risch de matar
> E la mort per tostemps se procurar.
> ¿Què farà si la pren tal que sera
> com a sepulcre daurat:
> defora bell e de dins pudirà?

[Whoever takes a wife he does not know is putting himself at risk of being killed and obtaining death for ever for himself. What shall he do; should he take her as she is, like a gilded tomb: beautiful on the outside and rotten within?]

Vienne presents her suitors with evidence of Eiximenis' warning against marrying a woman of unknown moral standing. As she has attempted to elope with her lover, and has pledged herself to him, she may indeed be considered to have diminished her value in the marital market. Paris, of course, knows Vienne well, so he can look into the gilded tomb and know that its rottenness is as cosmetic as her fine clothes.

Vienne's ironic manipulation of her observers' misogynistic fears may account for part of the success of the narrative, but (again) it is not the whole picture. The comic and dramatic impact of Vienne's aggression lies also in her deliberate misuse of cooked food. She refuses to eat it, and she secretes it not inside her body but beneath her clothing, under her armpits. The rotting chicken flesh is placed strategically in proximity to her courtly heart and desirable and nutritive breasts, while being radically removed from the acceptable social order of food that must be ingested and excreted. This food is entombed along with its consumer. Her refusal is framed by her father's determination to starve her into submission and by his own experience of starvation when he is imprisoned at Alexandria. Indeed, La Cépède subtly makes the Dauphin the agent of Vienne's stratagem, for when he uncovers her plan to persist in her love for Paris and to ignore his alternative marriage plans, he threatens to eat her: "Si te dy que ains que je consentisse ad ce que tu penses, je te destruiroye et defferoye de tous tes membres l'un après l'autre, et ta cher a beaux petis morceaux, et les mengeroye" (I tell you that before I consent to the thing you are thinking, I would [rather] kill you, and tear you limb from limb, [tear] your flesh into little pieces, and eat them) (Kaltenbacher, 530). La Cépède's Vienne projects this violence onto the meat she is given in preparation for her suitor's visit, as she feigns penance and fasting in obedience to her father's wishes; breaks the chicken carcass in two; and tears off segments of it, which she tucks between her breasts (551–52). Her second assault on food occurs on the eve of Paris' visit to her cell, and she repeats this gesture, this time on a piece of mutton (610). Vienne's father has threatened to reduce her to *cher* that he will consume, and she chooses to embody inedible food: "la cher fut aussi pugnayse comme charoyne" (The flesh stank like a corpse) (610), as if she were signaling that she is a consumable product on a par with other foodstuffs that are processed, dressed and served up, in her parents' kitchen.

When the friar repeats the Moor's offer of marriage, Vienne threatens to beat her head against the wall, "et je me feray issir les cervelles par la bouche" (and I shall make my brains come out of my mouth) (Kaltenbacher, 133). Vincensini interprets Vienne's graphic threats as another instance of the romance's disruption of the idyllic. It is also worth noting that Vienne is threatening to use her mouth not to speak or to ingest food, but to expel the thinking part of her body, and in so doing, to deny herself the ability to give both mental and verbal consent. Her threatened suicide underlines her value as an autonomous thinking being and as a living creature that both eats and vomits.

Good food may be contrasted with corrupt and corrupting language, especially the words that are cooked up in the malicious heart. Michel Jeanneret has traced the development, from fifteenth-century Italy outward, of an association between cooks and those who use Latin badly, the *culinaria lingua* criticized by early modern Latinists. This is a branch of a long-standing tradition of macaronic and dog Latin multilingual poetry, of "churchmen who cultivate their stomachs and talk about it in bad Latin," from the *Cena Cypriani* to multilingual collages of liturgy, *auctores* and carnival.[33] Monolingual vernacular examples are also extant that work on a contrast between good and bad food, such as the exchange of Occitan *coblas* by the Catalan Monk of Foissan (possibly Jofre de Foixà) and an anonymous respondent, in the later part of the thirteenth century:[34]

Hoc dixit monachus de Fuxano

Sobrefusa ab cabirol
Porc ab [un] unyó novell,

E gallina ab juxell,
E capó rostit d'un an
Vull que hom me pos denan,
E formatge torrador,
E vi rosat en Pascor,
E giroflat quan iverna.

[Strong sauce on kid, pork with fresh onions, and chicken with thick sauce, and a roasted yearling capon. I want all that set before me, and creamy cheese dessert, rosé wine at Eastertide, and wine with cloves in the wintertime.]

Responcio sibi facta

Truja vella morta a dol,
Et al ventre haja porcell,
E cols ab magre anyell,
. . . .
Vull que hom li pos denan
Aquel monge enganador,
E vi torbat part Martror,
E haja foc de lanterna.

[An old sow that died of grief, with a piglet in its belly, and cabbage with thin lamb. . . . I want all that set before him, that deceitful monk; and clouded wine at the feast of All Souls, and may he have lantern light.]

The monk's stanza lists foods that are associated with fertility, such as milk-fed kid, as well as rich sauces and desserts made with eggs. He adds the capon, a castrated cockerel, a noble food that peasants can only dream of eating. These foods are sophisticatedly produced with complex recipes. It is intriguing that the respondent uses carrion in the form of a compound image of a sow that is simultaneously old and pregnant, affected by the human emotion of grief. The kid is replaced with thin lamb, the fresh onions with cabbage. The *cobla* reaffirms the image of death with its reference to All Souls and cloudy wine drunk by lantern light. The monk's *cobla* called for festive wines at Easter and Christmas, as well as feast food of venison and roast capon. Feast food is set against impossible food, images of death and fertility intertwined. In the writings of Francesc Eiximenis, fatty chicken meat is a feast food that he contrasts to some comic effect with the traditional fare of a religious man.[35] In such poems, the cook and the kitchen become sites of renewed fertility, allowing for the cycle of birth, death, and consumption.[36] Vienne usurps the cook's prerogative, turns roast chicken from feast into debased famine, and by her actions transforms the required gestures and words of obedience and consent into a violent rejection of her social role as a marriageable daughter.

This detail also points to why Vienne is a "martirs d'amours," for the witnesses to her smell believe that she must be a saint to endure the stench of her ghastly disease and spread the rumor that she has become a holy woman (Kaltenbacher, 557–58). Pierre de La Cépède allots Vienne a standard renunciation of worldly love, one that is associated with mystery plays. Vienne says, "je veulh du tout le monde abandoner pour estre au service de Dieu" (I want to abandon the world entirely in order to put myself in the service of God) (Kaltenbacher, 611–12). Vienne's words are found in the mouth of the virgin martyr Agnes, the subject of a fourteenth-century mystery play composed in the region of Marseille:[37]

> Mais sapias ben que ieu non farai
> cest putage nil cosintrai,
> anz portarai a mo senor
> tostems mais de mon cor honor,
> si com bona moller deu far
> qe deu fort son marit onrar.
>
> (*Jeu de Sainte Agnès,* lines 65–70)

[But know well that I shall not act like a whore, nor consent to it; rather I shall always bear the honor of my heart for my lord, as a good wife should, who should honor her husband well.]

The *passio* of Saint Agnes pits the child saint's determination to stay betrothed to her spiritual groom against the authority of the Roman prefect, the father of her rejected suitor. As she has described marriage as akin to whoring, she is placed in a brothel (lines 281–344). The stinking sheets of the brothel are taken away by two archangels, who also cover her naked body with a white robe and tidy her cell (lines 403–509). Agnes's body erases the stench of the brothel and replaces it with divine perfume, and the prostitutes surrounding her are converted. Like Vienne's specially constructed prison cell within her parents' house, Agnes's cell juxtaposes a brothel, a prison, and a monastic retreat. She is both exposed and protected. The lustful prefect's son is struck down dead when he attempts to touch the child saint:

> *Filius prefecti dicit sibi sic ironice:*
>   Fora putan? Anz ti penrai
>   es am tu mal grat tieu jhairai,
>   que jha honor non volrai far
>   a cel dieu que ti vol gardar.
>
> (lines 556–59)

> *Modo venit versus lectum et credit ipsam accipere, et diabolus accipit ipsum ad gulam et stinxit eum et cadit in solum, et omnes diaboli veniunt et portant animam in infernum sibilando.*

> [The prefect's son says to himself with irony: "Here, whore? Now I shall take you and against your will I shall lie with you, for I do not want to honor that god that wishes to protect you." He goes toward the bed and wants to touch her, and a devil grabs him by the throat and chokes him; he falls down on the ground, and all the devils come and carry him off, hissing, into Hell.]

In La Cépède's text, Vienne's martyrdom is ironically patterned on such tales as this. She claims that she has consecrated her virginity to a hidden lover, and uses odor to repel her suitors, but in both instances she is following her physical desires (see also Kaltenbacher, 557):

> Lors Vienne ouvrit son som, dont il yssist une si grant pueur, qu'il sembloit que il y eust ung chien pourry, dont l'evesque et le frere commensarent a closre les nez et torner le visage aultre part. (611)

> [Then Vienne opened her bodice, from which there issued such a great stink that it seemed that there was a rotting dog in there. Thereupon the bishop and the friar began to pinch their nostrils and turn their faces away.]

In a construct far from the devil grabbing a lecherous suitor by the throat, it is Vienne's body odor that attacks the clergymen who approach her. There are no archangels in her cell, only her servant, who is condemned to suffering the same fate as hers, and it is she who spreads foulness to protect her virginity for worldly purposes. When Saint Agnes is handed over to torturers on suspicion of witchcraft, her silence is taken to indicate her guilt: "Il es vaudesa, so mi par, / Per que non nos vol mot sonar" (It seems to me she's a Waldensian, because she doesn't want to say a word to us) (lines 608–9). One of her tormentors suggests that she should be hanged by the tongue until it is ripped out as a punishment for necromancy (lines 600–607). Vienne's silence, by contrast, is a sign neither of heresy nor of witchcraft. It is associated with her use of olfactory language. Her smell gives the false impression that there is a rotting dog located somewhere, either in the cell or in her bodice. However, it is precisely looking that resolves the mystery of what exactly is rotten around Vienne's body, for when he is treated to the same olfactory assault as the friar and the bishop, Paris chooses to look where they have averted their eyes: "regardoit dans le seym de Vienne" (He looked into Vienne's bosom) (611).

La Cépède's Paris creeps into the cell, overhears her lament, then speaks to her "en langue latine" (615). This is his familiar *parler* and Vienne recognizes him by it, but it is not the vernacular (615–16). Later, his father mitigates this by saying he recognized Paris, as did his companions, by his voice (624). Paris' action is not separate from his ability to recognize a rotting stench for what it is: a subterfuge. Pierre de La Cépède's prologue to the romance cites a proverbial warning that one should be wary of the evidence of one's eyes (391). His version of the tale demonstrates that seeing and smelling are not always believing. If Vienne appears to be a martyr, it is only because she has donned a particularly effective disguise in order to preserve her chastity, not for God, but for her lover. Similarly, the smell of putrefaction does not automatically denote either a deadly disease or a corpse.

I would suggest a different reading to Vincensini, one that moves away from abjection as a disruption of generic patterns, in order to explore the cultural association that was made between the abject female body, food, and martyrdom. If Vienne's actions are read as an ironic parody of the abasement visited on virgin martyrs such as Agnes in mystery plays, this would compel a reader to interpret the tale less as a serious story of "martirs d'amours," and more as a gentle subversion of the very concept of suffering in love. Corruption touches on language as well as pieces of roasted chicken, for both are distorted from their true natures. Vienne's aggressive silence is a perfect complement to Paris' skilful manipulation of silence and speech.

The chicken stratagem may go beyond language itself. Laura Marks has noted that odors are particularly difficult to represent in aesthetic media and that perfume and stenches are both relegated to the minor arts that are the kitchen and perfumery. Unlike visual or aural material, scents cannot be symbolized. When Vienne stinks, her stratagem goes beyond any of the languages that narrate her tale; she is placed, at that moment, simultaneously in the kitchen and in the reader's earliest memories of food and disgust. To invoke smell is to invoke affect and to release the text at that moment from translation or interpretation into a realm that is purely subjective.[38] Every reader is alone with the associations he or she may make with food and decomposition, and this appeals to a personal idiom that lies beyond grammar or verbal interpretation. If La Cépède is viewed as one of the best readers of the β version, he draws from it the warning that when vernaculars and Latin *auctoritates* overlap, the result may not necessarily be a cacophony, as long as one keeps an eye on the affective, subjective, and associative material that is beyond spoken languages. It may be thanks to this pungent detail that the romance appealed to so many translators from the fifteenth to the seventeenth centuries, a period that precedes the change, wrought by the Enlightenment, in how odors were described and experienced in French, and ultimately Western, culture.[39]

Paris and Vienne was a multilingual phenomenon of the late fifteenth century. The romance emerged through translation and was diffused in an impressive number of idioms until the seventeenth century, but it seemed to lose its appeal thereafter. The *aljamiado-morisco* version seems especially relevant for Venuti's theory that "translation is scandalous because it can create different values and practices, whatever the domestic setting."[40] Paris acquires Arabic during his exile overseas; the Castilian printed text was rendered in Arabic script, probably by an *alfaquí*, for an Aragonese Morisco community. The text would have been illicit, as texts composed in Arabic script were suppressed by the Inquisition.[41] Here, the tale of *Paris and Vienne* acquires a symbolic value as a work of intercultural resistance, affirming the cultural and religious identity of a Castilian-speaking community that was banned from learning the Arabic that comes so easily to the protagonist.

By restoring the tale to its probable origins in Catalan and Occitan literature of the fourteenth century, it may be concluded that the romance appealed to a multilingual audience because of its diegetic engagement with language as the vehicle of illusions and as something that might be transcended through a singular conflation of the cultural constructions of smell, food, and martyrdom. In the following chapter I will examine a text that is very close to *Paris and Vienne*, but that explores language through a different treatment of both translation and alienation.

8

Pierre de Provence et La Belle Maguelonne

THE SUCCESS OF *Paris et Vienne* may have inspired its textual sibling, *Lystoire du chevalier Pierre de Provence et de La Belle Maguelonne* (c. 1453) (henceforward *La Belle Maguelonne*). The romance resembles *Paris et Vienne* in many ways and has often been studied alongside it, although surviving manuscripts do not preserve the two romances together.[1] Unlike *Paris and Vienne*, the romance makes no claims concerning its sources. All the late medieval versions that survive in Western Europe preserve the geographical setting in Provence and the kingdom of Naples, which would point to a single source for the European tradition. Surviving manuscripts point to patrons in northeastern France and Paris, as do the features of the narrative that are derived from the French romances of *L'Escoufle* and the Handless Maiden tradition. The romance was translated into German (1453) soon after its composition and later into Flemish (1510) and Castilian (1519). It was diffused in other languages during the sixteenth and seventeenth centuries.[2]

Synopsis

Pierre is the only son of the count of Provence and an heiress of Barcelona. He leaves his distraught parents, claiming to go on tournaments, but really to meet the daughter of the king of Naples, Maguelonne. His mother gives him three rings. Pierre, presenting himself as "le chevalier aux clefs," courts Maguelonne via meetings in church with her nurse, and he lures her in by refusing to tell her his name until she will meet him alone. He gives Maguelonne his three rings, one by one. Maguelonne disobeys the nurse and runs away with Pierre (who asked her permission to visit his parents) but they are separated in a seaside forest, as the start of a divine punishment for their presumption. Pierre has ripped open Maguelonne's bodice as she sleeps and removed a red silk cloth containing the three rings. A bird of prey thinks the red bundle is a piece of meat and steals it. Pierre runs after the bird, throwing stones at it; it drops the cloth onto a rock. He leaps into an abandoned skiff, but a storm whisks him off. Pierre is rescued by some corsairs, who give him to the sultan of Babylon, who adopts him and teaches him several languages. Maguelonne wakes up, climbs trees, sets their horses loose, and swaps her rich clothes for the rags of a woman pilgrim. She covers her face in earth and saliva and makes her way alone to Rome, Genoa, and Aigue-Mortes as a pilgrim; she founds a church and hospital. As "la saincte hospitaliere" of the island of Port Sarrasin, Maguelonne tends to the sick, enacts her penance for her elopement, and helps Pierre's parents grieve for their missing son. Pierre asks the sultan for permission to visit his parents and embarks on a Provençal ship bound for Aigues-Mortes with fourteen barrels filled with gold that he claims are a cargo of salt. Pierre is abandoned on an island, then hospitalized for nine months in a port. A big fish is brought to the count and countess and is found to contain the cloth and three rings. They go into mourning. Another Provençal ship takes Pierre to the hospital, now a shrine renamed Saint-Pierre-de-Maguelonne. There, Pierre and Maguelonne are reunited. She reunites Pierre with his parents. Their son rules both Naples and Provence.

Recurring claims have been made that *La Belle Maguelonne* shares the Catalan origins of *Paris et Vienne,* notably on the basis of a printed version of 1616.[3] However, this printed text is late, and it is believed to be a translation of a Castilian version of the French short version, so the claim is tenuous at best. It seems more convincing to view *La Belle Maguelonne* as a romance that was composed in French for a readership that appears to have had an informed interest in the Provençal island harbor and its maritime connection with both Genoa and Naples. As the narrative, as was said above, is quite dependent on northern French models, its earliest patrons may well have been connected to the court of Anjou.

La Belle Maguelonne presents itself as a foundation narrative for the Cathedral of Saint-Pierre at Villeneuve-lès-Maguelonne (Hérault). It narrates the complex courtship and the reunion after penitential suffering of the son of the count of Provence and Barcelona and the daughter of the king of Naples, which is possibly an allusion to René d'Anjou's claims over both the kingdom of Naples and the county of Provence. As Coville pointed out, the romance is explicitly embedded in a recognizable Provençal and a less reliable Neapolitan topography.[4] Its treatment of Catalan lands is very vague, something that weighs further against a Catalan source. Whereas Vienne and Genoa in *Paris et Vienne* are little more than place-names, *La Belle Maguelonne* is a text that insists on the heroine's physical as well as nominal connection with both her birthplace and her adult home, as the daughter of King Maguelon and as the founder of a hospital at Maguelonne.

However close the text's relationship may be to its geographical setting, its early readers appear to have received it in an international, multilingual context. A manuscript now in Coburg (dated 1453) is a copy of the French text with a complete interlinear translation into Latin and marginal glosses in German. Anna Maria Babbi has interpreted this as material evidence that the text was used as a teaching tool and that tutors sought to entertain their pupils by making them learn Latin versions of familiar works such as *Paris et Vienne* and *La Belle Maguelonne*.[5] She particularly noted the didactic and moral tone of some of the glosses on this luxury manuscript and the contrast that this makes with the comparatively poor quality of the surviving paper copies of the French text. Other scholars have suggested that the Coburg manuscript is evidence of a translator's method, in that he (or she) may have found it easier to translate French into German through the interpretative medium of Latin.[6]

Among the precise geographical and political references of *La Belle Maguelonne*, it comes as a surprise to find an allusion to Jason and Medea. I will argue in this earlier part of the chapter that there may be a direct relationship between this apparently classical allusion and the possible uses made of the text as schoolroom literature. In the first part of this chapter, I shall examine how this romance explores the (m)other tongue through its intertextual relationship with one of the most monstrous versions of this mythical narrative, one that is traceable to the French literary production in the kingdom of Naples and Italian developments from it.[7] The second part of the chapter concerns the romance's manipulation of both mother tongue and patronymics to suggest that "national" identity is elective rather than a matter of either geography or birth.

After their elopement, Maguelonne wakes up on a seashore to discover that Pierre has disappeared. While the reader is fully aware that Pierre has been abducted by pirates, Maguelonne leaps to the conclusion that he has made a new Medea of her. She exclaims, "Certes vous estes le second Jason et je suis la nouvelle Medee" (25v).[8] She argues that Pierre has deceived and misled her. Despite no wrongdoing on her part, for she has merely deceived her royal father by eloping with a knight errant, Maguelonne associates her predicament with her guilt, and she embarks on a penitential journey to Rome and Pierre's homeland.

Roger Dubuis suggested that the fleeting allusion to the myth of Jason and Medea is a negligible display of erudition on the part of the text's multiple redactors. Indeed, the allusion was dropped in the popular printed edition that circulated in France after the sixteenth century, which implies that its relevance declined after the rediscovery of Euripides' play.[9] This contrasts with the fact that in around 1519, a young Clément Marot appears to have responded to the allusion to Medea in an elegiac poem in which he treated Maguelonne as if she were one of the abandoned heroines of Ovid's *Heroides*. Marot's early sixteenth-century Maguelonne is likened repeatedly to Dido, possibly because he recognized the Medea allusion as a borrowing from the *Aeneid* (IV, lines 365–87), but also as a response to intertextual allusions that were already present in the prose romance.[10] Marot's poem, and the allusion itself, are arguably less about erudition than about the network of vernacular texts that underscore Maguelonne's predicament.

In histories of the Trojan War, Jason and Medea formed part of a historical narrative directly connected with dynastic ambitions in royal circles, especially those of France, and later the ducal court of Burgundy. Raoul Lefèvre's *Histoire de Jason* (1460), which was composed specifically for Duke Philip the Good, reflects the Burgundian courtly appropriation of the Golden Fleece as a court emblem of noble chivalry, as does Guillaume Fillastre's treatise, *La Toison d'Or* (1468, printed in 1516). Both Lefèvre and Fillastre reinscribe Jason's exploits within a Christian and Burgundian chivalric frame and depict Jason's ultimate reconciliation with Medea after her revenge, a detail taken from Boccaccio's *Genealogie deorum gentilium*.[11] Maguelonne's allusion, however, is neither to Burgundian texts nor to Catalan versions of Seneca's tragedy. It is traceable to the prose *Roman de Troie* tradition as it was transmitted in French and Italian texts from the thirteenth to the fifteenth centuries, a complex multilingual phenomenon that may well be described, in Rita Copeland's words, as "a fairly integrated textual system" of translations and independent developments. In this respect, *La Belle Maguelonne* may be viewed as an example of Copeland's concept of "secondary translations," apparently newly composed works that do not openly declare their relationship with their Latin or vernacular sources, unlike "primary translations," which do signal their derivative status.[12] What *La Belle Maguelonne* presents, within its humble form as a minor romance, is an intriguingly rich picture of what can emerge through a series of both interlingual and intralingual translations.

This Prose *Troie* "system" owes much to the verse poem of Benoît de Sainte-Maure, and very little to Benoît's Latin sources, but it acts also as a tributary of many different influences and texts.[13] On their return journey with the Golden Fleece and Medea, Jason and the Argonauts find themselves on an island. According to a Tuscan translation of Guido delle Colonne's

Historia destructionis Trojae, and its Venetian counterpart, Jason decides to abandon Medea as she lies asleep under a tent:

> E uno giorno sendo Medea adormentata sotto un padiglione, Gianson pensa dislealtade verso Medea di volerla lasciare in su questa isola, aceiò che niuna persona potesse dire chella detta vettoria avesse auta per lei e non per suo prodezza.[14]

> [One day as Medea was asleep beneath a pavilion, Jason planned a disloyal act toward Medea, thinking of leaving her on this island, so that no one might say that he owed his victory to her rather than to his own prowess.]

The Argonauts abandon her, unaware that she is pregnant with twins. Medea awakes and delivers a lengthy speech addressed to several Olympian gods, bewailing her fate and applying it to the common lot of humanity. She prays to Saturn: "Ma guarda cogli ochi tuoi pieni di misericordia la fragelità della nostra carne misera, la quale é sottoposta a tanta corruzione" (But look down with your eyes full of mercy on the fragility of this miserable flesh of ours, which is subject to so much corruption) (Gorra, 475) The animals of the island gather to look pityingly on her as she bewails her abandonment by Jason, who has left her "tradita e ingannata" (betrayed and deceived), and demands divine vengeance. The speech reflects a conflation of Medea with the abandoned Ariadne of the *Heroides* (X, lines 6–12), and it reflects into Maguelonne's speech, as she refers to the wild animals that threaten her now she is alone. There are other parallels with Maguelonne's abandonment, both her predicament on awakening and her own lengthy speech, in which she cries out to Fortune and the Virgin Mary. This passage is glossed in a marginal note to the trilingual Coburg manuscript as "Planctus et lamentatione Maguelone" (the *planctus* and lamentation of Maguelonne), noting that she blames herself for the ill fame that her elopement and Pierre's abandonment have brought on her.[15] The "nouvelle Medee" is a comprehensible and important allusion for this particular German reader and translator.

The Tuscan/Venetian Medea is marooned for three years on the island with her two infant sons, living on roots and grasses until they are rescued by a ship. She works her passage to Thessaly by deploying her talent as a storyteller. Once there, she lives incognito in a cave on the outskirts of the city and begs for food in the streets, where she occasionally catches sight of Jason's cavalcades. Jason marries the daughter of the king (named Creuso in the Venetian text, Pelleus in the Tuscan), and falls sick. Medea grasps the opportunity this presents for revenge. In the Tuscan version, she murders her two sons and carries their bodies into Thessaly in a sack. She dresses herself as a male physician, gains admission to the palace on the pretence of offering a cure for Jason (it is here that she murders their two sons in the Venetian version), and serves up their hearts at a banquet. Jason eats his medicinal dish unwittingly. In the Tuscan version, Medea narrates her story and her revenge to the assembled lords of the palace. They judge her actions to have been justified and let her go (Gorra, 479).

In the Venetian version, Medea's revenge is more comprehensive. She sends Jason to bed with a sleeping draught, pins the boys' corpses to the door of his chamber by thrusting daggers through their necks, and also affixes a written declaration of what she has done: "Sapia zaschuna persona che questi si e li fioli de Jaxon e de Medea; e Jaxon si manzo ieri al disnar li suo chuori e llo miedigo lo qual li li de fo Medea instessa" (May each person know that these are the sons of Jason and Medea. Jason ate their hearts last night at dinner, and the physician who did this was Medea in person).[16] She sets fire to the bed, kills the still-sleeping Jason in the conflagration, and flies off into clouds that drip blood. The Venetian Medea flees the scene and delegates her declaration of her actions to a written note. She does not give a motive for her actions. She eventually commits suicide by throwing herself down from the clouds that bore her away onto a sword blade that happens to be fixed upright in the ground. The Tuscan Medea is allowed to leave unharmed, and she continues her adventures in keeping with Guido delle Colonne's original text, but the Venetian antiheroine performs the grievous sin of self-murder with a subtle echo of the suicide of Dido. The conflation of Medea and Dido's death by the sword also occurs in the late fifteenth-century *Histoire de la destruction de Troye la Grant* (c. 1495–1500). However, this is a translation of Guido delle Colonne that may well also share a source with the same Venetian text. Marie Jacob has pointed out that this unusual version of the tale is definitely Italian, as it was also depicted on a fourteenth-century wall painting in Florence.[17] Given the strength of the evidence, it may well be more cogent to argue for the status as source of the extant Venetian tale than for a lost French original.

The grisly tale contrasts with the no less violent but far more faithful revenge scene in Raoul Lefèvre's Burgundian *Histoire de Jason* (1460). Here, Medea flies out of a chamber within the palace, seated on four dragons and carrying her naked son, to interrupt Jason's wedding feast. She tears the boy limb from limb and throws him into the laps of Jason and his wife, Creüsa, while the dragons destroy all those in attendance with fire and venom, with the exception of Jason, who is protected from these substances by the ointment that was originally given to him by Medea.[18]

Quite unlike Lefèvre's Medea, but like the Italian one, Maguelonne resorts to disguise (first as a beggar and then as a healer) in her pursuit of Pierre, albeit for ends that are the reverse of those of the classical antiheroine, as they are both curative and devout. Indeed, Maguelonne's adventures are presented as a penitential pilgrimage that expiates her foolish decision to elope with Pierre and makes amends through healing work. In this respect she does indeed appear to be presented as an "anti-Medea," much as Ruth Morse suggested could be the case with the tale of Griselda.[19]

Heinrich Morf and Léon Mallinger concluded that the abandonment-revenge Medea tale represents a conflation of Trojan material with Ovid's *Heroides* that can be observed in several other instances during the Middle Ages, notably from the way the Neapolitan tradition of the French Prose *Troie* text (versions 3 and 5) interpolate or append French versions of up to thirteen of these poems. Intriguingly, none of these transmits a translation of *Heroides* book 12 (Medea to Jason).[20] The Medea abandonment-revenge tale first appears in French in the mid-thirteenth century Prose *Troie* 1, which is the most widespread prose tradition and appears to originate from a French colony in Morea, possibly the city of Corinth.[21] It differs from the Tuscan and Venetian texts in several details that I have italicized below (Constans and Faral, § 23):

> Et en la parfin l'en mena Jason aveuc lui en son païs, dont elle fist grant follie, et mout s'en repenti après, *si comme li autor dit,* quar celi lassa sur une ille de mer, et si estoit grosse de dous enfans. Et puis fist elle tant que *elle se parti de l'isle et se delivra des enfans,* et tant quist Jason qu'ele le trova, et lors tua ses deus enfans, si en prist les cuers et les entrailles et les dona a mangier a Jason qui engendrés les avoit de sa char, et puis *après geta devant lui les piés et les mains des enfans et li dist que ce estoient les membres de ses filz que il avoit engendrés,* dont il avoit les entrailles mangiees, et qu'ele avoit cen fait en venjance de ce qu'ele l'avoit delivré de mort et il l'en avoit rendu aspre guerredon comme d'elle laissier en une ille sauvage. Por quoi les sages jugent que ceste fu la plus crüel mere qui onques fust.

> [In the end Jason took her with him, to his lands, in which she acted most foolishly, *as the authorities say,* for he left her on an island in the

sea, and she was pregnant with two children. *Then she succeeded in escaping from the island and giving birth to her sons,* and she sought out Jason so much that she found him, and then she killed her two children, took their hearts and entrails, and gave them to Jason to eat, for he had fathered them from his own flesh. Then she threw down the feet and hands of the children *and told him they were the limbs of the sons he had fathered, whose entrails he had eaten,* and that she had done this as revenge for she had saved him from certain death and he had given her a harsh reward by abandoning her on a desert island. Which is why wise men consider her to be the cruelest mother that ever lived.]

This version explains the cannibalistic act as the logical return to Jason of his own flesh. Intriguingly, the Valencian poet Joan Roís de Corella's version of Medea's story (after 1450) has her congratulate herself on her self-control for not having served up her sons to Jason as food.[22] However, there are no signs here of Medea's storytelling, or of her medical disguise, one that seems to be important if Maguelonne identifies herself coherently as Medea. The Tuscan and Venetian versions develop these two aspects from Medea's other widely disseminated roles as a witch and physician.[23]

None of this explains why an innocuous heroine such as Maguelonne should be likened to a marginal Medea tradition that is truly monstrous. As has been pointed out by Ruth Morse and Alessandro Ballor, fifteenth-century treatments in French of the tale of Jason and Medea reflect a number of contradictory discourses.[24] This tradition restores Medea's infanticidal aggression, but ties it to a premeditated and spectacular revenge, not to the spontaneous outpouring of bitterness and jealousy one might expect from a more explicit reception of the *Heroides*. Ruth Morse noted that it is Medea's function as traitor to several aspects of patriarchal authority that characterizes the reception of the myth in French literary works composed between the twelfth and fifteenth centuries. She suggests that the myth produced a literary type, the "Medean woman" who was associated with danger and destructiveness.[25] By comparison, Maguelonne is far from threatening to patriarchy. She is reunited with Pierre after she disguises herself as a beggar, a pilgrim, and a saintly nurse. Maguelonne's decision to identify herself as Medea signals the romance's association with a complex network of texts that are all tributaries of Benoît de Sainte-Maure's vernacular reworking of the matter of Troy. Her *planctus et lamentatione* is not so much an allusion to the *Heroides* as it is to a singular vernacular tradition, one that places the romance squarely within the interlingual politics of the vernaculars rather than in a deferential posture with respect to Latin learning.

Babbi's interpretation of the Coburg manuscript raises the possibilities that *La Belle Maguelonne* was read by children and that it was used for the acquisition of Latin. This might certainly explain why Clément Marot's juvenilia should include an otherwise eccentric treatment of Maguelonne as an Ovidian heroine. But if the text was received in the schoolroom, it was also intratextually determined by the harrowing exemplum of a Medea known through vernacular rather than Latin sources. Of course, Medea may be viewed as a figuration of the "cruelest mother that ever lived" in terms of the mother tongue. Where the mother tongue represents a reliable connection between nature, nurture, and genealogy (as lineage/language), the Medean mother is violently opposed to genealogy: she kills her ex-husband's sons as well as her brother, and so destroys two lines of male succession. Her relationship with nature is flawed, as she practices magic and manipulates cooking to produce poison. The Medean mother's treatment of her role as *nutrix* probably needs no further gloss. The vernacular developments play on Medea as storyteller and as the author of written documents. Joan Roís de Corella composed a letter-cum-dialogue by Medea is which she justifies herself to women readers. The vernacular versions also expand on the violence visited by Medea on her sons, rather than on Jason.

On a more global narrative level, *La Belle Maguelonne* is explicitly concerned with the oscillation between being foreign and familiar and with elopement as the moment of release from the maternal realm symbolized by Maguelonne's nurse. The prologue of the Coburg version states that the tale was put "en cestuy langaige" in honor of the shrine of Saint Pierre-de-Maguelonne in 1453 (Babbi, app. 1, § I). It is, then, appropriate to consider the text once again as one that is rooted in its geographical setting and its intertextual relationship with *Paris and Vienna*.

As Babbi has noted, *La Belle Maguelonne* reads like a complementary response to *Paris and Vienne*.[26] Paris and Vienne's companions Aduardo and Ysabel are replaced by a single go-between, Maguelonne's nurse. *Paris et Vienne* depicts Vienne's obstructive parents and Paris' passive, sick father, but *La Belle Maguelonne* allots considerable importance to both sets of parents, especially Pierre's mother, and treats the go-between as a maternal substitute. The relationship between the lovers is reversed: Maguelonne elopes with Pierre successfully but they are separated by accident. Unlike Paris, Pierre does not travel to Babylon of his own accord, but as a corsair's gift to the sultan. Pierre learns to speak "Moorish," Greek, and Persian, because the sultan regards him as an adoptive son, and does not make great use of his languages during his journey to Provence. It is Maguelonne who travels independently and uses both disguise and false identity to be reunited with her lover. The sickness motif is also reversed at the end of the text, where it is Pierre who is the patient and Maguelonne the physician.

The events recounted happened "when Christianity came into France," as well as in Provence, Languedoc, Guyenne, and Comminges (Babbi, I. 1–5).[27] Pierre is the son of the Provençal count Jehan de Cherisse and the daughter of Count Alvaro d'Albara (app. 1, § II) or Ilnaro d'Alboro (I.6–8). Pierre's parents are distressed when he wishes to travel to seek out both adventure and Maguelonne, because they fear that if their sole heir came to grief, "nostre conté et seigneurie seroit perdue" (II.31–32). The understated distinction made between "France" and the counties of Provence, Guyenne, and Comminges frames Pierre's decision to leave his home. As Pierre later identifies himself as "ung povre chevalier François qui serche le monde" (V.44) and "le seul filz au conte de Prouvence et suis nepveu au roy de France" (XIII.55–56), there is no intrinsic narratorial reason for making this distinction. However, toward the end of his adventures, Pierre meets some mariners who speak the "langaige de prouvence" and take him to Maguelonne's hospital at Aigues-Mortes. It is only in these closing stages of the tale, after Pierre has become a proficient linguist, and apparently lost his local knowledge, that a specific language is identified with this place (34v).

This narrator is more concerned with the importance of Pierre's position as a "jeune chevalier qui est estrangier" (VII.40) once he leaves his *pais* to join the ranks of the "chevaliers estranges" who wish to compete in King Maguelon's jousts (IV.38–39, V.13–15). Pierre has no need for interpreters on his travels in Europe but he experiences the city of Naples as a place where he has to set aside the "estranges viandes" served at dinner and feed his eyes on his love for Maguelonne instead (VI.20–23). He fights dressed in red and adorned with the keys of Saint Peter, as "le chevalier des clefs" (V.1–9, VI, 3). These arms reveal his name, yet no one seems able to read them, not even his own uncle (XVI.25–27, 93–94), as they persist in regarding him as a nameless knight. Perhaps, despite their geographical proximity to Rome and Maguelonne's rank as the most beautiful of Christian princesses, they do not have the "key" to his emblem. He refuses to declare his lineage, and this makes him a dangerous suitor for Maguelonne in the eyes of her nurse, who means specifically that they do not know if he is of noble rank or what his intentions might be (VII.36–42). The nurse does not see Pierre's assurance of his noble rank as sufficient reason to allow Maguelonne to love him, for his namelessness makes him still "ung estrangier" whose love would shame her. At this point, Maguelonne rejects the term altogether: "Ne me le nommez plus estrangier, car cestuy est mon seigneur et non autre. Par quoy n'est pas a moy estrangier, ne au monde n'ay plus chiere personne que luy, car je suis toute sienne ne jamais homme ne me muera de cestuy propos; par quoy je vous prie que jamais ne me vueillez dire semblables paroles se vous voullez avoir m'amour et ma grace" (IX.41–46). "Estrangier" has become an unacceptable term to Maguelonne, but she promptly dreams that she asks Pierre where he is from and what his name is (IX.69–73). Maguelonne's refusal to hear the term *estrangier* cannot withstand her obsession, even in dreams, with finding out his lineage. Once Pierre does reveal who he is, she is relieved because he argues (and she concludes) that he has left his homeland and parents solely in pursuit of her love (XIII.56–61, 79–80). Maguelonne's words and actions, particularly in her dialogue with her nurse, echo once again the tale of Medea's love for the foreign Jason in Ovid's *Metamorphoses* and offer an intriguing contrast with Raoul Lefèvre's *Histoire de Jason*. Lefèvre's Medea has an exchange with her nurse where the typical fear of the stranger is expressed as Rebecca Dixon has noted.[28]

> Quant la dame oy ces parolles, elle commença a plourer et dist: "Ma fille, hellas! Et qu'avez vous fait? Je suis bien deshonnouree par vous qui priez les estrangiers d'amours! Les estrangiers! O quel oultrage! Ilz s'en tromperont de vous, et, s'il est sceu, jamais honnouree ne serés." (Pinkernell, § 14.14)

> [When the lady heard these words, she began to weep and said, "Alas, daughter, what have you done? I am dishonored by you, for you are flirting with foreigners! Foreigners! Oh, how shocking! They will deceive you and, if it gets out, you will never be treated with honor."]

However, Medea's words do not offer any echo of the nurse's xenophobia. In her response, she emphasizes her role as a courtly lady moved by Pity to love a valorous knight (§ 14.14). The concept of Jason as a foreign threat to the stability of the kingdom of Colchos is dissolved, in keeping with Lefèvre's emphasis on Jason as the model of Burgundian knighthood. In the geographical and political worldview that underpins *La Belle Maguelonne*, Pierre's foreignness is important because his eventual match with Maguelonne will seal the otherwise unlikely Angevin union of Provence and Naples.

Maguelonne's identification of Pierre as a new Jason is fleeting, and she proposes that they have been separated by the devil as a punishment for their sinful love, with Pierre having been taken "en quelque estrange region pour son desplaisir et pour le mien" (into some foreign region for his displeasure and for mine) (XXIV.67–68). Her words echo those uttered to her by Pierre: "j'ay deliberé en moy de ne jamais partir de vostre païs que je verray la fin de vostre adventure, et j'ameroye plustost mourir que vous laisser ne vous faire ung seul desplaisir" (I have decided not to leave your land before I see the end of your adventure, and I would rather die than displease you even once) (XVIII.5–8). The abandoned Maguelonne reinterprets Pierre's reference to *desplaisir* as a possible reflection of his boredom with their unconsummated relationship (XVIII.20–21). "[P]our son desplaisir et le mien" becomes a double-edged idea. She is sorrowful to lose him to some foreign soil, "quelque estrange region," but she is also afraid that he may be unfaithful, and her quest for him becomes all the more urgent. Maguelonne's quest takes her through these *estranges regions,* first to Rome; next to Genoa; and finally to the port of Aigues-Mortes, where she asks a charitable woman if *estrangiers* such as she can travel safely in these lands (XXVI.65–66). She travels in order to become the *estrangiers* that her nurse initially rejected in Pierre. Pilgrimage deracinates Maguelonne and removed the name that denotes her connection to the kingdom of Naples ruled by Maguelon. She is no longer hostile to the concept of foreignness and has adopted it herself in her quest for her estranged Pierre. Maguelonne's new friend does not reply directly, but tells her that her safety is guaranteed because the count of Provence rules both Provence and Aragon safely, despite his sorrow over the disappearance of his son Pierre on his travels "de par le monde" (across the world) (68–80). To be a stranger in this vast territory is to enjoy a degree of safety that is not available in other regions, and it is here that Maguelonne reinterprets her own name, no longer as the daughter of the king of Naples, but now as the founder of a shrine and hospital, places of safety for travelers.

Maguelonne never equates *estrangiers* with linguistic difference. She needs no interpreter to speak to the women she encounters in the forest of Naples and in Provence. Maguelonne's travels are interesting for her ability to receive support from other women such as the pilgrim who gives her both a sermon and clothes, the woman who gives her a meal, and the countess of Provence. Although she founds the hospital initially to protect her chastity, there are no suitors or abductors in evidence during her travels. Unlike the traveling Paris, she seems able to use a common mother tongue, which is also that of her nurse. This is not a transparent language between women, however, for neither the woman pilgrim nor the hostess answers her questions directly (XXV.21–24, XXVI). Both answer more in terms of the narrative than of her proposed dialogue. Her extended dialogues with her nurse prior to her elopement may illuminate this feature of the text, because the nurse is associated with both the acquisition of speech and the maternal function. She initially addresses Maguelonne as "ma belle dame et chiere fille," and Maguelonne tells her, "ie vous vieulx obeir comme a ma chiere mere et nourrisse" (VII.24, XIV.35–36). The nurse acts as a surrogate maternal figure that ensures the connections between mothers and offspring. The nurse, a figure traditionally associated with the primary acquisition of language, is placed initially in a mediating role that allows the pair's courtship to emulate a conventional aristocratic betrothal: she distances Maguelonne from her own mother (who interrupts her first meeting with Pierre [VI.53–66]). She also precipitates both their elopement and their separation by giving Maguelonne the three rings that were given to Pierre by his mother, a gesture that echoes a betrothal by proxy.

Maguelonne effectively weans herself from the nurse by absconding into a world where she may emulate Pierre in traveling incognito through other linguistic regions. Once she is the "saincte hospitaliere," however, Maguelonne develops a close relationship with the countess of Provence and finds comfort for her own mourning for Pierre in soothing her maternal sorrow. Maguelonne's lack of language barriers and her flexible choices of name are also intriguing. In a text that places some stress on Pierre's name as a signifier that can be hidden and can become as powerless as a pebble thrown after a bird, the heroine's name shifts seamlessly. Maguelonne fleetingly attempts to rename herself "la nouvelle Medee," but prefers to don an anonymous pilgrim's clothing. She is known at Aigues-Mortes as "la belle hospitaliere." However, Maguelonne somehow imposes her patronymic as a toponym in her lover's homeland. It is not clear if, at the end, Pierre has reached a hospital, his homeland, or her body as metonymy for her ownership of the island of Maguelonne on the shore of Aigues-Mortes (a place-name that alludes both to salt production and to the paradoxically curative but inert waters of the Dead Sea).

If language is one issue for Maguelonne, the second aspect of the *nutrix*, nourishment, affects Pierre. The second part of the text describes Pierre's adventures in a world where food and bodies are confused, and he is repeatedly mistaken for food. When he wins King Maguelon's tournament, the court feasts their eyes on Pierre's white flesh, gray eyes and red gold hair and think, "bien euree estoit la mere qui avoit porté tant noble fruit" (The mother was fortunate who bore such noble fruit) (XVI.166–73). The "estranges viandes" (strange foodstuffs) served up on the king of Naples's table are ignored by Pierre, who prefers to consume Maguelonne's beauty with his eyes. Both fruit and flesh of his mother's body, Pierre prepares to elope with Maguelonne by packing enough food for two days (XIX.1–5). When their elopement is discovered, King Maguelon shows his grief by fasting for a whole day (XX.36–37). The scene is set for a separation predicated on nourishment. When Pierre and Maguelonne reach the shore and Maguelonne falls asleep, Pierre takes advantage of this opportunity and opens her bodice to feast on the sight of her breasts. He finds a bundle of red silk tucked into her bosom and unwraps it to find that it contains his mother's three rings. He places this treasure laden with maternal and erotic connotations on a rock (*une pierre*) (XXI.22). A passing bird of prey ("oysel vivant de rapine") thinks the red bundle is a piece of meat ("une piece de char") and swoops down to steal it (XXI.28–29). Pierre is disturbed to have lost Maguelonne's concealed treasure "et commença a suivre l'oisel et luy lanssoit pierre" until it lands on an offshore rock (this time, a *roche*). Pierre throws another *pierre* at the bird so it flies away and drops the bundle into the sea (XXII.4–12). Pierre tries to recapture the bundle by sailing out to the rock in a fisherman's abandoned boat, but he is lost at sea.

Much later, Pierre's mother is required to interpret the cloth and rings when they are found in an unusually large and beautiful fish that has been caught by fishermen and given to the count's cooks (XXVIII.1–11). She concludes that her innocent son has been eaten by fish: "quel mal avoit fait ceste innocente creature que les poissons aient mangié sa chair?" (What harm had this innocent creature done, for fish to have eaten his flesh?) (XXVIII.20–21). Pierre is by this point of the text reduced to a worthless commodity, no more than fish food and undigested maternal objects, his passing witnessed, says his mother, by "une creature inraisonnable et morte qui ne voit ne oyt ne sant" (a dead, irrational creature that can neither see nor hear, nor feel) (XXVIII.27–28). An innocent creature eaten by an irrational one, Pierre has been absorbed into inert matter. He is lost at sea on a boat that has been abandoned by fishermen because they thought it was worthless, and he reacquires some value only in commercial terms when he is rescued by corsairs, because his good looks and the gold chain he wears round his neck make him a worthy gift for a sultan anxious to recruit a young nobleman to serve at his table (XXII.21–23, XXIII.5–10). If Maguelonne flirts repeatedly with a new identity as Medea, Pierre is far less a new

Jason than a human version of the Golden Fleece: desired and valued both as a symbol and an object, but intrinsically a useless remnant of uncooked mutton.

Pierre's confused grasp of signs reaches its apex in Alexandria, where he is once again nameless and *estrangiers*. There are interpreters at this court to assist the sultan, and Pierre acquires proficiency in Moorish, Greek, and Persian within a year. He acquires great influence at court and the sultan loves him like a son (XXIII.14–15, XXX.2–10). Yet Pierre, unlike Paris, proves incapable of putting his language skills to subtle use. He insults the sultan's paternal love by asking for his permission to return to Provence to visit his mother and father (XXXI.3–10), and in so doing loses the inheritance that was about to fall to him (12–19). He attempts to return to Provence with fourteen barrels filled with gold, but presents these to the Provençal mariners as barrels of salt. They are perplexed by a traveler who wants to take salt to one of the most important centers of the saline industry of the northern Mediterranean, but they allow him his whim, as he has paid them handsomely (XXXI.49–70). Unfortunately for Pierre, the barrels of food-preserving salt appear to desiccate the ship's crew, as they are forced to stop on the island of Sangana to collect some fresh water (XXXII.73–76).[29] Pierre is seasick and goes ashore. He is distracted by the beauty of a flower on this island (where there is no food) into thinking of Maguelonne and falls asleep (XXXII). He, like she before him, is stranded, when the ship leaves without him, and only the worthless barrels of salt reach Maguelonne's hospital of "Saint Pierre de Maguelonne" (XXXII.29–40, XXXV). Pierre is far from classical allusion at this point. Far from being eaten by fish, a confused, parched, and starving Pierre is rescued once again and fed by fishermen (XXXV.49–55), and after nine months of hospitalization and good food in the port of Crapena meets yet more mariners who speak the "langaige de Prouvence" and take him to Saint-Pierre de Maguelonne, which has been miraculously enriched and enlarged, unbeknownst to him, thanks to his mislaid barrels of gold (XXXVI.59–24).

This narrative sequence plays on the paradoxes of salt, a product of the sea that was valued essentially for its peripheral role in preserving meat from rotting and for enhancing the taste of food, yet one that cannot be eaten in significant quantities and cannot be drunk. Salt is both dead and alive, a dispensable product, a treasured commodity, and a poison. It was subject to fierce commercial competition, yet it was literally as plentiful as the sea. Like salt, Pierre dissolves whenever he is tested by contact with water, and like salt, he is associated with fish and with food.

Pierre thus appears to metamorphose into a series of foodstuffs, as his reunion with Maguelonne is heralded and made possible by barrels of salt that could preserve the fish his mother believes have eaten him. Maguelonne has searched for him in Rome, the location he initially claimed as his by using the *armes parlantes* of the keys of Saint Peter. She is subsequently condemned to await his reappearance from the sea in a church she dedicates to Saint Peter. However, Pierre is never recognized by his first name or his lineage: he recognizes Maguelonne's name in the hospital, but fails to identify her. Rather, he fantasizes that she (or rather her attractive flesh) has been eaten by animals because of him: "Et suis cause que les bestes sauvages luy ont rompue et mangee sa chair, qui estoit tant belle et tant noble" (It is because of me that the savage beasts have torn and eaten her flesh, which was so beautiful and noble) (XXXVII.14–16).

However, as it is necessary to reunite the two protagonists so the tale may end, the narrative abandons Pierre's fixation on flesh as food and reverts to the concept initially raised by Maguelonne of what defines the *estrangier*. Pierre tells Maguelonne that he is the son of a nobleman who abandoned his parents because he had heard about the beauty of "une fille qui estoit en ung estrange pays" (XXXVIII.5–7). In retelling his tale and mentioning no names once he is back in Provence, Pierre reformulates the roles the two protagonists have played. Maguelonne is now redefined as the *estrangier*, as her elopement and disguise doubly mean that she now has neither a name nor a lineage. The toponym she has imposed on the island of Port Sarrasin has a dual function: it unites the names of the separated lovers as well as their two lineages, and it affirms Pierre's initial dedication to Saint Peter. A third function is also obvious in that the name makes a "Saracen" port of Provence into a Christian shrine named after the king of Naples.

La Belle Maguelonne stages a detailed alienation of both protagonists from their lineage and homeland, so that the category of *estrangiers* is redefined, from an intolerable or frustrating word signifying marital and social rejection, to an object of desire. Accordingly, Maguelonne dresses in royal clothing in order to unveil herself before him as the daughter of the king of Naples, the "estrange pays" that led Pierre to abandon every ounce of his identity as the son of the count of Provence, to the point that he became no more than a series of signs and substances (XIL.1–20), keys, rock, ring, and fish.

In many respects the tale again exhibits strong connections with *Paris et Vienne*, where the port of Aigues-Mortes is also exploited as a base for travel and return (XIX, XL). Pierre de La Cépède's statement that he has taken the name of Saint Peter also hints at the symbolic exploitation of Pierre's name: "Et c'il vous plaist savoir qui je suis: de Saint Piere j'ay prins le non, de la Cypede pour sournon" (And if you want to know who I am: I have taken the name of Saint Peter and the surname of La Cépède). To conclude, *La Belle Maguelonne* operates within a network of "secondary translations," texts that do not declare their relationship with their source and that display a competitive attitude toward contemporary or prior compositions in the vernacular. In terms of the romance's allusion to a classical source, it is embedded in a dense textual field encompassing French adaptations of the matter of Troy that were in turn translated into other French texts and give rise to Latin, Tuscan, and Venetian versions. As a vernacular romance, it explores the mother tongue and *nutrix* tongue through images of parentage and nourishment. In so doing, it appears to depict both ethnic and familial identities as elective concepts that are grounded in language. The romance is explicitly connected with the problematic claims to empire of the Angevin house of Anjou-Provence, and it is this complex multilingual court, in direct competition with the house of Aragon and Catalonia, that determines its geographical and linguistic ambiguities.

9

TRAVELS IN THE *Monolangue*

TRAVELERS IN ANY REGION AND HISTORICAL PERIOD are forced to engage in dialogue with unfamiliar languages. Such encounters are determined by the traveler's status and may be marked by all manner of cultural anxieties. A merchant will not have the same status abroad as a soldier or a migrant. As we saw in both *Paris and Vienne* and in the *Belle Maguelonne*, travel may estrange the masculine subject from his mother tongue or may prove the feminine subject's independence of it. Travel narratives may well be the locations of the most explicit explorations of the *monolangue*'s fragile, essentially phantasmatical basis. Derrida's statement concerning the monolangue as anything but a personal possession reemerges in this context as part of the cultural baggage taken by travelers as they leave one location (sometimes but not always their "home") in order to visit, explore, or colonize others. The strange location may refuse to let the traveler interpret its particular idiom in terms of his or her mother tongue, the signifying grid he or she strives to impose onto it.

Guillem de Torroella's *Faula* presents a bewildering journey (a "fable," after all) in which the dreaming narrator finds King Arthur entombed beneath Etna (lines 689–705), flanked by two weeping ladies, Amours and Valors.[1] Guillem travels eastward from Mallorca on the back of a great fish, escorted by a parrot (lines 75–79), and lands on an island where he encounters a Francophone snake in a tree (lines 121–25) and eats its mysterious fruit that he cannot name ("mas li pom so de tal figura / com son toronges o noronges" [lines 132–33]). A biblical apple is mixed with a new fruit purloined from Arab culture, the orange. The apple-orange hybrid from this new tree of knowledge enables him to find out from the snake (in French) that he is in an Arthurian realm (in fact, he is not: he is in Sicily, as the precise distance he has traveled would have told his audience). Morgan la Fay welcomes this visitor from overseas ("outra la mer" [line 497]), "en son lenguatge" (in her language) (line 491). Now Guillem's interlocutors on the island are as Francophone as the snake, although he continues to speak in Catalan. The Catalan traveler assures the entombed Arthur that he understands his language well enough, but is nevertheless aware of a significant gap in his knowledge and has to inquire if he is indeed the once and future king (lines 919–28). Arthur is offended by this ignorant traveler's failure to identify him as a king (lines 933–36), but Guillem explains that in the version of the death of Arthur that he has read, there is no entombment beneath Etna (lines 937–84). Sicily is transformed into a literary site where two competing versions of Arthur's final moments are compared, contrasted, and reconciled.

Guillem's journey ends when he travels back to Mallorca to tell of his adventures and the new insight he has acquired into a legend that he now realizes is well known. He can now assure his fellow countrymen (who may like him have been completely oblivious to the very idea) that Arthur will return to the world of the living. Guillem's complex journey expressly moves him from the familiar location of Mallorca, an island that was invaded and Christianized in the late thirteenth century, into a relatively recent Aragonese possession. Sicily is depicted as a strange literary environment that mixes the garden of Eden with Arthurian romance and Gervase of Tilbury's account of the tomb of Arthur under Etna. Guillem's literary invention (*inventio*) of Sicily allows him to explore translation's ability to revitalize "French" books, to domesticate them to the point that he might transfer them (in an act of *translatio*) back to his cultural starting point with the profitable result of turning him from a squire into a suitably chivalric knight. His text uses literary allusion to stage the absorption by the crown of Aragon of an island that was under Anglo-Norman rule some two centuries beforehand.

Literary models proved as pervasive for autobiographical accounts of travels. The account of the pilgrimage to Jerusalem by Philippe de Voisins, *seigneur* of the Gascon seat of Montaut (near Auch) was written in French in the 1490s by his squire Jehan de Belesta. It notes the linguistic marvel that is the southern Italian region of Puglia, "ou les genz parlent gascon audict lieu et aultres a l'environ; lesquelz se tienent sepparés de l'aultre nation du pais" (where people speak Gascon in that place and surrounding areas. They keep themselves separate from the other people in the region).[2] Gascon-speaking Pugliese may seem as ludicrous as Francophone snakes in Sicily, but there seems to have been a slim basis of fact, in that a Franco-Provençal dialect was spoken in isolated areas of Puglia.[3] If their travels to the Holy Land and back bring the lord and squire into contact with their mother tongue, it is notable that this is not the language of Belesta's written account. He writes in French. The mother tongue may be pleasurably rediscovered in southern

Italy, but it is not used within the *seigneur* of Montaut's own lands. Mother tongue becomes (m)other tongue, a sign of an unfamiliar familiarity.

This estranged mother tongue finds an echo in Belesta's account of the island of Cyprus as the site of contested literary as well as political authority. The lord of Montaut and his squire sail from Venice to the Venetian port of Baffa, only to find themselves in a location that they interpret as truly belonging to the French:

> Et y est la caverne ou feurent trouvés les sept dourmans, et Remondin, sieur de Lezinam, mary de Meluzine, y est ent[er]ré, a cause qu'un son filz feust roy dudict Chippre et y fist pourter le corps. Et de ceste generation sont descendus les rois de Chippre, jusques a present qu'ilz sont ausdicts Venitiens, qui leur est chose griefve et seroient volountiers ez mains des François, car ilz en ayment naturellement la nation. (25)

> [The cave is there where the seven sleepers were found, and Raymondin, the husband of Melusine, is buried there because his son was king of Cyprus and had his corpse taken there. The kings of Cyprus have descended from this lineage until the present day, when they [the Cypriots] are in the hands of the Venetians, which they do not like, and they would prefer to be in the hands of the French, because they are drawn by nature to love their people.]

If Belesta has traced signs of his mother tongue in Puglia, he ascribes a patrilinear loyalty (one he perceives as "natural") to the population of Cyprus on the basis of a literary fiction, albeit one that was enjoying very widespread success by the end of the fifteenth century. The romance of Melusine is given an immediate political purpose by its French reader and is used to perpetuate the claim that a distant island should be viewed as rightfully the property of one country rather than another. Between Cypriots who are naturally drawn to prefer French rulers over Venetians, and Gascon-speaking enclaves in Puglia, Belesta's apparently naive mapping of his travels begins to show signs of an interpretative grid that is both political and empire building. It lays claim to lands that have been under "French" (Angevin or Poitevin) rule at some point in their history and in so doing negates the equally flimsy claims of Aragonese or Venetian rulers.

Several decades earlier, the Gascon *seigneur* Nompar de Caumont wrote a description in French of his own pilgrimage to the Holy Land that he had undertaken in 1418–20, for the edification of his sons. He does not lay dynastic claims to any islands, and seems more keen to list the various souvenirs that he keeps in a single trunk, among them precious spices, amulets, a handful of relics, rings that have touched the Sepulcher, and a little water from the River Jordan (Noble, 80–82).[4] His preference for keeping his travels locked away is explained within the manuscript, as he prefaces his narrative with a fable in which an ageing wolf takes his cubs up to a mountaintop; shows them his lands; and warns them, now he is no longer able to travel, that they must learn from him that "on païs où vous vouldres fere vostre prise, ne fettes point votre maison ne habitacion, si vous vueillez vivre sans doubte" ([you should] never build your house or dwelling place in a region you want to capture, if you want to live without fear) (Noble, 21). Nompar warns his sons that invasion has its costs, before he gives them his detailed description of the sites he has visited. Nompar's pilgrimage is framed by paternal advice to maintain a cautious peace with neighboring lands, to cultivate the family lands without seeking to expand them, to acquire precious possessions that may be handed down, and to strive to lead an upstanding life. "Cest petit livre" is, he hopes, something that his sons will be able to read and emulate in adulthood (113v).

Nompar and the *seigneur* of Montaut both chose to have their memoirs written down in French, in keeping with their increasingly Francophone environment. Their very different travel narratives are couched in a single language that is not, presumably, that in which they expressed themselves on a daily basis. Nompar was raised at the court of the count of Foix, and it is plausible that his account was translated into French by its scribe, Johannes Ferriol. The contrast could not be greater between Nompar's memoir, which closes with a moralizing poem in French, and a vision poem composed only a half century before it by Bernat de So.[5]

Bernat was one of the most powerful noblemen of the Roussillon, attached to the king of Mallorca, and also a vassal of the count of Foix. He dedicates his work of 1382 to another vassal of the count, the Languedocian nobleman Bernat Serviers, and intends it to be read by Gaston Phébus, but he may also have destined the poem for the court of King Pere IV at Barcelona. His poem narrates the hallucinatory encounter between a traveler and an animated description of the world. His protagonist is traveling from the royal court of Barcelona to pay homage to the count of Foix in celebration of the end of the war between the houses of Foix and Armagnac. He and his men stop for a rest on the southernmost edge of the county of Comminges, at Saint-Gaudens (Haute-Garonne). They have crossed the Pyrenees (lines 37–43). Bernat decides to take a stroll on the banks of the Garonne, the river that flows from the Pyrenees via Toulouse to the Gironde estuary on the Atlantic Coast, one of the northernmost points of Occitania. He decides to go a little farther, perhaps to admire the river, "Que.m meses en un puy / Trop bell, don sens enuy / Pugey leumen lassus. / E, garden sus e jus" ([lacuna] that I should go to the top of a very attractive hill, which I climbed without any trouble. And, looking around high and low) (lines 55–59). There is no chance to admire the view, for at this moment a gigantic male figure rears out of the Garonne and lets forth three screams "aut e cujat" (loud and quick) in a terrifying voice (lines 60–71). Bernat says that he alone could see the giant. His horrified companions are unable to see the vision that he narrates. With each cry, the giant summons from the river's depths a series of satirical vignettes: corrupt clerics, unjust kings, oppressed merchants, and finally a long series of wars between the rulers of Europe. All are described with an alien eye, as if Bernat were an uninformed observer. It is only toward the end of the poem that he is able to speak to the "home gran" (great man) and ask him to give the names of the many individuals and peoples that have appeared momentarily from the river. He says very affably and with a smile that he is the World ("le Mon") in person (lines 1078–1101). Bernat unleashes his bitterness against the World's corruption, temptations, and endless violence (lines 1082–1134): "ell nos conffon, / e.ns tresex, e.ns affolla" (How it confounds us, and betrays us, and drives us mad), emulating the World's terrible voice, as he speaks "Ab guisca vots e folla" (in a harsh and wild voice) (lines 1082–85). The World reminds Bernat that it is merely the product of Creation, with no responsibility for what humans choose to make of it. The giant disappears and a disembodied voice, that not of the World, but of another figure speaking "per l'ome gran" (on behalf of the great man), briskly names the figures and countries that Bernat has seen.

Bernat's vision poem seems to stage an encounter between the uninformed viewer of a *mappa mundi* and its strange content: coats of arms, castles, crowned figures. He requires the assistance of a disembodied intermediary to interpret his words, much as the modern reader of the poem requires Amédée Pagès's editorial notes. The World refuses to be drawn into this decrypting process. He is concerned only with stating that unlike the bewildered human beings who inhabit it, it has no need of a code of either ethics or self-control. Nompar would preface his description of his travels in the world with a peaceful plain viewed from a hilltop, bathed in the warning words of an ageing father to his sons. Bernat's protagonist climbs a hill to admire the foothills of the Pyrenees, just as he is reaching the less arduous part of his journey (one that celebrates a newfound peace), and is shocked by a terrifying portrait of the world that contains his immediate, highly localized, field of vision. Here, the Occitan verse serves to cement the connections between the court of Barcelona, the count of Foix, and Bernat's home in the mountains of Roussillon, but the World displays ample evidence that this constitutes too narrow a point of view. Like the new peace that has been established between the counts of Foix and Armagnac, the Occitan poem is localized and limited. Bernat can see and hear the World, but his companions can only hear the dreadful noise that it makes. Once Bernat demands a verbal gloss on the things and peoples he has seen, the World vanishes from view. He is also left to contend with a disembodied interpreter that he cannot identify (this time by sight). Bernat is forced to contend with a global vision that is fragmented and unsatisfactorily glossed. He meets the World, only to realize that he can neither conquer it by sight or words nor overcome its fundamental disregard for human emotions.

Anxieties about the impossibility of encompassing the experience of the world by sight or words in Bernat's *Vesio* are echoed by Antoine de La Sale, the Provençal-born author who wrote initially for the Francophone Angevin court of Provence and Naples and later acquired some literary success in the ambit of the duke of Burgundy.[6] La Sale also depicts the volcanic regions near Sicily as the site of linguistic tensions. Throughout his writings, La Sale makes occasional appearances as the protagonist of short travel tales that he dates and situates within a fragmented autobiography. He depicts himself as a youth climbing Vulcano in 1407 and fighting at the siege of Ceuta (Morocco) in 1415. He seeks out the cave of the Sibyl in Umbria in 1420 and accompanies Duke Louis III on an excursion to the Flegrean fields and Pozzuoli in 1425. The same man is presented on his home turf as ducal *viguier* at Arles in 1429 and protective adviser to the ducal family during the siege of Naples by the Aragonese in 1437.[7] However, La Sale's travel tales are not autobiographies or continuous narratives. Rather, they are fragments inserted into these collections of extracts and exempla named after La Sale himself, and his readers are to travel figuratively through this written portrait of his own learning. His eyewitness accounts of journeys are scattered between other stories as if to point out the narrator's own shared store of experience acquired in body as well as in books.

Among the 167 exempla of *La Sale,* La Sale describes an excursion to the volcanic area of Pozzuoli with Duke Louis III of Anjou in 1425, which was an opportunity for his patron to enjoy the great marvels he has conquered with the kingdom of Naples. The Angevin courtiers are shown the thermal complex with its healing baths. The Frenchmen are shown a lake full of inedible fish and pause to stare at a beautiful Neapolitan noblewoman who has accompanied her husband, a leper, and tends to him in the baths with no regard for herself.[8] The narrator says that he rails at the woman's relatives for letting her ruin her beauty and health in this way. He learns from them that this woman sets a model of wifely devotion for the French conquerors' womenfolk, some of whom are prepared to leave sick husbands in search of other men. The French excursion is borrowed from the ceremonial practices of the Neapolitan royal court, which appreciated what Jesús Carrillo has termed "the classicist flavor of the elite ritual of visiting volcanoes and other natural portents,"[9] but it hints at a quest for a thrilling mixture of travelers' marvels and spiritual horror; after all, the region had long been regarded as the mouth of Hell.[10] Pozzuoli was accessible in the ducal library as well as on the ground, for Duke Louis III owned one of the many descriptions of the healing baths. Although we can assume that the historical La Sale could well have visited the Campi Flegrei, this anecdote, as with so many others, could be culled from purely written sources.

La Sale's narrator is notoriously unreliable in several of these first-person anecdotes, most notoriously in his geography of the world, which includes the short texts now titled *Le Paradis de la Reine Sibylle* and the *Excursion aux îles Lipari* (1437). *Le Paradis de la Reine Sibylle* is designed to correct Agnès de Bourbon's false knowledge, as he aims to show her how different the Monti Sibillini are from their depiction in a tapestry she owns:

> Pour ce vous envoie par escript et pourtrait les mons du lac de Pilate et de la Sibille, qui autrement sont que en vostre tapisserie ne sont faiz, et aussi tout ce que je ay peu veoir et moy informer par les gens du païs. (Desonay, C text, 63).

> [I send you in writing and image the mountains of the lake of Pilate and of the Sybil, which look different from the way they are depicted in your tapestry, as well as everything I was able to see and glean from the people of the region.]

This is to be a corrective gloss by a seasoned traveler of an image.[11] Agnès's manuscript and the printed versions of *La Salade* provide a map of the Monti Sibillini, allowing the reader to plot the travels and possibly to recreate them.

Several medievalists sought to reenact the climb in the nineteenth century and were disappointed to find that the journey plan had been subtly flawed and that even the detailed descriptions and sketches of two local plants were inaccurate.[12] The reader is given marvels that are commonplace (two local flowers), plus a misleading itinerary. According to Michèle Perret, even these learned refutations of La Sale's tale contribute to a trompe l'oeil narrative, one that is literally too good to be true.[13] The reader of La Sale's travel tales has to deal with a constantly shifting focus, moving from one vignette to another, led on by a verbal promise of authenticity that becomes increasingly tenuous. In this respect, La Sale's travel writing appears to destabilize the role of the interpreter-guide, a figure defined by Luigi Monga as "an essential facilitator who transfers notions and ideas from one culture to another." Monga goes on to note that seasoned travelers in turn become the "mediators and exegetes of a distant, inexplicable world," a task La Sale appears to stand on its head by distorting observable phenomena and explaining only that these other worlds are multiple and highly subjective.[14] This is all the more intriguing because of the ostensibly pedagogical function of both the geography and the *Salade,* which would imply that the authorial voice should be reliable.[15] As tutor and writer, La Sale presents himself as another interpreter-guide, the learned compiler who transfers knowledge from Latin to the vernacular, the past to the present.

The narrative of La Sale's journey to Lipari seems both more personal and less significant than the account of the Monti Sibillini, but it is the tale that raises the most questions about language.[16] Further, La Sale appears to destabilize the linguistic markers of authority throughout his anecdote and, in so doing, presents a meditation on the multilingual processes of the Angevins' empire building in the kingdom of Sicily. La Sale was criticized by his early editors and scholars for the poor quality of his French, as an uneducated author of Provençal origin. While he most probably had no formal tutoring in Latin, the Provencalisms and Italianisms in his writings are probably derived from both read and spoken knowledge. Indeed, La Sale's taste for multilingual neologisms and linguistic play is well attested and may provide a key for his narratorial treatment of his travel tales.[17]

The preceding section to the geography in *La Salade* consists of a series of extracts concerning *fallasseries* (deceits) and that he rubricates as translations from Valerius Maximus's *Facta et dicta memorabilia* (Desonay, 23–62). La Sale highlights the insufficiency of linguistic expression in this section and explains that "because they cannot be satisfactorily named in Latin or explained in French, the authors name them in Greek pronunciation, that is to say, *estrantegemens.*"[18] He traces his stratagems to Julius Frontinus's "Livre des Estrantegemens" (38, line 506), a book he says is difficult to find

(49, lines 838–40). The reader is compelled to trust La Sale as a resourceful compiler and translator, tracing inaccessible volumes in libraries full of newly rediscovered Greek and Latin learning. In fact, La Sale's direct source was no more than Simon de Hesdin's translation of Frontinus, which circulated independently of a shortened version he had inserted into book 7 of his French rendering of Valerius Maximus.[19] It is Simon de Hesdin, not La Sale, who advises his reader that he has translated a book that is otherwise quite elusive.

The "translateur" in this section of *La Salade* is variously the interpreter-translator of the Latin source (in reality, partial transcriptions of Simon de Hesdin's glosses) or a man who usurps the position of another through trickery (25–26). If *La Salade* is read as a book rather than a series of fragments, La Sale seems to preface his travel narratives with stratagems: tales of trickery, manipulation of religious faith, and translation. His own false claim to be the tales' translator adds a further edge of knowing deceit. In these exempla, Servius Tullius becomes king of Rome thanks to a priest of Diana who manipulates a sacrifice to ensure that Rome will benefit from a prophecy (23–24). Darius's servant Orbarès tricks a horse into neighing by making him sniff the scent of a mare's genitals, thus ensuring that the magi are given a sign of his right to become king of Persia (30). The duke of Thebes sits down fully armed on his chair before battle and it collapses. He laughs at his men's terrified faces and tells them that the gods have sent a good message, urging them to fight at once (56). These deceits and stratagems share certain features: they are short exempla of how ingenuity, linguistic dexterity, and prompt laughter can obtain political advantage. La Sale also advises Jean de Calabre on the value of tutors, noting that Alexander the Great benefited from all his tutors, including one who saved a city by advising him to destroy it, thus anticipating that his master would ignore his words (31–32):

> Assavoir est que Alixandre n'eust pas seullement Aristote a maistre, pour lui endoctriner, mais en eust pluisieurs. Car Phelipe, son pere, mist tresgrant cure a le faire endoctriner en science, avant qu'il preist les armes. Et de ses maistres, entre les aultres, fust ung appellé Damaximenès. Item, est assavoir que la cite de Lancasus fust saulvée par ung subtil dit de Danecienès. Car quant Alixandre s'en alloit, a tout son ost, moult impetueusement, pour la destruire, il vist hors des murs Maximenès, son maistre, venir vers lui, pour ce qu'il ne lui sembloit pas qu'il opposast ses prieres a la grant yre qu'il avoit; mais quant il le vist, sy jura qu'il ne feroit chose qu'il lui priast, sy hault

que Maximenès le oïst. Et tantost Maximenès lui dist: je vous prie que vous destruisiez Lancasus. Ceste hastive parolle de sagacité la noble et ancienne cité garda de destruction. (Desonay, 31–32)

[It should be known that Alexander did not only have Aristotle as his tutor, but had many others to teach him. For his father, Philip, took great care to teach him the sciences before he took up a military life. One of his masters among many was called Damaximenès. Item: it should be known that the city of Lancasus was saved by Danecienès' subtle words. For when Alexander was heading there most impetuously with his army, to destroy it, he saw Maximenès, his tutor, coming toward him outside the city walls, and he did not think he would confront [the king's] great rage with his entreaties. But when he saw him, he swore that he would do nothing that he asked for, [and he swore this] so loudly that Maximenès heard him. Then Maximenès said to him, "I beg you to destroy Lancasus." These quick, sagacious words saved the noble and ancient city from destruction.]

Aristotle would make a very useful tutor for any aspiring world conqueror, but the obscure tutor whose very name cannot be remembered accurately (is he Damacienès, Maximenès, Danecienès?) can be fruitful too, as long as both parties are mistrustful of language. The tutor's "subtil dit" consists in knowing when to lie and when to make use of his master's unwillingness to listen to his words. Later in the compilation, the reader is informed that battles are commonly won because the aggressor has used spies to discover the enemy's plans, ensured that they are hungry or anxious, and lowered their morale by dividing their opinions (242, § xxvi). The same idea is repeated twice in the *Excursion,* once as a tale told by a strange mariner, second as the youthful La Sale's own misadventure. The travel narrative echoes the warning that the young prince is to be wary of stratagems in the most unlikely locations.

La Sale prefaces his tale by noting that the islands of Stromboli and Vulcano are part of the kingdom of Sicily and the duchy of Calabria (140), which are destined to be ruled by his tutee and by Agnès de Bourbon's daughter. These then represent the mouth of Hell that is closest to home for his immediate readers, as well as for him, and his text stands as a useful survey of the future duke's least controllable possessions. He opens the text as an official report; dates his journey precisely; and lists his companions, as well as the names of the Catalan merchants who took them from Messina to the islands.

Comment soit chose vraie que, en l'an de Nostre Seigneur mil quatre cens et six et vingt jours avant Pasques, soient en la cite de Messine, en l'isle de Trinacle ditte l'isle de Sicile, messeigneurs messier Hugues de Chalun, frere chevalier de Saint Jehan, de Pruilli en Touroine, de La Tour en Enjou, de Sernasse en Enjou et pluseurs autres chevaliers et escuyers de ce royaume, dont je n'ay pas bien en memoire les noms, qui tous venoient d'outre mer, montasme en la naive de Miquel Sappin et de Jehan Boros, marchans de Quathelogne. (140–41)

[So I assert that in the year of Our Lord 1406, twenty days before Easter, there were in the city of Messina, on the island of Trinacle known as the island of Sicily, my lords Hugues de Chalun, a brother knight of St. John, of Prouilly in Touraine, of La Tour in Anjou, of Sernasse in Anjou, and several other knights and squires of this kingdom whose names I do not recall well, who all came from Outremer. We all embarked onto the ship owned by Miquel Sappin and Joan Boros, merchants from Catalonia.]

Despite La Sale's assertion that his account is "chose vraie," he hints that his memory may well fail him, as he has omitted names and locations he does not recall precisely. The men he remembers are from distant, nonvolcanic Anjou and Touraine. The ship stops in the Lipari islands and they encounter a sight that is strange indeed: Stromboli burns both night and day and throws out "les merveilleuses et grandes flambes de fumee rouge, noire, verte, jaune et de diverses couleurs" (marvelous great plumes of red, black, green, yellow, and multicolored smoke) (141). La Sale presents a first-person description of Vulcano as a depressed summit with a visible crater, containing four deep wells that produce "tresgrans et hydeux espiraux de fumee, tous entourtiglés, rouges, jaunes, vers, noirs et de diverses couleurs" (very big, hideous spirals of smoke, all curled up, red, yellow, green, black, and multicolored) (144). *Entourtiglés* is an Italianism, and it would have required some glossing for a French-speaking reader, enhancing the exoticism of the description.[20] There is a most terrible noise, "tresespoventables bruiz," like thunder. The crater also contains innumerable little funnels of smoke (fumaroles), which can be trodden upon, as they do not burn.

Rational observation gives way little by little to the irrational, as the travelers move nearer to the crater of Vulcano. The narrator and two fellow squires, François de La Tour and Guillelme le Secte, take three servants and set off to climb the crater "par occieuseté" (because of leisure), and because "folle jeunesse nous y fist aller" (foolish youth made us go there) (145).

The youths climb to a higher level but are chased downhill by billowing smoke, to the jeers of their audience. They are disturbed to find they have lost their swords (they had used them as sticks), and they determine to climb again to get them back. To their surprise, the swords have shifted. It would seem that the volcano is repelling these apprentice conquerors and playing subtle tricks on their senses.

Facts are called into question further by the arrival on a skiff of a mariner who tells them that despite many letters from many places to that effect, the *capitaine* (governor) of Lipari, Nicholo de Lussio, is alive (146–47). As Miquel Sappin writes a letter to his long-lost friend, the men scrutinize the mariner's extraordinary physique (149), for the man's appearance is systematically distorted: his eyes are too small, his smile too wide, his feet too broad, and his fingernails large and dirty. His colors are also muddled: he wears a dark, faded blue bonnet; his hair is a mixture of white and black; and even his eyeballs are off white. His clothes are a faded shade of gray. The volcano has spouted the heraldic colors red, yellow, and black, but once they were placed in a tangle of flames or stripes, noble colors (*entourtiglés*) could be synonymous with prostitution and felony.[21] The ugly mariner, however, is clad in mixed shades of black, gray, and blue, indicative of clouds, smoke, and illusion. Yet his presence is more vivid than that of the two craters, as La Sale adds: "Que vous diroie? Il me semble que je le voy, toutes les fois qu'il m'en souvient" (What could I tell you? It seems to me I see him every time I remember him) (150). La Sale has no trouble recalling the man's dirty fingernails, unlike the names of his traveling companions.

Such detailed descriptions, with no illustration to support them, draw the reader's attention to language and its potential to deceive. The mariner starts to gloss the place for its visitors and to undermine their certainties further. He tells them that the allegedly immemorial custom of protecting ships in the Lipari Islands by fixing crosses to masts was provoked by him. La Sale notes that he is reluctant to use the word "croix" and refers to crosses as "ce signal" (151), ignoring the local term, "le signe de la croix." The mariner seems to be at odds with the linguistic custom of the islands, although it should be obvious to the reader that the Sicilian-speaking Liparese probably do not speak French, so "le signe de la croix" cannot be a completely accurate rendering of a local term. In this respect the mariner is also at odds with a narrator whose monolingualism appears to blind him to obvious linguistic variations.

The mariner explains that during a recent war, he was asked by de Lussio to investigate twelve galleys that had landed at Vulcano, because he knew all the languages spoken on these seas (151). The people of the Lipari Islands were at war with the Sicilians, the Sardinians, the Corsicans, the Genoese, and the Provençaux. Clad only in a shirt and armed with a dagger, the mariner sailed in his skiff to the harbor, hid in the undergrowth, and spied on the men, but could not hear their language clearly because of the loud wind (152). He untied one galley from its moorings, but this did not make the men speak clearly enough to recognize their language. He tried again, and as they cried out, he heard them use Genoese, Provençal, and Catalan (151–52). It is only after he untied a fifth galley that the men of the first ran up to the rock behind which the mariner was hiding, and he was able to identify their true language. He does not say what language that was, just as he has not specified his own native tongue.

La Sale's companions, a trilingual assortment of Catalans, Angevins, and Provençaux, as well as men from an unspecified location in Outremer, overcome the mistrust the man's appearance inspires in them and decide to untie the three crosses on their ships. Their informant sails away with the letter for Nicholo de Lussio, but their trust turns out to have been misplaced, as in the night violent gusts of wind and smoke nearly drive the ships onto the rocks, and one man is almost killed when he leaps into the sea (154–55). The men realize that they have fallen victim to a trickster's stratagem and have been left vulnerable, hungry, and disorientated. However, the tale has a further twist when it turns out that the mariner has also told them the truth, for the next day, de Lussio turns up in person to rescue them with a hearty meal and much laughter at their expense. He informs the luckless victims that they have been gulled by one of the demons that haunt the Lipari Islands.

La Sale transfers the role of interpreter-guide at this point from the deformed mariner to de Lussio, an authority figure placed on the threshold between life and death, deceit and reality. The mariner and de Lussio are both marked as unstable figures, and both infiltrate the men's ships to laugh at the naïveté of visitors to their realm. De Lussio reportedly has been dead for two years and the letter sent to him by Sappin has not reached him, but he arrives in time to give them food and to rejoice at their misadventure (158). Similarly, in the *Paradis,* La Sale's informer at the Sybil's lake is a certain "don Anthon Fumato, c'est a dire missire Anthoine Fumé" (82), a lunatic priest whose tales cannot be trusted much of the time. This smoky, *sfumato* Antonio/Antoine echoes the two figures encountered on Vulcano, the graying, ragged mariner and the revenant captain. La Sale comments at the end that de Lussio told them many tall tales and could not be trusted either.

The mariner's anecdote is disturbing, as it depicts the island of Vulcano as a place inhabited by individuals who hide behind rocks and trees to spy on their visitors. In the Lipari Islands, every visitor is from overseas; the mariner's own speech appears to differ from that of the locals whose testimony and language are invoked, but who never intervene directly in the tale. The Catalan merchant writes a letter to the (Sicilian? Neapolitan?) governor of Lipari, but we are not told what language he uses. Similarly, we are not told what languages are used by the mariner and de Lussio when they tell tales to their multilingual guests (158). La Sale's narrator informs us that the locals use a French term for the sign of the cross and appears in so doing to be less than trustworthy himself, as he seems to assume that the monolingualism he shares with his readers is a universal fact. The text plays on the destabilizing effects of multilingual confusion and associates mastery of several languages with trickery.[22]

La Sale the tutor-narrator constructs an untried La Sale who learns to mistrust the tall tales of strangers. It seems that Vulcano teaches a lesson in revealing the thresholds that the traveler has taken for granted, setting the *otium* of youth against the learning of maturity. It also provides a location where a translated Latin anecdote can be retold, and subsequently experienced, in the reader's own world. Language itself cannot be relied upon, and authority is leached out of linguistic labels and signs by the three speakers, who are the narrator-tutor, his narrated younger self, and the mariner. A Francophone Angevin court seeking to reign over a multilingual empire could learn much from the lesson.

This tale of real and apparent ghosts has been described as the first example in French literature of the "fantastic."[23] As the elderly mariner vanishes into the night bearing letters for a man long thought dead, there are signs of a characteristic association of darkness and deformity with Hell. Accounts of the Lipari Islands included encounters with the souls of the dead, which were believed to reside beneath the craters; Vulcano and Stromboli lacked Etna's reassuringly fantastical alternative role as Arthur's tomb.[24] However, the Lipari Islands are the site of a juxtaposition of medieval beliefs concerning Hell and classical Hades, through the tale of Pluto's rape of Proserpine.[25] It may be argued that La Sale sets the medieval vision of Hell against the classical natural history that was beginning to enter ducal libraries, by using the volcano as an ambiguous object of knowledge. Lucretius's *De rerum natura* (before 55 B.C.E.) describes volcanic eruptions as the outcome of the heating movement of air against rocks and earth in the caves beneath the surface of the earth.[26] Volcanic eruptions such as those of Etna, according to his poem, are simply the interaction of earth, fire, and water with violent winds, resulting in vast telluric belches (bk. 1, lines 722–30). Lucretius's poem attacks those who ascribe religious and moral explanations to phenomena that are the work of neutral natural forces. Lucretius survived in medieval texts alongside Pliny the Younger's first-person account of the eruption of Vesuvius, one that may also have been read as an exemplum.[27] Pliny's two letters (ed. Stout, 6.16, and 20) concerning the eruption, which recounted the death of the naturalist Pliny the Elder, construct a powerful meditation on the dangers of intellectual curiosity.[28] His account includes three points of view: the learned scientist, the learned student (who is the first-person narrator), and the reported fears and illusions of the less learned around them. The letters offer a striking echo of the patterning of encounters with volcanoes as transitions between youth and maturity, especially the sense that the catastrophe marks the culmination of Pliny the Elder's gathering of knowledge about the world (ed. Stout, 6.16, p. 476). For all the nephew's praise of his heroic acts, he makes it clear that it is his very thirst for learning that blinds him to his own safety and endangers his companions. Pliny the Younger's narrative reports a transfer of authority from the elder Pliny, killed by his curiosity, to the younger man who survives to transcribe his own observations, with the burning mountain as both agent and mediator.

La Sale's text may, then, carry a subtle consideration of where authority lies, when it comes to observing and recording the activities of volcanoes. Vulcano grants a rite of passage for the young squire, who learns through its conquest that idle curiosity is potentially life threatening. La Sale's text also echoes Petrarch's famous narrative of his ascent of Mont Ventoux.[29] Petrarch in mid-ascent pauses to meditate on his reluctance to take the steepest path, which is called "Filiol" (little son, or godson). His topographical choice, between the path of the "son" and that chosen by the mature man, points to the underlying sense that an untried youth may be tutor or father to himself. Petrarch's narrator places his ascent at an exact midpoint, a decade after his studies and another decade before his anticipated death (177; Letter 4.1). By presenting a convincing temporal and geographical location in trompe l'oeil, the ascent of Mont Ventoux also provided a template for later descriptions of ascents.[30] It is plausible that Bernat de So's frustrated attempt to admire the Garonne from a hill that he climbs with remarkable ease, at a halfway point on his journey, is also modeled knowingly on Petrarch.

In La Sale's text, the three young men are impelled to climb Vulcano by boredom and sunshine, armed not with copies of Augustine's *Confessions*, but with swords. They have opted for the easier path, Vulcano, as Stromboli has steeper slopes covered in loose debris. They are jeered when they tumble downhill. Their decision to finish their climb the following day is explained as a joint decision to enjoy the good weather. Their triumphant return impels their companions to emulate them. By reducing the physical encounter with the volcano to a tale of spontaneous enjoyment, La Sale emphasizes that it is simply a fiery mountain. Their psychological encounter with deceptive tales and beliefs is foreshadowed by the message that the volcano is a mass of rock and fire that can be looked into and "conquered." This leaves the reader to suppose that the wind, not the devil or damned souls, blows smoke from the crater onto the ships by night, and that the men's panic may be the work of their own superstition—there is no loss of life, and they are rescued the following day.

The ascent of a mountain, especially one that burns, may well provoke moments of doubt in those who think they are enacting either a sacred gesture or a conquest. It is both knowable and a marvel, something that may be gazed upon, but that ultimately may not be controlled. Ascents are not simply a reflection of the pilgrimage narrative and its emphasis on spiritual transcendence; rather, such narratives may be moments of dynamic *translatio studii,* combining, scrutinizing, and assessing the authoritative texts that allow the traveler to interpret his or her observations. Antoine de La Sale rethinks an anecdote he has ostentatiously gleaned secondhand from Valerius Maximus and prompts his reader to reconsider the value of trust and the reliability of interpretation between languages and to confront the disorienting effect of traveling out of the familiar realm into one that is stranger yet somehow wiser than that of its monolingual visitors. Disorientation may make a victim of the traveler, but it also enables him to learn some valuable lessons.

As a final twist, the printed *Salade* of 1521 (which Desonay thought was derived from a lost autograph copy) offers a key lesson: the world as we represent it is an image of our body, and the infernal depths that we fear are in fact only our horror at our own excreted foulness. The head is the noblest limb, and all good things enter the body through it (159). Digestion produces gases and filth: "et toute l'ordure qui est en toy, que tu reçois des IIII elemens, viennent [de] la profondeur de ta personne; et en icelle fait espiraux, dont yssent pueurs et abhominables ordures" (All the ordure that is inside you, that you receive from the four elements, comes from the depths of your person. And within it, it [the ordure] makes spouts, from which flow stenches and abominable filth).[31] As all parts of the world are composed of four elements, the turbulent activity ascribed by Lucretius to the interaction of the elements can be reflected in the human body, which becomes a miniature volcano. Mariner and volcano collide, and the ugly corruption of one body is associated with the powerful natural forces seen in the other. By a trick of language (for the body is a microcosm only in linguistic convention, not observable fact), La Sale removes Hell from the picture and leaves his reader to ponder the extent to which he or she produces infernal emanations, be they words or gases. The forces spewed out by the burning mountain may be oracular, infernal, or mere flatus. His insistence on food in the *Excursion,* itself one of the leaves of a salad, hints at the risks posed by lessons that are poorly digested. The head cannot know fully what the body, in all its uncontrollable activity, is doing when it absorbs the stuff of the world, nor can it know what will become of it. Bernat de So's "gran home," a bellowing giant of a World, sneers at the little man's attempt to criticize its injustice, replying that it is merely an unfeeling, created artifact.

Antoine de La Sale as compiler and translator was in the position of go-between for an audience who expected to be given clear renditions of his sources in French, French from Latin, Latin and iconography. His stratagem in dealing with an apparently monolingual transfer of knowledge is to make it foreign, to introduce unreliable narrators and landscapes, so that even unavoidable facts, such as the existence of volcanoes, seem to be a matter of subjective experience and words. Translations and multilingual transmissions of knowledge are so unreliable that a book may not prove useful, once it is expressed in the mother tongue, unless it is systematically mistrusted. Derrida's statement "Je n'ai qu'une langue, ce n'est pas la mienne" may be reworked and applied to these complex relationships of power and desire. The mother tongue can only be effectively absorbed once it is divorced from the maternal and has become, thanks to numerous go-betweens, the (m)other tongue, producing new thoughts and texts in a process of hybridization and enrichment. The *monolangue* unmasks the fantasies that subtend the mother tongue as both an ideal and a nostalgic symbol of lost (pre-Babelian) communication. It makes its status as (m)other tongue explicit and exposes it as another example of the many myths concerning languages and multilingualism in the later Middle Ages.

NOTES

INTRODUCTION

1. MS Paris BNF lat. 3313A. Louis Carolus-Barré, "Peyre de Paternas, auteur du *Libre de sufficiencia e de necessitat*," *Romania* 67 (1942–43): 234. Discussed by Keith Busby, *Codex and Context: Reading Old French Verse Narrative in Manuscript* (New York: Rodopi, 2002), vol. I, 52–53.

2. "Palaytz de savieza," prologue to the *Elucidari de las proprietatz*, a fourteenth-century translation of Bartholomaeus Anglicus, *De proprietatibus rerum*, in *Denkmäler der provenzalischen Litteratur*, ed. Karl Bartsch (Stuttgart: Litterarischen Vereins, 1856; rpt., Geneva: Slatkine Reprints, 1966), reproduced in *Concordance de l'Occitan médiéval*, vol. II, *Les Troubadours: Les Textes narratifs en vers* (COM 2), ed. Peter T. Ricketts and Alan Reed (Turhout: Brepols, 2005).

3. A vehicular language (*langue véhiculaire*) is used here to describe literary Occitan as an example of a *lingua franca*, "language varieties used non-natively . . . across lines of native language difference." Joseph Errington, "Colonial Linguistics," *Annual Review of Anthropology* 30 (2001): 29. Vehicular languages are by definition used or acquired artificially or both, and are distinguished from vernaculars. Errington's paper critiques the value judgments of colonial linguistic analyses.

4. Kevin Brownlee, "The Conflicted Genealogy of Cultural Authority: Italian Responses to French Cultural Dominance in *Il Tesoretto*, *Il Fiore*, and *La Commedia*," in *Generation and Degeneration: Tropes of Reproduction in Literature and History from Antiquity to Early Modern Europe*, ed. Valerie Finucci and Kevin Brownlee (Durham: Duke University Press, 2001), 283.

5. On the complex definitions of modern Occitan as "langue dialectale" (Philippe Gardy), see James Thomas, "Fabre d'Olivet and Victor Gelu: Two Responses to the Symbolic Value of Occitan, 1815–1856" (M.Phil. diss., University of Bristol, 2005), 3–4, citing Philippe Gardy, *Langue et société en Provence au début du XIXe siècle: Le Théâtre de Carvin* (Paris: Presses Universitaires de France, 1978), 16.

6. Maurizio Perugi, *Trovatori a Valchiusa: Un frammento della cultura provenzale del Petrarca* (Padua: Antenore, 1985).

7. For crucial information about the literary texts of the period and a discussion of how Catalan and Occitan poets and patrons fit together, see François Zufferey, *Bibliographie des poètes provençaux des XIVe et XVe siècles* (Geneva: Droz, 1984).

8. Perugi, *Trovatori a Valchiusa*, 68.

9. "Un arbitrari provençalisme lingüístic que pesarà com una llosa sobre els lírics Catalans fins a l'aparició d'Ausias March." Martín de Riquer, *Historia de la literatura catalana* (Barcelona: Ariel, 1980), vol. II, 532, cited by Perugi, *Trovatori a Valchiusa*, 141–42.

10. *Ausiàs March: Poesies*, ed. Pere Bohigas (Barcelona: Barcino, 1951), vol. V; Riquer, *Historia de la literatura catalana*, vol. II. On March's multiple poetic influences, see M. J. Duffell, "The Metrics of Ausiàs March in a European Context," *Medium Aevum* 63 (1994): 287–300.

11. Miriam Cabré, *Cerverí de Girona and His Poetic Traditions* (Woodbridge, U.K.: Tamesis, 1999).

12. Such reassessments inevitably involve the role of Joan I's wife Violant/ Yolande; see Antonio Cortijo Ocaña, "Women's Role in the Creation of Literature: Catalonia at the End of the Fourteenth and Beginning of the Fifteenth Century," *La Corónica* (1999): 3–16.

13. Busby, *Codex and Context*, vol. II, 486–87, 596–634.

14. Rosanna Cantavella, "The Meaning of *destral* as 'Go-Between' in the Catalan *Facet* and in Old Occitan," *Medium Aevum* 67 (2004): 304–12. *Le "Breviari d'amor" de Matfre Ermengaud*, ed. Peter T. Ricketts, 5 vols. (now on COM 2); *Breviari d'amor: Manuscript valencià del segle XV (Biblioteca Nacional de Madrid) / Manuscrito valenciano del siglo XV (Biblioteca Nacional de Madrid)*, ed. Antoni Ferrando, 2 vols. (Valencia, 1980).

15. Paul Zumthor, *Langue et technique poétiques à l'époque romane (XIe–XIIIe siècles)* (Paris: Klincksieck, 1963) and his article "Un Problème d'esthétique médiévale: L'Utilisation poétique du bilinguisme," *Le Moyen Âge* 60 (1966): 301–36, 561–94. Renate Blumenfeld-Kosinski, "Introduction: The Middle Ages," in *The Politics of Translation in the Middle Ages and the Renaissance*, ed. Renate Blumenfeld-Kosinski, Luise von Flotow, and Daniel Russell (Tempe, Ariz.: Arizona Center for Medieval and Renaissance Studies; Ottawa: University of Ottawa Press, 2001), 17–27.

16. Furio Brugnolo, *Plurilinguismo e lirica medievale: Di Raimbaut de Vaqueiras a Dante* (Rome: Bulzoni, 1983). *The Poems of the Troubadour Raimbaut de Vaqueiras*, ed. Joseph Linskill (The Hague: Mouton, 1964). Alfred Pillet, *Bibliographie der Troubadours*, ed. Henry Carstens (Halle [Saale]: Niemeyer, 1933) (hereafter PC).

17. Brugnolo, *Plurilinguismo*, 71–103. See also William Burgwinkle, *Love for Sale: Materialist Readings of Troubadour Poetry* (New York: Garland, 1997).

18. Cabré, *Cerverí de Girona*, xi, 20–22, 31.

19. Raimon Vidal de Besalú, *The "Razos de trobar" of Raimon Vidal and Associated Texts*, ed. John Marshall (Oxford: Oxford University Press, 1972); Uc Faidit, *The "Donatz proensals" of Uc Faidit*, ed. John Marshall (Oxford: Oxford University Press, 1969).

20. María Rosa Menocal, *Shards of Love: Exile and the Origins of the Lyric* (Durham: Duke University Press, 1994).

21. Samuel Miklos Stern, *Hispano-Arabic Strophic Poetry: Studies*, ed. E. L. P. Harvey (Oxford: Clarendon Press, 1974); Vicenç Beltran, "Poesía popular antigua ¿Cultura cortés?" *Romance Philology* 55 (2002): 183–230.

22. María Rosa Menocal, *The Arabic Role in Medieval Literary History: A Forgotten Heritage* (Philadelphia: University of Pennsylvania Press, 1987), 71–114. For Menocal's defense of her theory of broad rather than specific influence, see *The Arabic Role*, 105n, and her extended study of intercultural exchange, *Shards of Love*.

23. *Marcabru: A Critical Edition*, ed. Simon Gaunt, Ruth Harvey, and Linda Paterson (Cambridge: D. S. Brewer, 2000), PC 293, 25, and 26, XXV, XXVI; Peire d'Alvernhe, "Rossinhol, en son repaire," in *Peire d'Alvernhe: Poesie*, ed. Aniello Fratta (Manziana, 1996), PC 323, 23, XIX; Christian Poché, *La Musique arabo-andalouse* (Paris: Actes Sud, 1995).

24. Stefano Asperti, "Flamenca e dintorni: Considerazioni sui rapporti fra Occitania e Catalogna nel XIV secolo," *Cultura Neolatina* 45 (1985): 59–104. In Catalan-speaking lands: Terramagnino da Pisa (resident in Sardinia), *Doctrina d'Acort*, Jofre de Foixà, *Regles de trobar*, *Doctrina de compondre dictats*, two treatises of the fourteenth century in MS Ripoll 129. In Raimon Vidal de Besalú, *The "Razos de trobar."* Manuel de Montoliu, *Un Escorç en la poesia i la novel.listica dels segles XIV i XV* (Barcelona: Editorial Alpha, 1961), 9–27.

25. Manuel de Montoliu, *La Llengua catalana i els trobadors* (Barcelona: Editorial Alpha, 1975), 18–19.

26. Simon Gaunt and Julian Weiss, "Cultural Traffic in the Medieval Romance World," in "Cultural Traffic in the Medieval Romance World," ed. Simon Gaunt and Julian Weiss, special issue, *Journal of Romance Studies* 4 (2004): 1–11.

27. Menocal, *Shards of Love* and *The Arabic Role*; Sahar Amer, *Ésope au féminin: Marie de France et la politique de l'interculturalité* (Atlanta: Rodopi, 1999). For the term *intercultural*, see also Laura U. Marks, *The Skin of the Film: Intercultural Cinema, Embodiment, and the Senses* (Durham: Duke University Press, 2000), 5–9.

28. "Entre los principios caballerescos no era el religioso el más dominante en el ánimo de los trovatores provenzales, ya fuese efecto de la común molicie, ya, como con menor probabilidad se

ha conjeturado, de epicúreas tradiciones galloromanas, ya del rechazo de las ideas propagandas por las sectas heterodoxas," Manuel Milá y Fontanals, *Obras de Manuel Milá y Fontanals*, vol. I, *De los trovadores en España* (Barcelona: Consejo Superior de Investigaciones Científica, Instituto Miguel de Cervantes, 1966), 40. Compare Stephen O'Shea: "The Perfect and the troubadours existed in the hearths of the Languedoc nobility. From the dualists' love your neighbour to the jongleurs' love your neighbour's wife all in the course of a day, the Occitan culture of piety and fine feeling was slipping the traces of traditional Christianity." O'Shea, *The Perfect Heresy: The Revolutionary Life and Death of the Medieval Cathars* (London: Profile Books, 2000), 43–44.

29. Amédée Pagès, *Ausias March et ses prédécesseurs* (Paris: Champion, 1915), and his *La Poésie française en Catalogne du XIIIe siècle à la fin du XVe* (Toulouse: Privat; Paris: Didier, 1936). Stefano Asperti, *Carlo I d'Angiò e i trovatori: Componenti 'provenzali' e angioine nella tradizione manoscritta della lirica trobadorica* (Ravenna: Longo, 1995), and his article "Flamenca e dintorni."

30. Regina Psaki, "The Traffic in Talk About Women," *Journal of Romance Studies* 4 (2004): 13–14.

31. Lola Badia, *De Bernat Metge a Joan Roís de Corella: Estudis sobre la cultura literària de la tardor medieval catalana* (Barcelona: Quaderns Crema, 1988).

CHAPTER I

1. Samuel Noah Kramer, "The 'Babel of Tongues': A Sumerian Version," *Journal of the American Oriental Society* 88 (1968): 111.

2. Frederick E. Greenspahn, "A Mesopotamian Proverb and Its Biblical Reverberations," *Journal of the American Oriental Society* 114 (1994): 33–38.

3. George Steiner, *After Babel: Aspects of Language and Translation*, 3rd ed. (Oxford: Oxford University Press, 1998), 61.

4. Isidore of Seville, *Étymologies, livre IX: Les Langues et les groupes sociaux*, ed., trans., and commentary by Marc Reydellet (Paris: Les Belles Lettres, 1984).

5. References are to book and chapter numbers.

6. The topic has been exhaustively studied by Arno Borst, *Der Turmbau von Babel: Geschichte der Meinungen über Ursprung und Viefalt der Sprachen und Völker*, 6 vols. (Stuttgart: Hiersemann, 1957–63).

7. Serge Lusignan, *Parler vulgairement: Les Intellectuels et la langue française aux XIIIe et XIVe siècles* (Paris: Vrin; Montreal: Presses de l'Université de Montréal, 1986).

8. *The Medieval French Roman d'Alexandre*, vol. I, *Text of the Arsenal and Venice Versions*, ed. Milan S. La Du, Elliott Monographs 36 (Princeton: Princeton University Press, 1937).

9. All quotations are from *La Chanson de Girart de Roussillon*, ed. Winifred Mary Hackett, 3 vols. (Paris: SATF, 1953–55). I use Hackett's parallel referencing of the laisses in the two extant complete texts. Roman numerals refer to the laisses in MS O; Arabic numerals refer to MS P.

10. Raymond S. Willis, *The Debt of the Spanish "Libro de Alexandre" to the French "Roman d'Alexandre,"* Elliott Monographs 33 (Princeton: Princeton University Press, 1935), 24–31. Willis identifies this passage as a translation of the Venice *Roman d'Alexandre*, 25–27.

11. Peter Low, "You Who Once Were Far Off: Enlivening Sculpture in the Main Portal at Vézelay," *Art Bulletin* 85 (2003): 469–89.

12. For interpretations of Berte's role in the poem, see Simon Gaunt, "Le Pouvoir d'achat des femmes dans *Girart de Roussillon*," *Cahiers de Civilisation Médiévale* 33 (1990): 305–16. Sarah Kay, *The Old French Chansons de Geste in the Age of Romance: Political Fictions* (Cambridge: Cambridge University Press, 1995).

13. There are strong parallels in the dynamics of translation between the Old French *Aliscans* and its German version; see Kathryn Starkey, "Traversing the Boundaries of Language: Multilingualism and Linguistic Difference in Wolfram von Eschenbach's *Willehalm*," *German Quarterly* 75 (2002): 20–34.

14. Simon Gaunt, "*Desnaturat son li Frances*: Language and Identity in the Twelfth-Century Occitan Epic," *Tenso: Bulletin of the Société Guilhem IX* 17 (2002): 10–31. Max Pfister, "Observations sur la langue de Girart de Roussillon," *Revue de Linguistique Romane* 34 (1970): 315–25. W. Mary Hackett, "Le manuscrit P de Girart de Roussillon," in *Mélanges de philologie et de litterature romanes offerts a Jeanne Wathelet-Willem*, ed. Jacques de Caluwé, Marche Romane (Liège: Cahiers de L'ARU, 1978), 207–18; "L'Auteur de *Girart de Roussillon*," in *Guillaume d'Orange and the Chanson de Geste*, ed. W. Van Emden, P. E. Bennett, and A. Kerr (Reading, U.K.: Société Rencesvals, 1984), 43–53.

15. Gaunt, "*Desnaturat*," 16–17.

16. Peter Noble, "Anti-clericalism in the Feudal Epic," in *The Medieval Alexander Legend and Romance Epic: Essays in Honour of David J. A. Ross*, ed. P. Noble, L. Polak, and C. Isoz (Millwood, N.Y.: Kraus, 1982), 149–58.

17. On the importance of this Ovidian text, see Suzanne C. Hagedorn, *Abandoned Women: Rewriting the Classics in Dante, Boccaccio, and Chaucer* (Ann Arbor: University of Michigan Press, 2004).

18. Kay, *The Old French Chansons de Geste*, and Gaunt, "Le Pouvoir d'achat des femmes."

19. "Tu autem, Domine, miserere nobis" concluded readings taken from most parts of the Bible. Kathleen G. Cushing, *Ritual, Text, and Law: Studies in Medieval Canon Law and Liturgy* (London: Ashgate, 2004), 79–80.

20. Occitan texts written in Hebrew script reflect the decline of Hebrew as a spoken language around the beginning of the thirteenth century. See Crescas du Caylar, *Roman de la Reine Esther*, in *Nouvelles Courtoises occitanes et francaises*, ed. Suzanne Thiolier-Mejean et Marie-Francoise Notz-Grob (Paris: Le Livre de Poche, 1997), 124–57.

21. Robert Chazan, *Daggers of Faith: Thirteenth-Century Christian Missionizing and Jewish Response* (Berkeley and Los Angeles: University of California Press, 1989).

22. Dietmar Rieger, "'E trait sos meillors omes ab un consel': Emotion, mise-en-scène et *consilium* féodal dans *Girart de Roussillon*," *Zeitschrift für romanische Philologie* 114 (1998): 628–50. See also André Labbé, *L'Architecture des palais et des jardins dans les chansons de geste: Essai sur le thème du roi en majesté* (Paris: Champion; Geneva: Slatkine, 1987), 107–12, 223–28, 293–95.

23. Nicole Bériou, "The Right of Women to Give Religious Instruction in the Thirteenth Century," in *Women Preachers and Prophets Throughout Two Millennia of Christianity*, ed. Beverly Maine Kienzle and Pamela J. Walker (Berkeley and Los Angeles: University of California Press, 1998), 134–45.

24. Nicholas Watson, "Introduction: King Solomon's Tablets," in *The Vulgar Tongue: Medieval and Postmedieval Vernacularity*, ed. Fiona Somerset and Nicholas Watson (University Park: Pennsylvania State University Press, 2002), 1–13.

25. The noun *ataïna*, "souci," or the verb *ataïnar*, "empêcher; irriter; inquiéter." Emil Levy, *Petit dictionnaire provençal-français* (Heidelberg: Carl Winter Universitätsverlag, 1973), 31.

26. Clare M. Waters, "Talking the Talk: Access to the Vernacular in Medieval Preaching," in *The Vulgar Tongue*, ed. Somerset and Watson, 34.

27. Susan S. Eberly, "A Thorn Among the Lilies: The Hawthorn in Medieval Love Allegory," *Folklore* 100 (1989): 41–52.

28. Citations are from Alberto Colunga and Laurencio Turrado, *Biblia Sacra iuxta Vulgatam Clementinam, nova editio* (Madrid: Biblioteca de Autores Cristianos, 1985); *The New English Bible* (London: Collins, 1970).

CHAPTER 2

1. Alberto Limentani, *L'eccezione narrativa: La provenza medievale e l'arte del racconto* (Turin: Einaudi, 1977), 110–19.

2. All quotations are taken from *Le Livre des aventures de Monseigneur Guilhem de la Barra*, ed. and trans. Gérard Gouiran (Paris: Champion, 1997). MS Chantilly, Musée Condé 594.

3. James Buchanan Given, *Inquisition and Medieval Society: Power, Discipline, and Resistance in Languedoc* (Ithaca: Cornell University Press, 1997), 70, 75, 143. Given uses Bernard Gui's *Liber sententiarum*, a record of 907 sentences passed in Toulouse from 1308 to 1323, including forty-one executions.

4. Most influentially, Jean-Charles Huchet, *Le Roman occitan médiéval* (Paris: Presses Universitaires de France, 1990).

5. Sophia Menache, *Clement V* (Cambridge: Cambridge University Press, 1998), 33–34, 46, 48–53. Uzeste was one of the fiefs of Clement V's father, Béraud de Got (6).

6. Menache, *Clement V*, 6.

7. *Guilhem de la Barra*, 19.

8. Jehan Maillart, *Le Roman du comte d'Anjou*, ed. Mario Roques (Paris: CFMA, 1931).

9. Annette Palès-Gobillard, *L'Inquisiteur Geoffroy d'Ablis et les cathares du comté de Foix, 1308–1309* (Paris: CNRS, 1984); Given, *Inquisition and Medieval Society*, 74.

10. *Lo Libre dels Set Savis de Roma*, ed. Andrea Giannetti (Bari: Adriatica, 1996), possibly a fourteenth-century version of an Occitan verse poem derived from the Old French prose L tradition, 32–38. The *Leys d'Amors* gives a summary of a similar *Roman dels .vii. savis* in the first redaction (prior to 1356), *Las Flors del Gay Saber, ester dichas las Leys d'Amors*, ed. M. Gatien-Arnoult, 3 vols. (Toulouse: Privat, 1845), III.288 (all Gatien-Arnoult references are to volume and page numbers). The stepmother's failed seduction is quite different both in its motivation and its narration, *Libre des Set Savis*, lines 378–443.

11. Peter Biller, "The Cathars of Languedoc and Written Materials," in *Heresy and Literacy, 1000–1530*, ed. Peter Biller and Anne Hudson (Cambridge: Cambridge University Press, 1994), 66–70; Given, *Inquisition and Medieval Society*, 67n6.

12. Cyril Hershon, *Faith and Controversy: The Jews of Mediaeval Languedoc* (Birmingham: University of Birmingham, AIEO, 1999), 163–66. William Chester Jordan, "Home Again: The Jews in the Kingdom of France, 1315–1322," in William Chester Jordan, *Ideology and Royal Power in Medieval France: Kingship, Crusade, and the Jews*, Variorum Reprints (Aldershot, U.K.: Ashgate, 2001), xiv. Yves Dossat, "Les Juifs à Toulouse: Un Demi-siècle d'histoire communautaire," in "Juifs et Judaïsme du Languedoc," *Cahiers de Fanjeaux* 12 (1977): 122, 124.

13. Yosef Hayim Yerushalmi, "Inquisition and the Jews of France in the Time of Bernard Gui," *Harvard Theological Review* 63 (1970): 360–63. William Chester Jordan, "Marian Devotion and the Talmud Trial of 1240," in *Ideology and Royal Power in Medieval France*, xi. Robert Chazan, *Barcelona and Beyond: The Disputation of 1263 and Its Aftermath* (Berkeley and Los Angeles: University of California Press, 1992), 48–50.

14. Alfred Jeanroy, *Les Joies du Gai Savoir* (Toulouse: Privat, 1914), I.

15. Levy, *Petit dictionnaire*, 342, 40.

16. References to Anglade are to volume and page numbers or to volume, book, and page numbers. Volume and book numbers are in Roman numerals (uppercase and lowercase, respectively); pages are in Arabic numbers.

17. Peter Biller, "Heresy and Literacy: Earlier History of the Theme," in *Heresy and Literacy*, ed. Peter Biller and Anne Hudson (Cambridge: Cambridge University Press, 1994), 7–8, plate 1 and n22.

18. Yerushalmi, "Inquisition and the Jews of France," 328–30, 341.

19. Biller, "Cathars," 70–71, 74.

20. *Compendi historial de la Biblia que ab lo titol de Genesi de Scriptura, trelladá del provençal a la llengua catalana mossen Guillem Serra en l'any M.CCCCLI, y ara ha fet estampar per primera vegada En Miquel Victoriá Amer* (Barcelona: Llibreria Alvar Verdaguer, 1873), 35–36. The date of 1451 corresponds to Guillem Serra's copy, not to the text; see Pere Bohigas, "El repertori dels manuscrits catalans de la Fundació Patxot. Missió a Paris. Biblioteca Nacional (1920–1927)," *Estudis Universitaris Catalans* 15 (1930): 215–17, and (on a newly discovered fourteenth-century fragment) Jaume de Puig i Olivier, "Més nous textos catalans antics de la 'Biblioteca Capitular y Colombina' de Sevilla," *Arxiu de Textos Catalans Antics* 20 (2001): 453–510.

21. Mieke Bal, *Loving Yusuf: Conceptual Travels from Present to Past* (Chicago: University of Chicago Press, 2008), 37–38.

22. Bal, *Loving Yusuf*, 13–14.

23. On the names and namelessness of "Mrs Potiphar," see Bal, *Loving Yusuf*, 31–32; Shalom Goldman, *The Wiles of Women / The Wiles of Men: Joseph and Potiphar's Wife in Ancient Near Eastern, Jewish, and Islamic Folklore* (New York: State University of New York Press, 1995), 37–46. There is a variant on Zuleikha in the *aljamiado-morisco* poem of Yusuf; see *La Leyenda de Yusuf, ein Aljamiadotext*, ed. Ursual Klenk (Tübingen: Niemeyer, 1972). She is called Zenobia in Micael de Carvajal's sixteenth-century *Tragedia Josephina*, ed. Joseph E. Gillet, Elliott Monographs 28 (Princeton: Princeton University Press; Paris: Presses Universitaires de France, 1932), lines 1824–71.

24. Goldman, *The Wiles of Women*, 39–40.

CHAPTER 3

1. Marie Balmary, *Le Sacrifice interdit: Freud et la Bible* (Paris: Grasset, 1986), 86–103.

2. Daniel Heller-Roazen, *Echolalias: Essays on the Forgetting of Language* (Berkeley, Calif.: Zone Books, 2005), 219–20, 226–28.

3. *The Works of Flavius Josephus, Whiston's Translation, Revised by the Rev. A. R. Shilleto, Antiquities of the Jews* (London: George Bell and Sons, 1889), vol. I, 1.4.1–4. References in Arabic numbers are to book, chapter, and line.

4. Balmary, *Le Sacrifice interdit*, 91, 93–94.

5. MS British Library Egerton 1500. André Vernet, "Une Version provençale de la *Chronologia magna* de Paulin de Venise," *Bibliothèque de l'École des Chartes* 104 (1943): 115–36. Bernhard Degenhart and Annegrit Schmitt, "Marino Sanudo und Paolino Veneto: Zwei Literaten des 14. Jahrhunderts in ihrer Wirkung auf Buchillustrierung und Kartographie in Venedig, Avignon und Neapel," *Römische Jahrbuch für Kunstgeschichte* 14 (1973): 1–137.

6. The debate concerning medieval *pueritia* is not relevant here, but see Karen K. Jambeck, "The *Tretiz* of Walter of Bibbesworth: Cultivating the Vernacular," in *Childhood in the Middle Ages and the Renaissance: The Results of a Paradigm Shift in the History of Mentality*, ed. Albrecht Classen (Amsterdam: Walter de Gruyter, 2005), 159–84, esp. 161n7.

7. Lucy Freeman Sandler, "John of Metz, *The Tower of Wisdom*," in *The Medieval Craft of Memory: An Anthology of Texts and Pictures*, ed. Mary Carruthers and Jan Ziolkowski (Philadelphia: University of Pennsylvania Press, 2002), 215–25. An example of this tower is reproduced in Pierre Riché and Danielle Alexandre-Bidon, *L'Enfant au Moyen Âge* (Paris: Seuil, Bibliothèque nationale de France, 1994), 96.

8. Jambeck, "The *Tretiz*," 168.

9. Giorgio Agamben, *Infancy and History: The Destruction of Experience*, trans. Liz Heron (New York: Verso, 2007), 54–59.

10. Agamben, *Infancy*, 8, 59–60.

11. Agamben, *Infancy*, 60.

12. See the famous printed image of Grammar leading a boy into his school "tower" reproduced in Riché and Alexandre-Bidon, *L'Enfant*, 128.

13. "Quod aqua Maris Mortui e ventis non movetur, et in se nichil vivere patitur, fit ex fontibus bituminis, quibus edificate est Babel turris. Bituminis autem natura resistit aque et non dividitur nisi menstruo sanguinis." Valerie I. J. Flint, "Honorius Augustodunensis, *Imago Mundi*," *Archives d'Histoire Doctrinale et Littéraire du Moyen Âge* 49 (1982): 7–153, 1.55.

14. Heller-Roazen, *Echolalias*, 225.

15. Gary P. Cestaro, *Dante and the Grammar of the Nursing Body* (Notre Dame: University of Notre Dame Press, 2003), 9–48.

16. Jacques Heers, *Esclaves et domestiques au Moyen Âge dans le monde méditerranéen* (Paris: Fayard, 1981), 98–108, 199–203; Heers, *Les Barbaresques: La Course et la guerre en Méditerranée, XIVe–XVIe siècles* (Paris: Perrin, 2001), 215–17.

17. Cestaro, *Dante*, 2–39, quotation at 2.

18. Valerie Fildes, *Wet Nursing: A History from Antiquity to the Present* (Oxford: Blackwell, 1987), 17, 33, 38–41. Cestaro, *Dante*, 99.

19. Joan Copjec, "Vampires, Breast-Feeding, and Anxiety," *October* 58 (1991): 24–43.

20. Balmary, *Le Sacrifice interdit*, 87–88.

21. Luce Irigaray, *Éthique de la différence sexuelle* (Paris: Éditions de Minuit, 1984), 41–59.

22. Jill Ross, *Figuring the Feminine: The Rhetoric of Female Embodiment in Medieval Hispanic Literature* (Toronto: University of Toronto Press, 2008), 109–17.

23. Serge Lusignan, *La Langue des rois au Moyen Âge: Le Français en France et en Angleterre* (Paris: Presses Universitaires de France, 2004), 40, 46, 74–79, 97–99, 140–44. See also my article "Languages in Conflict in Toulouse: *Las Leys d'Amors*," *Modern Language Review* 103, no. 2 (2008): 383–96.

24. John Hine Mundy, notably *The Repression of Catharism at Toulouse (the Royal Diploma of 1279)* (Toronto: PIMS, 1985); Nicole M. Schulman, *When Troubadours Were Bishops: The Occitania of Folc of Marseille, 1150–1231* (New York: Routledge, 2001). Richard Schneider, *Public Life in Toulouse, 1463–1789: From Municipal Republic to Cosmopolitan City* (Ithaca: Cornell University Press, 1990).

25. Alfred Jeanroy, *Histoire sommaire de la poésie occitane des origines à la fin du XVIIIe siècle* (Toulouse: Privat, 1945); Jeanroy, "La Poésie académique à Toulouse au XIVe et XVe siècles, d'après le 'Registre de Galhac,'" *Revue des Pyrénées* 26 (1914): 273–94; Jeanroy, *La Poésie lyrique des troubadours* (Toulouse: Privat, 1934), vol. II, 347–64. See also Dom Claude Devic and Dom J. Vaissète, eds., *Histoire générale de Languedoc avec des notes et les pieces justificatives*, vol. X (Toulouse: Privat, 1885), 177–208.

26. The earlier draft in five books (formerly MS Toulouse Archives de l'Académie des Jeux Floraux 500.007, now cataloged as Toulouse BEP MS 2884), was edited by Gatien-Arnoult. See Beatrice Fedi, "Per un'edizione critica delle 'Leys d'Amors,'" *Studi medievali* 40 (1999): 43–118, and "Il canone assente: L'esempio metrico nelle 'Leys d'Amors' fra citazione e innovazione," *Quaderni di filologia romanza* 14 (1999): 159–86. The second draft in three books (formerly 500.006, now Toulouse BEP MS 2883) was edited by Anglade. The verse epitome of the first redaction, extant in a manuscript in Barcelona, is *Las Flors del Gay Saber*, ed. Joseph Anglade (Barcelona: Institut d'Estudis Catalans, 1926).

27. Anglade, *Leys d'Amors* (hereafter *LA*), I.i.9–13.

28. Gérard Gros, *Le Poète, la Vierge et le Prince du Puy: Étude sur les Puys marials de la France du Nord, du XIVe siècle à la Renaissance* (Paris: Klincksieck, 1992) and *Le Poème du Puy Marial: Étude sur le serventois et le chant royal du XIVe siècle à la Renaissance* (Paris: Klincksieck, 1996).

29. *LA*, IV.40, citing *Histoire de Languedoc*, VIII, col. 1187.

30. Jean Batany, "Une Boutade renardienne au XIVe siècle: Les Clercs et la langue romane," in "Grammaires du vulgaire: Normes et variations de la langue française," ed. Christopher Lucken and Mireille Séguy, *Médiévales* 45 (2003): 90. Lusignan, *Parler vulgairement*, 35–47.

31. Justine Landau, "Figures of Grammar and Rhetoric in *Las Leys d'Amors*," *Tenso: Bulletin of the Société Guilhem IX* 19 (2005): 1–18.

32. Toulouse BEP MS 2884, 105r.

33. Olga Weijers, *Dictionnaires et répertoires au Moyen Âge: Une Étude de vocabulaire* (Turnhout: Brepols, 1991), 87–88. See Fedi, "Il canone assente," 162n.

34. *Improprietas*; see Weijers, *Dictionnaires*; Anne Grondeux, *Le "Graecismus" d'Évrard de Béthune à travers ses gloses: Entre grammaire spéculative et grammaire positive du XIIIe au XIVe siècle*, Studia Artistarum 8 (Turnhout: Brepols, 2000), 368. *Graecismus*, ed. Johannes Wrobel (Hildesheim: Georg Olms, 1987).

35. John H. Marshall, "Observations on the Sources of the Treatment of Rhetoric in the *Leys d'Amors*," *Modern Language Review* 44 (1969): 39.

36. Anglade, I.137; Gatien-Arnoult, III.264. Anglade discusses the sources: IV.65–66 and 83–85. On these and other sources, Nicoló Pasero, "Sulle fonti del libro primo delle *Leys d'Amors*," *Studj Romanzi* 34 (1965): 125–85. A "derivation" is a method, and the reference may be to Peter Helias's *Liber derivationum*, but Uguccione was also known as "derivator"; see also "textus derivarii" for the *Magnae Derivationes* in a source dated 1350, Weijers, *Dictionnaires*, 56n, 76–78.

37. Uguccione da Pisa, *Derivationes*, ed. Enzo Cecchini, Guido Arbizzoni, et al., Edizione nazionale dei testi mediolatini 11 (Florence: SISMEL, Edizioni del Galluzzo, 2004), vol. II, 42, for *allon* (A 140 2): "et ab allon et thesis, quod est positio, dicitur hec allotheta." Bernard Colombat and Irène Rosier, "L'Allothète et les figures de construction dans le *Catholicon* de Johannes Balbi," *Archives et Documents de la Société d'Histoire et d'Épistémologie des Sciences du Langage*, 2nd ser., 4 (1990): 96. Less popular texts such as Conrad of Mure's *Graecismus novus* (c. 1244) might have contained neologisms. Grondeux, *Le "Graecismus,"* 28.

38. Colombat and Rosier, "L'Allothète," 159–61.

39. Vivien Law, "Why Write a Verse Grammar?" *Journal of Medieval Latin* 9 (1999): 46–76. Grondeux, *Le "Graecismus,"* 14–17. Elsa Marguin-Hamon, *L' "Ars lectoria Ecclesie" de Jean de Garlande: Une Grammaire versifiée du XIIIe siècle et ses gloses*, Studia Artistarum 2 (Turnhout: Brepols, 2003), 3–11, 63–66.

40. See Landau, "Figures of Grammar"; Marshall, "Observations," 40.

41. Marguin-Hamon cites similar schemes in *Ars lectoria Ecclesie*, copied from Henry of Avranches' *Comoda gramatice* (c. 1214), such as the daughters of Grammar (lines 1414–28) and the triumph of Syntax over her sisters (lines 1406–13), 95–110, 121–22, 291–98.

42. *LA*, Gatien-Arnoult, III.22–24.

43. William Russell, "*Transsumptio*: A Rhetorical Doctrine of the Thirteenth Century," *Rhetorica* 5 (1987): 369–410.

44. Grondeux, *Le "Graecismus,"* 250; see also 330.

45. Zrinka Stahuljak, "Jean Froissart's *Chroniques*: *Translatio* and the Impossible Apprenticeship of Neutrality," in *The Politics of Translation in the Middle Ages*, ed. Blumenfeld-Kosinski, von Flotow, and Russell, 121–42.

46. Marshall, "Observations," 50–52, citing Gatien-Arnoult, III.36.

47. Rainier Grutman, "La Logique du plurilinguisme ou, une langue en vaut-elle une autre?" in *Literarische Mehrsprachigkeit: Multilinguisme littéraire*, ed. Georg Kremnitz and Robert Tanzmeister (Vienna: Belvedere Druck, 1995), 53–65.

48. Cestaro, *Dante*, 28.

CHAPTER 4

1. Stahuljak, "Jean Froissart's *Chroniques*."

2. Antoni Rubió y Lluch, *Documents per l'história de la cultura catalana mig-eval*, 2 vols. (Barcelona: Institut d'Estudis Catalans, 1908–21). Lola Badia, "L'Humanisme catalá: Formació i crisi d'un concepte historiogràfic," in *Actes del V Col.loqui Internacional de Llengua i Literatura Catalanes, Andorra, 1–6 d'octubre de 1979*, ed. J. Bruguera and J. Massot i Muntaner (Santa Creus: Publicacions de l'Abadia de Montserrat, 1980), 41–70.

3. Lawrence Venuti, *The Scandals of Translation: Towards an Ethics of Difference* (New York: Routledge, 1998), 67–68, 78–84.

4. Venuti, *Scandals of Translation*, 84.

5. Josep-David Garrido i Valls, "La traducció catalana medieval de las *Heroides* d'Ovidi," *Faventia* 24, no. 2 (2002): 39.

6. Carlos Alvar, "Una veintena de traductores del siglo XV: Prolegómenos a un repertorio," in *Essays on Medieval Translation in the Iberian Peninsula*, ed. Tomàs Martínez Romero and Roxana Recio (Castelló: Publicacions de la Universitat Jaume I; Omaha: Creighton University, 2000), 13–44.

7. Gemma Avenoza, "Antoni Canals, Simon de Hesdin, Nicolas de Gonesse, Juan Alfonso de Zamora y Hugo de Urriés: Lecturas e interpretaciones de un clásico (Valerio Máximo) y de sus comentaristas (Dionisio de Burgo Santo Sepulcro y Fray Lucas)," in *Essays on Medieval Translation in the Iberian Peninsula*, ed. Martínez Romero and Recio, 45–73.

8. Alvar, "Una veintana," 25–29, 42.

9. Francesca Ziino, "Una traduzione latina del *Boezio* catalano," *Romania* 119 (2001): 465–82.

10. Amédée Pagès, "*La Belle Dame sans merci* d'Alain Chartier: Texte français et traduction catalane," *Romania* (1936): 483–531.

11. Stefano Cingolani, "Traducció litèraria i traducció cultural," in *Essays on Medieval Translation in the Iberian Peninsula*, ed. Martínez Romero and Recio, 134.

12. Dominique de Courcelles, "Traduire et citer les évangiles en Catalogne à la fin du XVe siècle: Quelques enjeux de la traduction et de la citation dans la *Vita Cristi* de Sor Isabel de Villena," in *Essays on Medieval Translation in the Iberian Peninsula*, ed. Martínez Romero and Recio, 173–90. See de Puig i Olivier, "Més nous textos catalans," 499–500.

13. Alvar, "Una veintana," 15.

14. All quotations, unless stated otherwise, are taken from Bernat Metge, *Obras de Bernat Metge,* ed. Martín de Riquer (Barcelona: Facultad de Filosofia y Letras, 1959). On the Hispanic "querelle des femmes," see Robert Archer, "La tradición del vituperio de las mujeres antes y después de Ausiàs March," in *Ausiàs March y las literaturas de su época*, ed. Lourdes Sánchez Roderigo (Granada: Universidad de Granada, 2000), 151–65, and Archer, "Formes del desamor: Blasme de dona i maldit," *Ausiàs March i el món cultural del segle XV*, ed. Rafael Alemany (Alicante: Universitat d'Alacant, Institut Interuniversitari de Filologia Valenciana, 2000), 59–75; Dominique de Courcelles, "Recherches sur les livres et les femmes en Catalogne aux XIVe et XVIe siècles: Figures de lectrices," in *Des Femmes et des livres: France et Espagnes, XIVe–XVIIe siècle*, ed. Dominique de Courcelles and Carmen Val Julián (Paris: Champion; Geneva: Droz, 1999), 95–98.

15. Metge, *Obras de Bernat Metge*, 84–126.

16. Regina Psaki, "The Play of Genre and Voicing in Boccaccio's *Corbaccio*," *Italiana* 5 (1993): 41–54; Psaki, "Women Make All Things Lose Their Power: Women's Knowledge, Men's Fear in Boccaccio's *Decameron* and the *Corbaccio*," *Heliotropia* 1, no. 1 (2003): n.p.

17. Stefano Maria Cingolani, *Lo Somni de una cultura: "Lo Somni" de Bernat Metge* (Barcelona: Quaderns Crema, 2002). See also his articles "Bernat Metge i els poetes de *Lo Somni*," *Revue d'Études Catalanes* 3 (2000): 121–50, and "Política, societat i literatura: Claus per a una interpretació de *Lo Somni* de Bernat Metge," *Revista de Catalunya* 150 (2000): 85–105.

18. *Valter e Griselda*, in Metge, *Obras de Bernat Metge*, 118–55.

19. Nicole Loraux, *Les Expériences de Tirésias: Le Féminin et l'homme grec* (Paris: Gallimard, 1989), 253–71.

20. Giuseppe Tavani, "Tolosa i Barcelona: Dos consistoris per a una poesia," in *Actes del vuite col.loqui internacional de llengua I literatura catalanes* (Barcelona: Abadia de Montserrat: Associació Internacional de Llengua; Literatura Catalares, 1989), vol. I, 297–324.

21. Antonio Cortijo Ocaña, *La evolución genérica de la ficción sentimental de los siglos XV y XVI* (London: Tamesis, 2001), 31–34.

22. Psaki, "The Traffic in Talk About Women."

23. Psaki, "The Traffic in Talk About Women."

24. Rosi Braidotti, *Nomadic Subjects: Embodiment and Sexual Difference in Contemporary Feminist Theory* (New York: Columbia University Press, 1994), 12–13.

25. Venuti, *Scandals of Translation*, 94.

26. Homi K. Bhabha, *The Location of Culture* (London: Routledge, 1994), 218.

27. *Frondino e Brisona*, ed. Annamaria Annicchiaro (Bari: Adriatica, 1990), text at 85–129. Frondino seems to be the precursor of Castilian sentimental romances; see Cortijo Ocaña, *Evolución genérica*, 17–21.

28. Pagès, *La Poésie française en Catalogne*, 49, 106, 143–60.

29. Cortijo Ocaña, *Evolución genérica*, 27–38.

30. Ramon Llull, *The Book of the Lover and the Beloved: Lo Libre de amich e amat, Librum amici et amati*, ed. and trans. Mark D. Johnston (Warminster, Wilts.: Aris and Phillips Ltd.; Bristol: Centre for Mediterranean Studies, 1995), § 27, pp. 14–15.

31. MS Musée Condé 388, reproduced and discussed by Patricia Stirnemann, "Histoire d'amour sans paroles," *L'Art de l'enluminure* 5 (June–August 2004), 37–57.

32. Stirnemann, "Histoire d'amour," 5–6; Bal, *Loving Yusuf*, 77–94.

33. Stirnemann, "Histoire d'amour," 50–57, citing Jacqueline Cerquiglini, *"Un Engin si soutil": Guillaume de Machaut et l'écriture au XIVe siècle* (Paris: Champion, 1985), 169–70.

34. Jean Lemaire de Belges, *Épîtres de l'amant vert*, ed. Jean Frappier (Lille: Giard; Geneva: Droz, 1948).

35. Frances de Morlas inserts a French motto in "Plus que martir, jos los pes de tristessa," Anglade, *Flors del Gay Saber*, 235–38, stanza 3.

36. Alfredo Arteaga, *Chicano Poetics: Heterotexts and Hybridities* (Cambridge: Cambridge University Press, 1997): "The Chicano subject is not so much the subject of a language as the subject of language" (17).

CHAPTER 5

1. All citations from Suzanne Thiolier-Méjean, *Une Belle au Bois Dormant Médiévale* (Paris: Presses de l'Université de Paris-Sorbonne, 1996). The same edition is reproduced in *Nouvelles courtoises occitanes et françaises*.

2. Carles Mas i Garcia, "*Baixa dansa* in the Kingdom of Catalonia and Aragon in the Fifteenth Century," *Historical Dance* 3 (1992): 15.

3. Asperti, "Flamenca e dintorni."

4. Stith Thompson, *Motif-Index of Folk-Literature*, 6 vols. (Copenhagen: Rosenkilde and Bagger, 1955–58); see also D 1960.3–4. *Blandin de Cornouaille: Introduction, édition diplomatique, glossaire*, ed. Cornelis H. M. Van der Horst (The Hague: Mouton, 1974).

5. *Perceforest: Troisième partie*, ed. Gilles Roussineau (Geneva: Droz, 1993), vol. III, xxii. All references in the text and notes are to vol. III. Marc Soriano, *Les Contes de Perrault: Culture savante et traditions populaires* (Paris: Gallimard, 1968), 76–77, 125–34.

6. Sylvia Roubaud-Bénichou, *Le Roman de chevalerie en Espagne: Entre Arthur et Don Quichotte* (Paris: Champion, 2000), 157.

7. Bruno Bettelheim, *The Uses of Enchantment: The Meaning and Importance of Fairy Tales* (Harmondsworth, U.K.: Penguin, 1982), 225–36. *Perceforest*, xxvi.

8. Holly Tucker, *Pregnant Fictions: Childbirth and the Fairy Tale in Early Modern France* (Detroit: Wayne State University Press, 2003), 55–70, 106–14.

9. Soriano, *Les Contes de Perrault*, 129–30. Chariton, *Callirhoe*, ed. G. P. Goold, Loeb Classical Library 481 (Cambridge, Mass.: Harvard University Press, 1995), 10–11, referring to 1.6–1.9.

10. Huchet, *Roman occitan*. Rafael Beltran Llavador, *Tirant lo Blanc: Evolució i revolta en la novel. la de cavalleries* (Valencia: Institució Alfons el Magnànim, Diputació de Valencia, 1983).

11. Cabré, *Cerverí de Girona*.

12. Asperti, *Carlo I d'Angió e i trovatori*, 47–48.

13. Suzanne Thiolier-Méjean, "Virgile et Prêtre Jean dans la nouvelle *Frayre de Joy e Sor de Plaser*," in *Études de langue et de littérature médiévales offertes à Peter T. Ricketts à l'occasion de son 70ème anniversaire*, ed. Dominique Billy and Ann Buckley (Turnhout: Brepols, 2005), 93–105; Thiolier-Méjean, "Le Motif du perroquet dans deux nouvelles d'Oc," in *Miscellanea Mediaevalia: Mélanges offerts à Philippe Ménard*, 2 vols., ed. Jean-Claude Faucon, Alain Labbé, and Danielle Quéruel (Paris: Champion, 1998), vol. II, 1355–75. Hélène Charpentier and Patricia Victorin, eds., *Le Conte du Papegau: Roman arthurien du XVe siècle* (Paris: Champion, 2004), 253–73.

14. James Brundage, *Law, Sex, and Christian Society in Medieval Europe* (Chicago: University of Chicago Press, 1986), 187–91; Brundage, "Implied Consent to Intercourse," in *Consent and Coercion*

to *Sex and Marriage in Ancient and Medieval Societies,* ed. Angeliki E. Laiou (Washington, D.C.: Dumbarton Oaks Research Library and Collection, 1993), 245–56; John W. Baldwin, "Consent and the Marital Debt: Five Discourses in Northern France Around 1200," in *Consent and Coercion to Sex and Marriage,* 257–70; Irven M. Resnick, "Marriage in Medieval Culture: Consent Theory and the Case of Joseph and Mary," *Church History* 69 (2000): 352–71.

15. Baldwin, "Consent," 258. Resnick, "Marriage," 359.
16. Resnick, "Marriage," 362–63.
17. Resnick, "Marriage," 361.
18. Menocal, *Shards of Love*; Kathleen Biddick, *The Shock of Medievalism* (Durham: Duke University Press, 1997), 96–98.
19. Hélène Cixous and Mireille Calle-Gruber, *Rootprints: Memory and Life Writing* (London: Routledge, 1997), 9.
20. Maria Bendinelli Predelli, "The *Fier Baiser* Motif Between Literature and Folklore," in *Studies for Dante: Essays in Honor of Dante Della Terza,* ed. Franco Fido, Rena A. Syska-Lamparska, and Pamela D. Stewart (Fiesole: Cadmo, 1998), 467–84.
21. Jacques Monfrin, "Le Roman de Belris," in *Études de philologie romane* (Geneva: Droz, 2001), 451–92, and "Le Roman de Belris, Le Bel Inconnu, Carduino," in *Études de philologie romane,* 455. Peter Wunderli and Günter Holtus, "La 'Renaissance' des études franco-italiennes: Rétrospective et prospective," in *Testi, cotesti e contesti del franco-italiano: Atti del 1o simposio franco-italiano (Bad Homburg, 13–16 aprile 1987),* ed. Günter Holtus, Henning Krauss, and Peter Wunderli (Tübingen: Niemeyer, 1989), 14. Busby, *Codex and Context,* vol. II, 597–604.
22. Monfrin, "Le Roman de Belris, Le Bel Inconnu," 500–502.
23. Monfrin, "Le Roman de Belris, Le Bel Inconnu," 509–10. See also Francis Gingras, *Érotisme et merveilles dans le récit français des XIIe et XIIIe siècles* (Paris: Champion, 2002), 120–37.
24. Francesco Branciforti, *Il Canzoniere di Lanfranco Cigala* (Florence: Olschki, 1954).
25. "Ni sabs d'Aiolz / com anec solz, / ni de *Machari* lo felon; / ni d'Anfelis, / ni d'Anseis, / ni de Guillaumes lo baron (Nor do you know about Aiol, how he traveled alone, nor about the wicked Macaire; nor about Anfelis, nor Anseïs, nor Guillaume the baron) (st. IX). See the discussion of this poem in my *Between Sequence and Sirventes: Aspects of Parody in Troubadour Lyric* (Oxford: EHRC, Legenda, 2000). Andrea da Barberino, *Le storie nerbonesi, romanzo cavalleresco del secolo XIV,* ed. Ippolito Gaetano Isola, 4 vols. (Bologna: Romagnoli, 1877–91). André Moisan, *Répertoire des noms propres de personnes et de lieux cités dans les chansons de geste françaises et les oeuvres étrangères dérivées* (Geneva: Droz, 1980), vol. I, § 1; vol. II, § 3.
26. *La Geste Franc or di Venezia: Edizione integrale del Codice XIII del Fondo francese della Marciana,* ed. Aldo Rosellini, Pubblicazioni del Centro Linguistica dell'Università cattolica, Saggi e monografie 6 (Brescia: La Scuola, 1986). Busby, *Codex and Context,* vol. II, 627–33.
27. *La Chevalerie de Judas Macchabee de Gautier de Belleperche (et de Pieros du Riés),* ed. J. M. Smeets, 2 vols. (Assen: Van Gorcum, 1991).
28. Stefano Maria Cingolani, "Innovazione e parodia nel Marciano XIII (*Geste Francor*)," *Romanistisches Jahrbuch* 38 (1987): 61–77. Busby, *Codex and Context,* vol. II, 605–8.
29. Beltran, "Poesía popular antigua," 201.

CHAPTER 6

1. *Richars li Biaus,* ed. Anthony J. Holden (Paris: Champion, 1983), 5–12, 17–19. Linda M. Rouillard, "Rape and Marriage in *Richars li Biaus,*" *Medieval Perspectives* 13 (1998): 121–35. Walter Prevenier and Thérèse de Hemptinne, "La Flandre au Moyen Âge: Un Pays de trilinguisme administratif," in *La Langue des Actes: Actes du XIe Congrès International de diplomatique, Troyes, 11–13 septembre 2003,* ed. Olivier Guyotjannin, Editions en ligne de l'École des chartes (ELEC), 7, § 2: "Confins et contacts."

2. *Lion de Bourges: Poème épique du XIVe siècle,* ed. William W. Kibler, Jean-Louis Picherit, and Thelma S. Fenster (Geneva: Droz, 1980), vol. I, cviii–xxi. *Perceforest,* 335.

3. Elizabeth Archibald, *Incest and the Medieval Imagination* (Cambridge: Cambridge University Press, 2001), 130–31, 195–96.

4. *Tobler-Lommatzsch Altfranzösisches Wörterbuch*, ed. Adolf Toblers and Erhard Lommatzsch, rev. Hans-Helmut Christmann (Stuttgart: Neudruck, 1954), vol. VIII, cols. 945–49; *Französisches etymologisches Wörterbuch*, ed. W. von Wartburg, rev. M. Hoffert, J.-P. Chambon and J.-P. Chauveau (Basel: Zbinden, 1976–2001) (hereafter *FEW*), vol. VI, 153; vol. VIII, 445. Pregnant women were believed to be fond of eating blackberries (*Tobler-Lommatzsch*, vol. VI, col. 266).

5. Tucker, *Pregnant Fictions*, 109–10, 117–18, 174n.

6. *Tydorel*, in *Les Lais anonymes des XIIe et XIIIe siècles*, ed. Prudence Mary O'Hara Tobin (Geneva: Droz, 1976).

7. Gautier d'Arras, *Eracle*, ed. Guy Raynaud de Lage (Paris: Champion, 1976), lines 2969–5092.

8. On ritual sprinkling of newborns with salt, see David Cressy, *Birth, Marriage, and Death: Ritual, Religion, and the Life-Cycle in Tudor and Stuart England* (Oxford: Oxford University Press, 1997), 81.

9. Joan Brumlik, "Incest and Death in Marie de France's *Deus Amanz*," in *The Court Reconvenes: Selected Papers from the Ninth Triennial Congress of the International Courtly Literature Society, 1998*, ed. Barbara K. Altmann and Carleton W. Carroll (Cambridge: D. S. Brewer, 2003), 169–77. Archibald, *Incest*, 145–91, 233–35.

10. Archibald, *Incest*, 187, citing *Le Roman de Tristan en Prose*, ed. Renée L. Curtis (Munich: Max Hüber, 1963), vol. I, § 98 (p. 76).

11. On its intertextuality, see *Lion de Bourges*, vol. I, xcii–xcvi, xcix–ciii; Archibald, *Incest*, 178–79.

12. Yin Liu, "Incest and Identity: Family Relationships in *Emaré*," in *The Court Reconvenes*, ed. Altmann and Carroll, 180.

13. Archibald, *Incest*, 29.

14. Catherine M. Jones, "Rape, Redemption, and the Grateful Dead: *Richars li Biaus*," in *Gender Transgressions: Crossing the Normative Barrier in Old French Literature*, ed. Karen Taylor (New York: Garland, 1998), 3–19.

15. *Perceforest*, L, LI, LII, LIX, LX. In this and subsequent references to this work, unless shown otherwise, uppercase Roman numerals refer to chapters and lowercase Roman numerals and Arabic numbers to pages.

16. *Perceforest*, xviii–xxix.

17. L.59, lines 77–79, 265–68; LII.79, lines 12–17.

18. *Perceforest*, xxv–vi. See also textual note to 91, line 441.

19. J. C. McKeown, *Ovid: Amores; Text, Prolegomena, and Commentary in Four Volumes* (Leeds: Francis Cairns, 1998), vol. III, commentary on 2.19 with reference to 3.4.

20. Ovid, *Les Amours*, ed. Henri Bornecque (Paris: Les Belles Lettres, 1961).

21. McKeown, *Ovid: Amores*, vol. III, commentary on 2.19 with reference to 3.4.

22. Horace, *Odes*, 3.16. 1–2. M. L. Stapleton, *Harmful Eloquence: Ovid's "Amores" from Antiquity to Shakespeare* (Ann Arbor: University of Michigan Press, 1996), 28–29, 120–21. Cathy Santore, "Danaë: The Renaissance Courtesan's Alter Ego," *Zeitschrift für Kunstgeschichte* 54 (1991): 412–13.

23. Variant in MS C of *Perceforest*, Roussineau, 318–20, 326; for main text, 210, lines 19, and 213, lines 144ff.

24. Variant, MS C, 319–20: "Mais se le dieu Marc l'estoit venue veoir, il avoit bien peu emporter sa verge."

25. On the text's play on *raiere*, "a split or furrow," see Roussineau's textual notes.

26. "Adont amours, qui avoit dormy dedens son cœur ung an, s'esveilla, et ce avoit procedé par l'inconvenient de sa maladie" (Then Love, which had been asleep in her heart for a year, awoke, and this had happened through the obstacle caused by her illness) (p. 318, note to p. 213, line 144, variant text of C).

27. Hélène Cixous, *L'Heure de Clarice Lispector* (Paris: des femmes, Antoinette Fouque, 1979).
28. Cixous, *Vivre l'orange* (Paris: des femmes, 1979), 41. See also Cixous, "*The Apple in the Dark*: The Temptation of Understanding," in Cixous, *Reading with Clarice Lispector*, ed. and trans. Verena Andermatt Conley (London: Harvester Wheatsheaf, 1990), 60–97.

CHAPTER 7

1. Jacques Derrida, *Le Monolinguisme de l'autre: La Prothèse d'origine* (Paris: Galilée, 1996), quotation at 14.
2. Derrida, *Monolinguisme,* 47, 50–51, 60–71, 112–14.
3. All quotations are from the following editions: Pierre de La Cépède, French version: Robert Kaltenbacher, "Der altfranzösische Roman *Paris et Vienne,*" *Romanische Forschungen* 15 (1904): 321–688; French *"Paris et Vienne": Romanzo cavalleresco del XV secolo. Parigi. Bibliothèque nationale, MS. fr. 20044,* ed. Anna Maria Babbi (Milan: Franco Angeli, 1992); *Història de París i Viana: Edició facsímil de la primera impressió catalana (Girona, 1495),* ed. Pedro Cátedra (Girona: Diputació de Girona, 1986).
4. Boethius, *Le Livre de Boece de Consolacion,* ed. Glynnis M. Cropp (Geneva: Droz, 2006).
5. Cited by Babbi, *Paris et Vienne,* 14n. On related issues, see my article "Maternal *Consolatio*: Antoine de La Sale's *Réconfort de Madame de Fresne,*" in *The Erotics of Consolation: Desire and Distance in the Late Middle Ages,* ed. Catherine E. Léglu and Stephen J. Milner (New York: Palgrave Macmillan, 2008), 263–91.
6. MS Carpentras, Bibliothèque municipale Inguimbertine, 1792. Kaltenbacher, 630; Babbi, 11–12.
7. Kaltenbacher, "Der altfranzösische Roman *Paris et Vienne,*" 338–39. Compare Gilles Corrozet, who describes himself as "simple translateur" for his adaptation of a French poem into prose, *"Richard Sans Peur": Edited from the "Romant de Richart" and from Gilles Corrozet's "Richart sans Paour,"* ed. Denis Joseph Conlon, Studies in the Romance Languages and Literatures 192 (Chapel Hill: University of North Carolina Department of Romance Languages, 1977), 12–13.
8. Alfred Coville, *La Vie intellectuelle dans les domaines d'Anjou-Provence, de 1380 à 1435* (Paris: Droz, 1941), 480–91.
9. *Paris and Vienne, Translated from the French and Printed by William Caxton,* ed. MacEdward Leach, Early English Text Society (New York: Oxford University Press, 1957), xv–xvii. For the Castilian and *aljamiado-morisco* texts, see *Historia de los amores de París y Viana,* ed. Alvaro Galmés de Fuentes (Madrid: Gredos, 1970).
10. Babbi, *Paris et Vienne,* 36–53. The Italian tradition differs from the French in several ways that it is not possible to discuss here; see *Paris e Vienne, romanzo cavalleresco,* ed. Anna Maria Babbi (Venice: Marsilio, 1991). Hebrew alphabet edition of the Yiddish version: *Pariz un' Viene: Mahadura biqortit bezeruf mavo, he'arot venispahim,* ed. Chone Shmeruk, with Erika Timm (Jerusalem: Israel Academy of Sciences and Humanities, 1996). For a review of Shmeruk's edition, and an explanation of how his conclusions about attribution differ from those of both Babbi and other editors, see Jerold C. Frakes, in *Speculum* 73, no. 1 (1998): 258–60.
11. Babbi, *Paris et Vienne,* 22–36.
12. Antoine de La Sale, *Jehan de Saintré,* ed. Joël Blanchard, Lettres Gothiques (Paris: Le Livre de Poche, 1995), chap. 1, 34–36: "Et le deuxieme livre traittera des tresloyalles amours de Mademoiselle Vyenne d'Allençon et de Paris de Rousillon, comme les plus martirs d'amours que je aye leu ne oÿ dire."
13. [Fra] Rocabertí, *The "Gloria d'Amor" of Fra Rocabertí: A Catalan Vision-Poem of the Fifteenth Century,* ed. H. C. Heaton (New York: AMS Press, 1966), canto VII, lines 952–92.

14. Cátedra, *Història de París i Viana*, 21–22; see, for example, Leach, *Paris and Vienne*, xviii–xx.
15. Cátedra, *Història de París i Viana*, 24–25.
16. Coville, *La Vie intellectuelle*, 482–83.
17. Cátedra, *Història de París i Viana*, 30–31.
18. Cortijo Ocaña, *Evolución genérica*, 43–48.
19. Cátedra, *Història de París i Viana*, 32–35.
20. Babbi, *Paris et Vienne*, 20–22.
21. Gaston III, count of Foix [Gaston Fébus], *Le Livre de la Chasse*, ed. Gunnar Tilander (Karlshamn, Sweden: Johanssons, 1971): "Ma langue n'est pas si bien duite de parler le franssois comme mon propre langayge" (My tongue is not as adept at speaking French as my own language) (epilogue, 290–91).
22. See the Introduction in the present volume.
23. Cortijo Ocaña, *Evolución genérica*, 183–92.
24. In this and subsequent references to Babbi, unless otherwise indicated, Roman numerals are section numbers and Arabic numbers are page numbers.
25. Robert Muchembled, *L'Invention de l'homme moderne* (Paris: Fayard, 1988), 19–20.
26. On the resistance of olfactory signals to intellectualization, see Didier Anzieu, *Le Moi-Peau* (Paris: Dunod, 1995), 203–12.
27. Jean-Jacques Vincensini, "Désordre de l'abjection et l'ordre de la courtoisie: Le Corps abject dans *Paris et Vienne* de Pierre de la Cépède," *Medium Aevum* 68 (1999): 292–304.
28. The term is used by William T. Cotton, "Fidelity, Suffering, and Humour in *Paris and Vienne*," in *Chivalric Literature: Essays on Relations Between Literature and Life in the Later Middle Ages*, ed. Larry D. Benson and John Leyerle (Kalamazoo: Medieval Institute, 1980), 91–100.
29. *Historia de los amores*, 45–46, citing Clemente Sánchez de Vercial, *Libro de los exenplos por a.b.c.*, ed. John E. Keller and Connie L. Scarborough (Madrid: Ars Libris, 2000), exemplum 246 (177), pp. 207–8.
30. *Paris and Vienne*, editorial notes.
31. Françoise Bériac, *Des Lépreux aux cagots: Recherches sur les sociétés marginales en Aquitaine médiévale* (Bordeaux: Fédération historique du Sud-Ouest, Université de Bordeaux III, 1990), cites a warning of 1575 that *cagots* (descendants of lepers) may look handsome but have foul breath and body odour (9). *Jaufre*, lines 2313–33.
32. Francesc Eiximenis, *Lo libre de les dones*, ed. Frank Naccarato under the direction of Joan Coromines, rev. Curt Wittlin and Antoni Comas, 2 vols. (Barcelona: Departament de Filologia Catalana, Curial Edicions Catalanes, 1981), "Tractat de pendre muller," chap. 28.
33. Michel Jeanneret, *A Feast of Words: Banquets and Table Talk in the Renaissance*, trans. Jeremy Whiteley and Emma Hughes (London: Polity Press, 1991), 200–209.
34. Pierre Bec, *Burlesque et obscenité chez les troubadours: Pour une approche du contre-texte médiéval* (Paris: Stock, 1984), 18.
35. Francesc Eiximenis, *Com usar de beure e menjar: Norms morals contingudes en el "Terç del Crestià" per Francesc Eiximenis*, ed. Jorge E. Gracia (Barcelona: Curial, 1977), letters exchanged between a gluttonous churchman and his physician, chaps. XI–XIII, 43–48. Chicken is winter food as well as "carns precioses" (chap. XXII, 71).
36. Bridget Ann Henisch, *Feast and Fast: Food in Medieval Society* (University Park: Pennsylvania State University Press, 1976), 59–65, 127–28.
37. *Le Jeu de Sainte Agnès: Drame provençal du XIVe siècle*, ed. Alfred Jeanroy (Paris: Champion, 1931). Nadine Henrard, *Le Théâtre religieux médiéval en langue d'Oc* (Geneva: Droz, 1998).
38. Marks, *The Skin of the Film*, 210–23. See also Anzieu, *Le Moi-Peau*, 203–12.
39. Alain Corbin, *Le Miasme et la jonquille: L'Odorat et l'imaginaire social, XVIIIe–XIXe siècles* (Paris: Flammarion, 1982), 67–83.
40. Venuti, *Scandals of Translation*, 84.

41. Vincent Barletta, *Covert Gestures: Crypto-Islamic Literature as Cultural Practice in Early Modern Spain* (Minneapolis: University of Minnesota Press, 2005), 133–36.

CHAPTER 8

1. All quotations in this chapter, unless declared otherwise, are from *Pierre de Provence et La Belle Maguelonne,* ed. Anna Maria Babbi (Soveria Mannelli: Rubbettino, 2003). An alternative version is edited by Babbi in the same volume (222–66). *L'Ystoire du vaillant chevalier Pierre filz du conte de Provence et de La Belle Maguelonne: Texte du manuscrit S IV 2 de la Landesbibliothek de Cobourg, XVe siècle,* ed. Régine Colliot, Senefiance, Cahiers du CUER-MA 4 (Paris: Champion, 1977). For the text's possible sources, see Babbi, v–xvii. Coville, *La Vie intellectuelle,* 462–81.
2. Babbi, *Pierre de Provence,* app. 2, 267–96.
3. Cortijo Ocaña, *Evolución genérica,* 50–53, 269. *Historia de Pierres de Provença y de la gentil Magalona: Ara novament publicada segons les edicions de 1616 y 1650,* ed. Ramon Miquel i Planas (Barcelona: n.p., 1908). This might be the Catalan source proposed for the Greek version by Elizabeth M. Jeffreys and Michael J. Jeffreys, "'Imberios and Margarona': The Manuscripts, Sources, and Edition of a Byzantine Verse Romance," in E. M. Jeffreys and M. J. Jeffreys, *Popular Literature in Late Byzantium,* I (Aldershot: Ashgate Variorum Reprints, 1983), 135, 139, 156–57. Beaton, *Medieval Greek Romance,* 135–36.
4. Babbi, *Pierre de Provence,* x. Coville, *La Vie intellectuelle,* 475.
5. MS Coburg Landesbibliothek, MS 4, ed. Colliot, *L'Ystoire*; Babbi, *Pierre de Provence,* xxiv–vii. Anna Maria Babbi, "La prima ricezione tedesca del 'Pierre de Provence et La Belle Maguelonne,'" in *Filologia romanza, filologia germanica: Intersezioni e diffrazioni; Convegno internazionale, Verona, 3–5 aprile 1995,* ed. Anna Maria Babbi and Adele Cipolla (Verona: Edizioni Fiorini, 1997), 437–48.
6. On the importance of the Coburg manuscript as evidence of a translator at work, see Babbi, *Pierre de Provence,* xxiv–vii.
7. For a longer discussion of this point, see my article "A 'New Medea' in Late-Medieval French Narratives," in *Medea: Transformations and Transmutations of a Myth,* ed. Heike Bartel and Anne Simon (Oxford: MHRA, forthcoming).
8. "Certes vous estes le second Jason et je suis la seconde Medee" in the bilingual Coburg version (Colliot, *Ystoire,* 36).
9. Roger Dubuis, "Les Formes narratives brèves," in *Grundriss der romanischen Literaturen des Mittelalters,* vol. VIII, no. 1 (Heidelberg: Carl Winter Universitätsverlag, 1988), 189–91. Bibliothèque bleue version: *Histoire de Pierre de Provence & de La Belle Maguelonne* (Nouvelle Bibliothèque bleue de Troyes) (Villiers-sur-Marne: Phénix Éditions, 2003), 33. Babbi discusses the popular printed versions in *Pierre de Provence,* xiv–xvii.
10. *Epistre de Maguelonne à son Amy Pierre de Provence, elle estant en son Hospital,* in Clément Marot, *Oeuvres lyriques,* ed. C. A. Mayer (London: Athlone Press, 1964), 114–24. "Ne suis je pas la seconde Medée? / Certes ouy, à bonne raison / Dire te puis estre l'aultre Jason," lines 110–12.
11. Ruth Morse, *The Medieval Medea* (Cambridge: D. S. Brewer, 1996), 148–84.
12. Rita Copeland, *Rhetoric, Hermeneutics, and Translation in the Middle Ages* (Cambridge: Cambridge University Press, 1991), 127–29.
13. Copeland, *Rhetoric, Hermeneutics,* 127. Marc-René Jung, *La Légende de Troie en France au Moyen Âge* (Basel: Francke Verlag, 1996), 440–562.
14. Egidio Gorra, *Testi inediti di storia trojana, preceduti da uno studio sulla leggenda trojana in Italia* (Turin: Löscher, 1887), 458–80. Heinrich Morf, "Notes pour servir à l'histoire de la légende de Troie en Italie et en Espagne," *Romania* 21 (1892): 18–38, 88–107; see also Morf, "Notes pour servir à l'histoire de la légende de Troie en Italie (suite et fin)," *Romania* 24 (1895): 174–96. Léon Mallinger, *Médée: Étude de littérature comparée* (Geneva: Slatkine Reprints, 1971), 205–8. Quotation from Gorra, *Testi,* Tuscan version, chap. xv, 474.

15. "Jam Magelone se ipsam increpat propter malas opiniones de recessu Petri conceptas." Colliot, *Ystoire*, 36n.

16. Morf, "Notes pour servir" (1895), 182.

17. Marie Jacob, "L'Ekphrasis en images: Métamorphoses de la description dans *l'Histoire de la destruction de Troye la Grant* enluminée par l'atelier des Colombe à la fin du XVe siècle (BnF. NvAcq.Fr. 24920)," in *Conter de Troye et l'Alexandre: Pour Emmanuèle Baumgartner*, ed. Laurence Harf-Lancner, Laurence Mathey-Maille, and Michelle Szkilnik (Paris: Presses de la Sorbonne Nouvelle, 2006), 294–97.

18. Raoul Lefèvre, *Histoire de Jason*, ed. Gert Pinkernell (Frankfurt, 1971), 227–28, § 18.5.

19. Morse, *Medieval Medea*, 293; see also Lynn Shutters, "Griselda's Pagan Virtue," *The Chaucer Review* 44, no. 1 (2009): 82.

20. Hagedorn, *Abandoned Women*; Jung, *La Légende de Troie*, 507–8.

21. *Le "Roman de Troie" de Benoît de Sainte-Maure*, ed. Léopold Constans (Paris: SATF, 1912), vol. VI, 329–33, and *Le Roman de Troie en Prose*, ed. Léopold Constans and Edmond Faral (Paris: Champion, 1922), vol. I, § 23 [vol. II was never published]. Jung, *La Légende de Troie*, 440–98 (location of Prose *Troie* 1, 441–44).

22. Joan Roís de Corella, "Scriu Medea a les dones la ingratitude e desconexença de Jàson, per dar-los exemple de honestament viure," in Roís de Corella, *Joan Roís de Corella: Proses mitològiques*, ed. Josep-Lluís Martos (Alicante: Universitat d'Alacant, 2001), 207–36.

23. On the importance of these aspects of Medea in the *Ovide moralisé*, see Marylène Possamaï-Pérez, *L'Ovide moralisé: Essai d'interprétation* (Paris: Champion, 2006), 446–48. *"Ovide moralisé": Poème du commencement du quatorzième siècle*, ed. Cornelis de Boer (Amsterdam: Johannes Müller, 1915–38), bk. 7, and *Ovide moralisé en prose (texte du quinzième siècle)*, ed. Cornelis de Boer (Amsterdam: N. V. Noord-Hollandsche Uitgevers Mij., 1954), 201–12. Renate Blumenfeld-Kosinski, *Reading Myth: Classical Mythology and Its Interpretations in Medieval French Literature* (Stanford: Stanford University Press, 1997), 90–170.

24. Alessandro Ballor, "Il mito di Giasone e Medea," *Studi francesi* 44 (2000): 455–71; Ballor, "Il mito di Giasone e Medea nel Quattrocento francese," *Studi francesi* 47 (2003): 3–22.

25. Morse, *Medieval Medea*, 204–8.

26. Anna Maria Babbi, "Il romanzo francese del Quattrocento: *Pierre de Provence* e dintorni," *Critica del testo* 2 (2004): 341–55.

27. In this and subsequent references to this edition, Roman numerals refer to chapters, and Arabic numbers to lines.

28. Rebecca Dixon, "'Homs sui je Dame, vraiement': Sex, Chivalry, and Identity in *Jehan d'Avesnes*," *French Studies* 61 (2007): 141–54.

29. Coville, *La Vie intellectuelle*, suggests that Sangana/Sangona is Sardinia and Crapana/Trapana may be Trapani in Sicily (475).

CHAPTER 9

1. Isabel de Riquer, "Lo 'Maravilloso' y lo cotidiano en *La Faula* de Guillem de Torroella," *Revista de filologia románica* 22 (2005): 175–82. *La Faula*, ed. Anna Maria Compagna, RIALC, 179, 2001.

2. *Voyage à Jérusalem de Philippe de Voisins, seigneur de Montaut*, ed. Philippe Tamizey de Larroque (Paris: H. Champion and Cocharaux Frères, 1883), 40–41. On the author, see 45.

3. *Voyage à Jérusalem*, 50–53.

4. *Le Voyatge d'Oultremer en Jherusalem de Nompar, seigneur de Caumont*, ed. Peter S. Noble (Oxford: Blackwell, 1975).

5. Nompar's poem: MS BL Egerton 890, 113r–32v. *La "Vesio" de Bernat de So et Le "Débat entre Honor et Delit" de Jacme March*, ed. Amédée Pagès (Toulouse: Privat, 1945), 3–91. Peter S. Noble, "La Disparition de l'occitan en Agenais au XVe siècle," in *Studia Occitanica in memoriam Paul Remy*, ed. Hans-Erich Keller (Kalamazoo: Medieval Institute, 1986), vol. II, 391–99.

6. Simonetta Cochis, "Antoine de La Sale's Delightful Teachings: Literature and Learning in His Late Medieval Books for Princes" (Ph.D. diss., New York University, 1998), 28–35, 42–44. *Antoine de La Sale, Oeuvres complètes, tome I: La Salade; tome II: La Sale,* ed. Fernand Desonay (Liège: Faculté de Philosophie et Lettres, Liège-Droz, 1935–41).

7. La Sale, *Le Réconfort de Madame de Fresne,* ed. Ian Hill (Exeter: Exeter University Press, 1979); La Sale, *La Sale,* 134–37 and 242–44; La Sale, *La Salade,* 63–130, 137–58.

8. La Sale, *La Sale,* 134–36.

9. Jesús Carrillo, "From Mt Ventoux to Mt Masaya: The Rise and Fall of Subjectivity in Early Modern Travel," in *Voyages and Visions: Towards a Cultural History of Travel,* ed. Jás Elsner and Joan-Pau Rubiés (London: Reaktion Books, 1999), 57–73.

10. Coville, *La Vie intellectuelle;* see also Simonetta Cochis, "The Sailor Demon of Vulcano in Antoine de La Sale's Geography of the Demonic, *L'Excursion aux îles Lipari,*" in *Demons: Mediators Between This World and the Other,* ed. Ruth Petzoldt and Peter Neubauer (Frankfurt: Peter Lang, 1998), 65.

11. Cochis, "The Sailor Demon," 70; see also Cochis, "Antoine de La Sale's Delightful Teachings," 100–139.

12. Jeanne Demers, "La Quête de l'anti-Graal, ou un récit fantastique: *Le Paradis de la Reine Sibylle,*" *Le Moyen Âge* 83 (1977): 469–92.

13. Michèle Perret, "L'Invraisemblable Vérité: Témoignage fantastique dans deux romans du XIVe et XVe siècles," *Europe: Revue Littéraire Mensuelle* 654 (October 1983): 29–30.

14. C.-A. Knudson Jr., "Une Aventure d'Antoine de La Sale aux îles Lipari," *Romania* 54 (1928): 101. Luigi Monga, "Translating the Journey: A Literary Perspective on Truth in Cartography," in *Cross-Cultural Travel: Papers from the Royal Irish Academy International Symposium on Literature and Travel, National University of Ireland, Galway, November 2002,* ed. Jane Conway (New York: Peter Lang, 2003), 12.

15. Cochis, "The Sailor Demon"; Demers, "La Quête de l'anti-Graal"; Perret, "L'Invraisemblable Vérité."

16. Patrice Uhl, "L'Excursion aux îles Lipari d'Antoine de La Sale: Anecdote récréative ou nouvelle fantastique?" in *L'Imaginaire du volcan,* ed. M.-F. Bosquet and F. Sylvos (Rennes: Presses Universitaires de Rennes, 2005).

17. Paul Demarolle, "A propos du vocabulaire d'Antoine de La Sale: Nature et portée des faits de syntaxe lexicale," *Travaux de Linguistique* 25 (1992): 13–24. Sylvie Lefèvre, "Salade et 'jambon'": Deux italianismes chez Antoine de La Sale, ou petites histoires de langue et de bouche," in *Pour acquerir honneur et pris: Mélanges de Moyen Français offerts à Giuseppe di Stefano,* ed. Maria Colombo Timelli and Claudio Galderisi (Montreal: CERES, 2004), 539–48.

18. "De laquelle les faiz et oeuvres, pour ce que on ne les puelt bonnement nommer en lattin ne exposer en françoiz, les acteurs les nomment en prononciacion greque, c'est assavoir estrantegemens" (p. 36, lines 445–48).

19. Frontinus, *Strategemata,* trans. Simon de Hesdin, *notice* in Frédéric Duval and Françoise Vieillard, *Le Miroir des classiques,* Éditions en ligne de l'École des chartes (ELEC) 17 (2003). Marcel Lecourt, "Une Source d'Antoine de La Sale: Simon de Hesdin," *Romania* 76 (1955): 39–83, 183–211.

20. See Demarolle, "A propos du vocabulaire d'Antoine de La Sale" and Lefèvre, "Salade et 'jambon.'"

21. Michel Pastoureau, *L'Etoffe du diable: Une Histoire des rayures et des tissus rayés* (Paris: Seuil, 1991).

22. Jose Vincenzo Molle, "*L'Asnerie:* Un esempio (periferico) di Sottie bilingue rinascimentale; Francese e patois borgognone nel repertorio teatrale della *Mère-Folle* di Digione (c. 1576–1643)," in *Nuovi saggi sul plurilinguismo letterario,* ed. Vincenzo Orioles (Rome: Editrice "Il Calamo," 2001), 209n.

23. Cochis rejects this view in "Antoine de La Sale's Delightful Teachings," 119–23.

24. Uhl, "L'Excursion aux îles Lipari," citing Jacques Le Goff, *La Naissance du Purgatoire* (Paris: Gallimard, 1981), 241–56.

25. Le Goff, *Naissance du Purgatoire,* 273–81.

26. Lucretius, *De rerum natura,* trans. W. H. D. Rouse (London: Heinemann; Cambridge, Mass.: Harvard University Press, 1943), bk. 6, lines 680–702.

27. Isidore of Seville's *De rerum natura* derives its description of Mount Etna in part from Lucretius. Bede's *De natura rerum* draws on both Isidore and Pliny; see Evelyn Edson, *Mapping Time and Space: How Medieval Mapmakers Viewed Their World* (London: British Library, 1997), 39, 50–51.

28. *Pliny: Letters,* trans. William Melmoth, rev. W. M. L. Hutchinson, 2 vols. (London: Heinemann; New York: Macmillan, 1927); Selatie Edgar Stout, *Plinius, Epistulae: A Critical Edition* (Bloomington: Indiana University Press, 1962), 1–30. According to Stout, Pliny's letters were plundered for "flores" in the High Middle Ages (7–11).

29. See Carrillo, "From Mt Ventoux to Mt Masaya," 57–59.

30. Carrillo, "From Mt Ventoux to Mt Masaya." See the short discussion of this article with reference to La Sale in Elsner and Rubiés's introduction to *Voyages and Visions,* 48.

31. "Et toute l'ordure qui est en toy, que tu reçois des IIII elemens, viennent [de] la profondeur de ta personne; et en icelle fait espiraux, dont yssent pueurs et abhominables ordures."

BIBLIOGRAPHY

PRIMARY SOURCES

Paris and Vienne

Historia de los amores de París y Viana. Edited by Alvaro Galmés de Fuentes. Madrid: Gredos, 1970.
Història de París i Viana: Estudi literari i tipogràfic de Pedro M. Cátedra; Estudi lingüístic de Modest Prats. Girona: Diputació de Girona, 1986.
Kaltenbacher, Robert. "Der altfranzösische Roman *Paris et Vienne*." *Romanische Forschungen* 15 (1903): 321–668.
Paris and Vienne, Translated from the French and Printed by William Caxton. Edited by MacEdward Leach. Early English Text Society. New York: Oxford University Press, 1957.
Paris et Vienne: Romanzo cavalleresco del XV secolo. Edited by Anna Maria Babbi. Verona: Franco Angeli, 1992.
"Paris et Vienne": Romanzo cavalleresco del XV secolo. Parigi. Bibliothèque nationale, ms. fr. 20044. Edited by Anna Maria Babbi. Milan: Franco Angeli, 1992.
Paris e Vienne, romanzo cavalleresco. Edited by Anna Maria Babbi. Venice: Marsilio, 1991.
Pariz un' Viene: Mahadura biqortit bezeruf mavo, he'arot venispahim. Edited by Chone Shmeruk, with Erika Timm. Jerusalem: Israel Academy of Sciences and Humanities, 1996.

Pierre de Provence and La Belle Maguelonne

Babbi, Anna Maria. "La prima ricezione tedesca del 'Pierre de Provence et La Belle Maguelonne.'" In *Filologia romanza, filologia germanica: Intersezioni e diffrazioni; Convegno internazionale, Verona, 3–5 aprile 1995,* ed. Anna Maria Babbi and Adele Cipolla, 437–48. Verona: Edizioni Fiorini, 1997.
———. "Il romanzo francese del Quattrocento: *Pierre de Provence* e dintorni." *Critica del testo* 2 (2004): 341–55.
Histoire de Pierre de Provence & de la Belle Maguelonne. Facsimile edition. Nouvelle Bibliothèque bleue de Troyes. Villiers-sur-Marne: Phénix Éditions, 2003.

Pierre de Provence et la belle Maguelonne. Edited by Anna Maria Babbi. Soveria Mannelli: Rubettino, 2003.

L'Ystoire du vaillant chevalier Pierre filz du conte de Provence et de La Belle Maguelonne: Texte du manuscrit S IV 2 de la Landesbibliothek de Cobourg, XVe siècle. Edited by Régine Colliot. Sénéfiance, Cahiers du CUER-MA 4. Paris: Champion, 1977.

Other Works

Alexandre de Paris. *The Medieval French Roman d'Alexandre.* 6 vols. Vol. I: *Text of the Arsenal and Venice Versions.* Edited by Milan S. La Du. Elliott Monographs 36. Princeton: Princeton University Press, 1937. Vol. II: *Version of Alexandre de Paris.* Edited by E. C. Armstrong, D. L. Buffum, Bateman Edwards, and L. F. H. Lowe. New York: Kraus Reprint, 1965.

Andrea da Barberino. *Le storie nerbonesi, romanzo cavalleresco del secolo XIV.* Edited by Ippolito Gaetano Isola. 4 vols. Bologna: Romagnoli, 1877–91.

Arnaut Vidal de Castelnaudary. *Le Livre des aventures de Monseigneur Guilhem de la Barra.* Edited and translated by Gérard Gouiran. Paris: Champion, 1997.

Ausiàs March, Poesies. Edited by Pere Bohigas. 5 vols. Barcelona: Barcino, 1951.

Une Belle au Bois Dormant Médiévale: Frayre de Joy e Sor de Plazer. Edited by Suzanne Thiolier-Méjean. Paris: Presses de l'Université de Paris-Sorbonne, 1996.

Benoît de Sainte-Maure. *Le "Roman de Troie" de Benoît de Sainte-Maure.* Edited by Léopold Constans. 6 vols. Paris: SATF, 1912.

———. *Le Roman de Troie en Prose.* Edited by Léopold Constans and Edmond Faral. Paris: Champion, 1922. [Vol. 1 only—the second volume was never published.]

Bernat de So. *La "Vesio" de Bernat de So et Le "Débat entre Honor et Delit" de Jacme March.* Edited by Amédée Pagès. Toulouse: Privat, 1945.

Blandin de Cornouaille: Introduction, édition diplomatique, glossaire. Edited by Cornelis H. M. Van der Horst. The Hague: Mouton, 1974.

Blandin de Cornualha i altras narracions en vers. Edited by Arseni Pacheco. Barcelona: Edicions 62 I "La Caixa," 1986.

Boethius. *Le Livre de Boece de Consolacion.* Edited by Glynnis M. Cropp. Geneva: Droz, 2006.

I cantari di Carduino giuntovi quello di Tristano e Lancielotto . . . Poemetti cavallereschi. Edited by Pio Rajna. Bologna, 1873.

Carvajal, Micael de. *Tragedia Josephina.* Edited by Joseph E. Gillet. Elliott Monographs 28. Princeton: Princeton University Press; Paris: Presses Universitaires de France, 1932.

Chariton. *Callirhoe.* Edited by G. P. Goold. Loeb Classical Library 481. Cambridge, Mass.: Harvard University Press, 1995.

Charpentier, Hélène, and Patricia Victorin, eds. *Le Conte du Papegau.* Paris: Champion, 2004.

La Chevalerie de Judas Macchabee de Gautier de Belleperche (et de Pieros du Riés). Edited by J. M. Smeets. 2 vols. Assen: Van Gorcum, 1991.

Corrozet, Gilles. *"Richard Sans Peur": Edited from the "Romant de Richart" and from Gilles Corrozet's "Richart sans Paour."* Edited by Denis Joseph Conlon. Studies in the Romance Languages and Literatures 192. Chapel Hill: University of North Carolina Department of Romance Languages, 1977.

Eiximenis, Francesc. *Com usar de beure e menjar: Norms morals contingudes en el "Terç del Cristia" per Francesc Eiximenis*. Edited by Jorge E. Gracia. Barcelona: Curial, 1977.

———. *Lo libre de les dones*. Edited by Frank Naccarato under the direction of Joan Coromines; revised by Curt Wittlin and Antoni Comas. 2 vols. Barcelona: Departament de Filologia Catalana, Curial Edicions Catalanes, 1981.

Everhard of Béthune. *Graecismus*. Edited by Johannes Wrobel. Hildesheim: Georg Olms Reprints, 1987.

Frondino e Brisona. Edited by Annamaria Annicchiaro. Bari: Adriatica, 1990.

Gaston III, Count of Foix [Gaston Fébus]. *Le Livre de la Chasse*. Edited by Gunnar Tilander. Karlshamn: Johanssons, 1971.

Gautier d'Arras. *Eracle*. Edited by Guy Raynaud de Lage. Paris: Champion, 1976.

Genesi de Scriptura: Compendi historial de la Biblia que ab lo titol de Genesi de Scriptura, trelladá del provençal a la llengua catalana mossen Guillem Serra en l'any M.CCCCLI, y ara ha fet estampar per primera vegada En Miquel Victoriá Amer. Barcelona: Llibreria Alvar Verdaguer, 1873. Available online: Alicante, Biblioteca Virtual Joan Lluís Vives, 2000. http://www.lluisvives.com/.

La Geste Francor di Venezia. Edizione integrale del Codice XIII del Fondo francese della Marciana. Edited by Aldo Rosellini. Pubblicazioni del Centro Linguistica dell'Università cattolica. Saggi e monografie 6. Brescia: La Scuola, 1986.

Girart de Roussillon, chanson de geste. Edited by W. Mary Hackett. 4 vols. Paris: Picard, 1953–55.

Isidore of Seville. *Étymologies, livre IX: Les Langues et les groupes sociaux*. Edited by Marc Reydellet. Paris: Les Belles Lettres, 1984.

Le Jeu de Sainte Agnès: Drame provençal du XIVe siècle. Edited by Alfred Jeanroy. Paris: Champion, 1931.

Les Lais anonymes des XIIe et XIIIe siècles. Edited by Prudence Mary O'Hara Tobin. Geneva: Droz, 1976.

La Sale, Antoine de. *Antoine de La Sale, Oeuvres complètes, tome I: La Salade; tome II: La Sale*. Edited by Fernand Desonay. Liège: Faculté de Philosophie et Lettres, Liège and Droz, 1935–41.

———. *Jehan de Saintré*. Edited by Joël Blanchard. Lettres Gothiques. Paris: Le Livre de Poche, 1995.

———. *Le Réconfort de Madame de Fresne*. Edited by Ian Hill. Exeter: Exeter University Press, 1979.

Lefèvre, Raoul. *Histoire de Jason*. Edited by Gert Pinkernell. Frankfurt, 1971.

Lemaire de Belges, Jean. *Épîtres de l'amant vert*. Edited by Jean Frappier. Lille: Giard; Geneva: Droz, 1948.

La Leyenda de Yusuf, ein Aljamiadotext. Edited by Ursual Klenk. Tübingen: Niemeyer, 1972.

Lo Libre dels Set Savis de Roma. Edited by Andrea Giannetti. Bari: Adriatica, 1996.

Lion de Bourges: Poème épique du XIVe siècle. Edited by William W. Kibler, Jean-Louis Picherit, and Thelma S. Fenster. 2 vols. Geneva: Droz, 1980.

Llull, Ramon. *The Book of the Lover and the Beloved: Lo Libre de amich e amat, Librum amici et amati*. Edited and translated by Mark D. Johnston. Warminster, Wilts.: Aris and Phillips Ltd.; Bristol: Centre for Mediterranean Studies, 1995.

Lucretius. *De rerum natura*. Translated by W. H. D. Rouse. London: Heinemann; Cambridge, Mass.: Harvard University Press, 1943.

Maillart, Jehan. *Le Roman du comte d'Anjou*. Edited by Mario Roques. Paris: CFMA, 1931.
Marcabru: A Critical Edition. Edited by Simon Gaunt, Ruth Harvey, and Linda Paterson. Cambridge: D. S. Brewer, 2000.
Marie de France. *Les Lais de Marie de France*. Edited by Karl Warnke. Lettres Gothiques. Paris: Le Livre de Poche, 1990.
Marot, Clément. *Oeuvres lyriques*. Edited by C. A. Mayer. London: Athlone Press, 1964.
Matfré Ermengaud. *Breviari d'amor: Manuscript valencià del segle XV (Biblioteca Nacional de Madrid)/Manuscrito valenciano del siglo XV (Biblioteca Nacional de Madrid)*. Edited by Antoni Ferrando. 2 vols. Valencia, 1980.
———. *Le "Breviari d'amor" de Matfre Ermengaud*. Edited by Peter T. Ricketts. Vol. V. Leiden: E. J. Brill; London: AIEO, Westfield College, 1976–2004.
Metge, Bernat. *Obras de Bernat Metge*. Edited by Martín de Riquer. Barcelona: Facultad de Filosofia y Letras, Universidad de Barcelona, 1959.
Molinier, Guilhem. *Las Flors del Gay Saber*. Edited by Joseph Anglade. Barcelona: Institut d'Estudis Catalans, 1926.
———. *Les Leys d'Amors: Manuscrit de l'Académie des Jeux Floraux*. 4 vols. in 2. Edited by Joseph Anglade. Toulouse: Privat, 1919–20.
———. *(Leys d'Amors), Las Flors del Gay Saber, estier dichas Las Leys d'Amors*. Edited by M. Gatien-Arnoult. 3 vols. Paris: Silvestre-Bon; Toulouse: Privat, 1841–43. Reprinted in 2 volumes. Geneva: Slatkine Reprints, 1977.
Nouvelles courtoises occitanes et françaises. Edited and translated by Suzanne Thiolier-Méjean and Marie-Thérèse Notz-Grob. Paris: Le Livre de Poche, 1997.
Nouvelles occitanes du Moyen Âge. Edited by Jean-Charles Huchet. Paris: Garnier Flammarion, 1992.
Novel.les amoroses i morals. Edited by Arseni Pacheco and August Bover i Font. Barcelona: Edicions 62 i "La Caixa," 1982.
Ovid: Amores. Text, Prolegomena, and Commentary in Four Volumes. Edited by J. C. McKeown. Leeds: Francis Cairns, 1998.
Ovide: Les Amours. Edited by Henri Bornecque. Paris: Les Belles Lettres, 1961.
"Ovide moralisé": Poème du commencement du quatorzième siècle. Edited by Cornelis de Boer. Amsterdam: Johannes Müller, 1915–38.
Ovide moralisé en prose (texte du quinzième siècle). Edited by Cornelis de Boer. Amsterdam: N. V. Noord-Hollandsche Uitgevers Mij., 1954.
Peire d'Alvernhe: Poesie. Edited by Aniello Fratta. Manziana: Vecchiarelli, 1996.
Perceforest: Troisième partie. Edited by Gilles Roussineau. Vol. III. Geneva: Droz, 1993.
Perceforest: Troisième partie, tome II. Edited by Gilles Roussineau. Geneva: Droz, 1991.
Plinius, Epistulae: A Critical Edition. Edited by Selatie Edgar Stout. Bloomington: Indiana University Press, 1962.
Pliny: Letters. Translated by William Melmoth. Revised by W. M. L. Hutchinson. 2 vols. London: Heinemann; New York: Macmillan, 1927.
Raimon Vidal de Besalú. *The "Razos de trobar" of Raimon Vidal and Associated Texts*. Edited by John Marshall. Oxford: Oxford University Press, 1972.
Renaut de Bâgé/Beaujeu. *Le Bel Inconnu*. Edited by G. Perrie Williams. Paris: CFMA, 1929.
Richars li Biaus. Edited by Anthony J. Holden. Paris: Champion, 1983.

[Fra] Rocabertí. *The "Gloria d'Amor" of Fra Rocabertí: A Catalan Vision-Poem of the Fifteenth Century*. Edited by H. C. Heaton. New York: AMS Press, 1966.
Roís de Corella, Joan. *Joan Roís de Corella: Proses mitològiques*. Edited by Josep-Lluís Martos. Alicante: Universitat d'Alacant, 2001.
Le Roman d'Enéas. Edited by Aimé Petit. Paris: Le Livre de Poche, 1997.
Le Roman de Perceforest: Première partie. Edited by Jane H. M. Taylor. Geneva: Droz, 1979.
Storie nerbonesi: Romanzo cavalleresco del secolo XIV. Edited by I. G. Isola. Bologna, 1877–80.
Uc Faidit. *The "Donatz proensals" of Uc Faidit*. Edited by John Marshall. Oxford: Oxford University Press, 1969.
Uguccione da Pisa. *Derivationes*. Edited by Enzo Cecchini, Guido Arbizzoni, et al. 2 vols. Edizione nazionale dei testi mediolatini 11. Florence: SISMEL, Edizioni del Galluzzo, 2004.
Voyage à Jérusalem de Philippe de Voisins, seigneur de Montaut. Edited by Philippe Tamizey de Larroque. Paris: Champion, Cocharaux Frères, 1883.
Le Voyatge d'Oultremer en Jherusalem de Nompar, seigneur de Caumont. Edited by Peter S. Noble. Oxford: Blackwell, 1975.

ONLINE ANTHOLOGIES AND OTHER RESOURCES

Concordance de l'Occitan médiéval. Vol. II, *Les Troubadours: Les Textes narratifs en vers* [COM 2]. Edited by Peter T. Ricketts and Alan Reed. Turhout: Brepols, 2005.
Duval, Frédéric, and Françoise Vieillard. Le Miroir des classiques. Éditions en ligne de l'École des chartes [ELEC], 17 (2003). http://elec.enc.sorbonne.fr/miroir/.
Repertorio informatizzato della letteratura catalana [RIALC]. Università di Napoli Federico II. www.rialc.unina.it.
Repertorio informatizzato dell'antica letteratura trobadorica e occitanica [RIALTO]. Università di Napoli Federico II. www.rialto.it.

SECONDARY SOURCES

Agamben, Giorgio. *Infancy and History: On the Destruction of Experience*. Translated by Liz Heron. New York: Verso, 2007.
Alvar, Carlos. "Una veintena de traductores del siglo XV: Prolegómenos a un repertorio." In *Essays on Medieval Translation in the Iberian Peninsula*, ed. Tomàs Martínez Romero and Roxana Recio, 13–44. Castelló: Publicacions de la Universitat Jaume I; Omaha: Creighton University, 2000.
Amer, Sahar. *Ésope au féminin: Marie de France et la politique de l'interculturalité*. Atlanta: Rodopi, 1999.
Anzieu, Didier. *Le Moi-Peau*. 2nd rev. ed. Paris: Dunod, 1995.
Archer, Robert. "Formes del desamor: Blasme de dona i maldit." In *Ausiàs March i el món cultural del segle XV*, ed. Rafael Alemany, 59–75. Alicante: Universitat d'Alacant, Institut Interuniversitari de Filologia Valenciana, 2000.

———. "La tradición del vituperio de las mujeres antes y después de Ausiàs March." In *Ausiàs March y las literaturas de su época,* ed. Lourdes Sánchez Roderigo, 151–65. Granada: Universidad de Granada, 2000.

Archibald, Elizabeth. *Incest and the Medieval Imagination.* Cambridge: Cambridge University Press, 2001.

Arteaga, Alfredo. *Chicano Poetics: Heterotexts and Hybridities.* Cambridge: Cambridge University Press, 1997.

Asperti, Stefano. *Carlo I d'Angiò e i trovatori: Componenti 'provenzali' e angioine nella tradizione manoscritta della lirica trobadorica.* Ravenna: Longo, 1995.

———. "*Flamenca* e dintorni: Considerazioni sui rapporti fra Occitania e Catalogna nel XIV secolo." *Cultura neolatina* 45 (1985): 59–104.

Avenoza, Gemma. "Antoni Canals, Simon de Hesdin, Nicolas de Gonesse, Juan Alfonso de Zamora y Hugo de Urriés: Lecturas e interpretaciones de un clásico (Valerio Máximo) y de sus comentaristas (Dionisio de Burgo Santo Sepulcro y Fray Lucas)." In *Essays on Medieval Translation in the Iberian Peninsula,* ed. Tomàs Martínez Romero and Roxana Recio, 45–73. Castelló: Publicacions de la Universitat Jaume I; Omaha: Creighton University, 2000.

Badia, Lola. *De Bernat Metge a Joan Roís de Corella: Estudis sobre la cultura literària de la tardor medieval catalana.* Barcelona: Quaderns Crema, 1988.

———. "L'Humanisme català: Formació i crisi d'un concepte historiogràfic." In *Actes del V Col.loqui Internacional de Llengua i Literatura Catalanes, Andorra, 1–6 d'octubre de 1979,* ed. J. Bruguera and J. Massot i Muntaner, 41–70. Santa Creus: Publicacions de l'Abadia de Montserrat, 1980.

Bal, Mieke. *Loving Yusuf: Conceptual Travels from Present to Past.* Chicago: University of Chicago Press, 2008.

Baldwin, John W. "Consent and the Marital Debt: Five Discourses in Northern France Around 1200." In *Consent and Coercion to Sex and Marriage in Ancient and Medieval Societies,* ed. Angeliki E. Laiou, 257–70. Washington, D.C.: Dumbarton Oaks Research Library and Collection, 1993.

Ballor, Alessandro. "Il mito di Giasone e Medea." *Studi francesi* 44 (2000): 455–71.

———. "Il mito di Giasone e Medea nel Quattrocento francese." *Studi francesi* 47 (2003): 3–22.

Balmary, Marie. *Le Sacrifice interdit: Freud et la Bible.* Paris: Grasset, 1986.

Barbieri, Luca. *Le "Epistole delle dame di Grecia" nel "Roman de Troie" in prosa: La prima traduzione francese delle 'Eroidi' di Ovidio.* Tübingen: A. Francke Verlag, 2005.

Barletta, Vincent. *Covert Gestures: Crypto-Islamic Literature as Cultural Practice in Early Modern Spain.* Minneapolis: University of Minnesota Press, 2005.

Batany, Jean. "Une Boutade renardienne au XIVe siècle: Les Clercs et la langue romane." In "Grammaires du vulgaire: Normes et variations de la langue française," ed. Christopher Lucken and Mireille Séguy, *Médiévales* 45 (2003): 85–98.

Beaton, Roderick. *The Medieval Greek Romance.* Cambridge: Cambridge University Press, 1989.

Bec, Pierre. *Burlesque et obscenité chez les troubadours: Pour une approche du contre-texte médiéval.* Paris: Stock, 1984.

Beltran, Vicenç. "Poesía popular antigua ¿Cultura cortés?" *Romance Philology* 55 (2002): 183–230.

Beltran Llavador, Rafael. *Tirant lo Blanc: Evolució i revolta en la novel.la de cavalleries.* Valencia: Institució Alfons el Magnànim, Diputació de Valencia, 1983.

Bendinelli Predelli, Maria. "The *Fier Baiser* Motif Between Literature and Folklore." In *Studies for Dante: Essays in Honor of Dante Della Terza,* ed. Franco Fido, Rena A. Syska-Lamparska, and Pamela D. Stewart, 467–84. Fiesole: Cadmo, 1998.

Bériac, Françoise. *Des Lépreux aux cagots: Recherches sur les sociétés marginales en Aquitaine médiévale.* Bordeaux: Fédération historique du Sud-Ouest, Université de Bordeaux III, 1990.

Bériou, Nicole. "The Right of Women to Give Religious Instruction in the Thirteenth Century." In *Women Preachers and Prophets Throughout Two Millennia of Christianity,* ed. Beverly Maine Kienzle and Pamela J. Walker, 134–45. Berkeley and Los Angeles: University of California Press, 1998.

Bettelheim, Bruno. *The Uses of Enchantment: The Meaning and Importance of Fairy Tales.* Harmondsworth, U.K.: Penguin, 1982.

Bhabha, Homi H. *The Location of Culture.* New York: Routledge, 1994.

Biddick, Kathleen. *The Shock of Medievalism.* Durham: Duke University Press, 1997.

Biller, Peter. "The Cathars of Languedoc and Written Materials." In *Heresy and Literacy, 1000–1530,* ed. Peter Biller and Anne Hudson, 61–82. Cambridge: Cambridge University Press, 1994.

———. "Heresy and Literacy: Earlier History of the Theme." In *Heresy and Literacy: 1000–1530,* ed. Peter Biller and Anne Hudson, 1–18. Cambridge: Cambridge University Press, 1994.

Boase, Roger. *The Troubadour Revival: A Study of Social Change and Traditionalism in Late Medieval Spain.* London: Routledge and Kegan Paul, 1978.

Bohigas, Père. "El repertori dels manuscrits Catalans de la Fundació Patxot. Missió a París. Biblioteca Nacional (1920–1927)." *Estudis universitaris catalans* 15 (1930): 215–17.

Borm, Jan. "Defining Travel: On the Travel Book, Travel Writing, and Terminology." In *Perspectives on Travel Writing,* ed. Glenn Hooper and Tim Youngs, 13–26. Aldershot: Ashgate, 2004.

Borst, Arno. *Der Turmbau von Babel: Geschichte der Meinungen über Ursprung und Vielfalt der Sprachen und Völker.* 6 vols. Stuttgart: Hiersemann, 1957–63.

Blumenfeld-Kosinski, Renate. "Introduction: The Middle Ages." In *The Politics of Translation in the Middle Ages and the Renaissance,* ed. Renate Blumenfeld-Kosinski, Luise von Flotow, and Daniel Russell, 17–27. Tempe, Ariz.: Arizona Center for Medieval and Renaissance Studies; Ottawa: University of Ottawa Press, 2001.

———. *Reading Myth: Classical Mythology and Its Interpretations in Medieval French Literature.* Stanford: Stanford University Press, 1997.

Braidotti, Rosi. *Nomadic Subjects: Embodiment and Sexual Difference in Contemporary Feminist Theory.* New York: Columbia University Press, 1994.

Brisson, Luc. *Le Mythe de Tirésias: Essai d'analyse structurale.* Leiden: Brill, 1976.

Brownlee, Kevin. "The Conflicted Genealogy of Cultural Authority: Italian Responses to French Cultural Dominance in *Il Tesoretto, Il Fiore,* and *La Commedia.*" In *Generation and Degeneration: Tropes of Reproduction in Literature and History from Antiquity to Early Modern Europe,* ed. Valerie Finucci and Kevin Brownlee, 262–86. Durham: Duke University Press, 2001.

Brugnolo, Furio. *Plurilinguismo e lirica medievale: Di Raimbaut de Vaqueiras a Dante.* Rome: Bulzoni, 1983.

Brumlik, Joan. "Incest and Death in Marie de France's *Deus Amanz.*" In *The Court Reconvenes: Selected Papers from the Ninth Triennial Congress of the International*

Courtly Literature Society, 1998, ed. Barbara K. Altmann and Carleton W. Carroll, 169–77. Cambridge: D. S. Brewer, 2003.

Brundage, James. "Implied Consent to Intercourse." In *Consent and Coercion to Sex and Marriage in Ancient and Medieval Societies*, ed. Angeliki E. Laiou, 245–56. Washington, D.C.: Dumbarton Oaks Research Library and Collection, 1993.

———. *Law, Sex, and Christian Society in Medieval Europe*. Chicago: University of Chicago Press, 1986.

Burgwinkle, William. *Love for Sale: Materialist Readings of Troubadour Poetry*. New York: Garland, 1997.

Busby, Keith. *Codex and Context: Reading Old French Verse Narrative in Manuscript*. 2 vols. New York: Rodopi, 2002.

Cabré, Miriam. *Cerverí de Girona and His Poetic Traditions*. Woodbridge, U.K.: Tamesis, 1999.

Calaresu, Melissa. "Looking for Virgil's Tomb: The End of the Grand Tour and the Cosmopolitan Ideal of Europe." In *Voyages and Visions: Towards a Cultural History of Travel*, ed. Jás Elsner and Joan-Pau Rubiés, 138–61. London: Reaktion Books, 1999.

Cantavella, Rosanna. "The Meaning of *destral* as 'Go-Between' in the Catalan *Facet* and in Old Occitan." *Medium Aevum* 67 (2004): 304–12.

Carolus-Barré, Louis. "Peyre de Paternas, auteur du *Libre de sufficiencia e de necessitat*." *Romania* 67 (1942–43): 217–39.

Carrillo, Jesús. "From Mt Ventoux to Mt Masaya: The Rise and Fall of Subjectivity in Early Modern Travel." In *Voyages and Visions: Towards a Cultural History of Travel*, ed. Jás Elsner and Joan-Pau Rubiés, 57–73. London: Reaktion Books, 1999.

Cerquiglini, Jacqueline. *"Un Engin si soutil": Guillaume de Machaut et l'écriture au XIVe siècle*. Paris: Champion, 1985.

Cestaro, Gary P. *Dante and the Grammar of the Nursing Body*. Notre Dame: University of Notre Dame Press, 2003.

Chazan, Robert. *Barcelona and Beyond: The Disputation of 1263 and Its Aftermath*. Berkeley and Los Angeles: University of California Press, 1992.

———. *Daggers of Faith: Thirteenth-Century Christian Missionizing and Jewish Response*. Berkeley and Los Angeles: University of California Press, 1989.

Cingolani, Stefano Maria. "Bernat Metge i els poetes de *Lo Somni*." *Revue d'Études Catalanes* 3 (2000): 121–50.

———. "Innovazione e parodia nel Marciano XIII (*Geste Francor*)." *Romanistisches Jahrbuch* 38 (1987): 61–77.

———. "Política, societat i literatura: Claus per a una interpretació de *Lo Somni* de Bernat Metge." *Revista de Catalunya* 150 (2000): 85–105.

———. *Lo Somni de una cultura: "Lo Somni" de Bernat Metge*. Barcelona: Quaderns Crema, 2002.

———. "Traducció literària i traducció cultural." In *Essays on Medieval Translation in the Iberian Peninsula*, ed. Tomàs Martínez Romero and Roxana Recio, 129–52. Castelló: Publicacions de la Universitat Jaume I; Omaha: Creighton University, 2000.

Cixous, Hélène. "*The Apple in the Dark:* The Temptation of Understanding." In *Hélène Cixous, Reading with Clarice Lispector*, ed. and trans. Verena Andermatt Conley, 60–97. London: Harvester Wheatsheaf, 1990.

———. *L'Heure de Clarice Lispector*. Paris: des femmes, Antoinette Fouque, 1979.

———. *Vivre l'orange*. Paris: des femmes, 1979.

Cixous, Hélène, and Mireille Calle-Gruber. *Rootprints: Memory and Life Writing*. New York: Routledge, 1997.
Clanchy, Michael. *From Memory to Written Record*. 2nd ed. Oxford: Blackwell, 1992.
Clément-Dumas, Gisèle. *Des Moines aux troubadours, IXe–XIIIe siècle: La musique médiévale en Languedoc et en Catalogne*. Montpellier: Presses du Languedoc, 2004.
Cochis, Simonetta. "Antoine de La Sale's Delightful Teachings: Literature and Learning in His Late Medieval Books for Princes." Ph.D. diss., New York University, 1998.
———. "The Sailor Demon of Vulcano in Antoine de La Sale's Geography of the Demonic, *L'Excursion aux îles Lipari*." In *Demons: Mediators Between This World and the Other*, ed. Ruth Petzoldt and Peter Neubauer, 65–73. Frankfurt: Peter Lang, 1998.
Colombat, Bernard, and Irène Rosier. "L'Allothète et les figures de construction dans le *Catholicon* de Johannes Balbi." *Archives et Documents de la Société d'Histoire et d'Épistémologie des Sciences du Langage*, 2nd ser., 4 (1990): 69–161.
Copeland, Rita. *Rhetoric, Hermeneutics, and Translation in the Middle Ages*. Cambridge: Cambridge University Press, 1991.
Copjec, Joan. "Vampires, Breast-Feeding, and Anxiety." *October* 58 (1991): 24–43.
Corbin, Alain. *Le Miasme et la jonquille: L'Odorat et l'imaginaire social, XVIIIe–XIXe siècles*. Paris: Flammarion, 1982.
Coromines, Joan. *Entre dos llenguatges*. 3 vols. Barcelona: Curial, 1976.
Cortijo Ocaña, Antonio. *La Evolución genérica de la ficción sentimental de los siglos XV y XVI*. London: Tamesis, 2001.
———. "Women's Role in the Creation of Literature: Catalonia at the End of the Fourteenth and Beginning of the Fifteenth Century." *La Corónica* (1999): 3–16.
Cotton, William T. "Fidelity, Suffering, and Humour in *Paris and Vienne*." In *Chivalric Literature: Essays on Relations Between Literature and Life in the Later Middle Ages*, ed. Larry D. Benson and John Leyerle, 91–100. Kalamazoo: Medieval Institute, 1980.
Courcelles, Dominique de. "Les Bibles en Catalogne à la fin du Moyen Âge, ou l'occultation de la lettre sacrée." *Revue de l'Histoire des Religions* 1 (2001): 65–82.
———. "Recherches sur les livres et les femmes en Catalogne aux XIVe et XVIe siècles: Figures de lectrices." In *Des Femmes et des livres: France et Espagnes, XIVe–XVIIe siècle*, ed. Dominique de Courcelles and Carmen Val Julián, 95–114. Paris: Champion; Geneva: Droz, 1999.
———. "Traduire et citer les évangiles en Catalogne à la fin du XVe siècle: Quelques enjeux de la traduction et de la citation dans la *Vita Cristi* de Sor Isabel de Villena." In *Essays on Medieval Translation in the Iberian Peninsula*, ed. Tomàs Martínez Romero and Roxana Recio, 173–90. Castelló: Publicacions de la Universitat Jaume I; Omaha: Creighton University, 2000.
Coville, Alfred. *La Vie intellectuelle dans les domaines d'Anjou-Provence, de 1380 à 1435*. Paris: Droz, 1941.
Cressy, David. *Birth, Marriage, and Death: Ritual, Religion, and the Life-Cycle in Tudor and Stuart England*. Oxford: Oxford University Press, 1997.
Cushing, Kathleen G. *Ritual, Text, and Law: Studies in Medieval Canon Law and Liturgy*. London: Ashgate, 2004.
Degenhart, Bernhard, and Annegrit Schmitt, "Marino Sanudo und Paolino Veneto: Zwei Literaten des 14. Jahrhunderts in ihrer Wirkung auf Buchillustrierung und

Kartographie in Venedig, Avignon und Neapel." *Römische Jahrbuch für Kunstgeschichte* 14 (1973): 1–137.
Demarolle, Paul. "A propos du vocabulaire d'Antoine de La Sale: Nature et portée des faits de syntaxe lexicale." *Travaux de linguistique* 25 (1992): 13–24.
Demers, Jeanne. "La Quête de l'anti-Graal, ou un récit fantastique: *Le Paradis de la Reine Sibylle.*" *Le Moyen Âge* 83 (1977): 469–92.
de Puig i Olivier, Jaume. "Més nous textos catalans antics de la 'Biblioteca Capitular y Colombina' de Sevilla." *Arxiu de textos catalans antics* 20 (2001): 453–510.
Derrida, Jacques. *Le Monolinguisme de l'autre: La Prothèse d'origine.* Paris: Galilée, 1996.
Dossat, Yves. "Les Juifs à Toulouse: Un demi-siècle d'histoire communautaire." In "Juifs et Judaïsme du Languedoc," *Cahiers de Fanjeaux* 12 (1977): 117–39.
Duffell, M. J. "The Metrics of Ausiàs March in a European Context." *Medium Aevum* 63 (1994): 287–300.
Eberly, Susan S. "A Thorn Among the Lilies: The Hawthorn in Medieval Love Allegory." *Folklore* 100 (1989): 41–52.
Edson, Evelyn. *Mapping Time and Space: How Medieval Mapmakers Viewed Their World.* London: British Library, 1997.
Errington, Joseph. "Colonial Linguistics." *Annual Review of Anthropology* 30 (2001): 19–39.
Fedi, Beatrice. "Il canone assente: L'esempio metrico nelle 'Leys d'Amors' fra citazione e innovazione." *Quaderni di filologia romanza* 14 (1999): 159–86.
———. "Per un'edizione critica delle 'Leys d'Amors.'" *Studi medievali* 40 (1999): 43–118.
Fildes, Valerie. *Wet Nursing: A History from Antiquity to the Present.* Oxford: Blackwell, 1987.
Flint, Valerie I. J. "Honorius Augustodunensis, *Imago Mundi.*" *Archives d'Histoire Doctrinale et Littéraire du Moyen Âge* 49 (1982): 7–153.
Garrido i Valls, Josep-David. "La traducció catalana medieval de las *Heroides* d'Ovidi." *Faventia* 24 (2002): 37–53.
Gaunt, Simon. "*Desnaturat son li Frances:* Language and Identity in the Twelfth-Century Occitan Epic." *Tenso: Bulletin de la Société Guilhem IX* 17 (2002): 10–31.
———. "Le Pouvoir d'achat des femmes dans *Girart de Roussillon.*" *Cahiers de Civilisation Médiévale* 33 (1990): 305–16.
Gaunt, Simon, and Julian Weiss. "Cultural Traffic in the Medieval Romance World." In "Cultural Traffic in the Medieval Romance World," ed. Simon Gaunt and Julian Weiss. Special issue, *Journal of Romance Studies* 4 (2004): 1–11.
Gingras, Francis. *Érotisme et merveilles dans le récit français des XIIe et XIIIe siècles.* Paris: Champion, 2002.
Given, James Buchanan. *Inquisition and Medieval Society: Power, Discipline, and Resistance in Languedoc.* Ithaca: Cornell University Press, 1997.
Goldman, Shalom. *The Wiles of Women/The Wiles of Men: Joseph and Potiphar's Wife in Ancient Near Eastern, Jewish, and Islamic Folklore.* New York: State University of New York Press, 1995.
Gorra, Egidio. *Testi inediti di storia trojana, preceduti da uno studio sulla leggenda trojana in Italia.* Turin: Löscher, 1887.
Greenspahn, Frederick E. "A Mesopotamian Proverb and Its Biblical Reverberations." *Journal of the American Oriental Society* 114 (1994): 33–38.

Grondeux, Anne. *Le "Graecismus" d'Évrard de Béthune à travers ses gloses: Entre grammaire spéculative et grammaire positive du XIIIe au XIVe siècle*. Studia Artistarum 8. Turnhout: Brepols, 2000.
Gros, Gérard. *Le Poème du Puy Marial: Étude sur le serventois et le chant royal du XIVe siècle à la Renaissance*. Paris: Klincksieck, 1996.
———. *Le Poète, la Vierge et le Prince du Puy: Étude sur les Puys marials de la France du Nord, du XIVe siècle à la Renaissance*. Paris: Klincksieck, 1992.
Grutman, Rainier. "La Logique du plurilinguisme littéraire ou, une langue en vaut-elle une autre?" In *Literarische Mehrsprachigkeit: Multilinguisme littéraire*, ed. Georg Kremnitz and Robert Tanzmeister, 53–65. Vienna: Belvedere Druck, 1995.
Hackett, W. Mary. "L'Auteur de *Girart de Roussillon*." In *Guillaume d'Orange and the Chanson de Geste*, ed. W. Van Emden, P. E. Bennett, and A. Kerr, 43–53. Reading, U.K.: Société Rencesvals, 1984.
———. "Le Manuscrit P de Girart de Roussillon." In *Mélanges de philologie et de litterature romanes offerts a Jeanne Wathelet-Willem*, ed. Jacques de Caluwé, 207–18. Marche Romane. Liège: Cahiers de L'ARU, 1978.
Hagedorn, Suzanne C. *Abandoned Women: Rewriting the Classics in Dante, Boccaccio, and Chaucer*. Ann Arbor: University of Michigan Press, 2004.
Heers, Jacques. *Les Barbaresques: La Course et la guerre en Méditerranée, XIVe–XVIe siècles*. Paris: Perrin, 2001.
———. *Esclaves et domestiques au Moyen Âge dans le monde méditerranéen*. Paris: Fayard, 1981.
Heller-Roazen, Daniel. *Echolalias: Essays on the Forgetting of Language*. Berkeley, Calif.: Zone Books, 2004.
Henisch, Bridget Ann. *Feast and Fast: Food in Medieval Society*. University Park: Pennsylvania State University Press, 1976.
Henrard, Nadine. *Le Théâtre religieux médiéval en langue d'Oc*. Geneva: Droz, 1998.
Hershon, Cyril. *Faith and Controversy: The Jews of Mediaeval Languedoc*. Birmingham: University of Birmingham, AIEO, 1999.
Histoire générale de Languedoc avec des notes et les pièces justificatives. Edited by Dom Claude Devic and Dom J. Vaissète. Vol. X. Toulouse: Privat, 1885.
Holtus, Günter. "Aspects linguistiques du franco-italien." In *Essor et fortune de la chanson de geste dans l'Europe et l'Orient latin. Actes du IXe Congrès international de la Société Rencesvals pour l'étude de l'épopée romane, Padoue-Venise, 29 août–4 septembre 1982*, ed. Alberto Limentani et al., vol. II, 806–9. Modena: Mucchi, 1984.
Huchet, Jean-Charles. *Le Roman occitan médiéval*. Paris: Presses Universitaires de France, 1991.
Irigaray, Luce. *Le Temps de la différence*. Paris: Grasset, 1990.
Jacob, Marie. "L'Ekphrasis en images: Métamorphoses de la description dans *l'Histoire de la destruction de Troye la Grant* enluminée par l'atelier des Colombe à la fin du XVe siècle (BnF. NvAcq.Fr. 24920)." In *Conter de Troye et l'Alexandre: Pour Emmanuèle Baumgartner*, ed. Laurence Harf-Lancner, Laurence Mathey-Maille, and Michelle Szkilnik, 291–308. Paris: Presses de la Sorbonne Nouvelle, 2006.
Jambeck, Karen K. "The *Tretiz* of Walter of Bibbesworth: Cultivating the Vernacular." In *Childhood in the Middle Ages and the Renaissance: The Results of a Paradigm Shift in the History of Mentality*, ed. Albrecht Classen, 159–84. Amsterdam: Walter de Gruyter, 2005.

Jeanneret, Michel. *A Feast of Words: Banquets and Table Talk in the Renaissance,* translated by Jeremy Whiteley and Emma Hughes. London: Polity Press, 1991.
Jeanroy, Alfred. *Histoire sommaire de la poésie occitane des origines à la fin du XVIIIe siècle.* Toulouse: Privat, 1945.
———. "La Poésie académique à Toulouse au XIVet XVe siècles, d'après le 'Registre de Galhac.'" *Revue des Pyrénées* 26 (1914): 273–94.
———. *La Poésie lyrique des troubadours.* 2 vols. Toulouse: Privat, 1934.
Jeffreys, Michael, and Elizabeth M. Jeffreys. "'Imberios and Margarona': The Manuscripts, Sources, and Edition of a Byzantine Verse Romance." In *Popular Literature in Late Byzantium,* ed. E. M. Jeffreys and M. J. Jeffreys. London: Variorum Reprints, 1983.
Jones, Catherine M. "Rape, Redemption, and the Grateful Dead: *Richars li Biaus.*" In *Gender Transgressions: Crossing the Normative Barrier in Old French Literature,* ed. Karen J. Taylor, 3–19. New York: Garland, 1998.
Jordan, William Chester. *Ideology and Royal Power in Medieval France: Kingship, Crusade, and the Jews.* Variorum Reprints. Aldershot, U.K.: Ashgate, 2001.
Jung, Marc-René. *La Légende de Troie en France au Moyen Âge.* Basel: Francke Verlag, 1996.
Kay, Sarah. *The Old French Chansons de Geste in the Age of Romance: Political Fictions.* Cambridge: Cambridge University Press, 1995.
Kline, Naomi Reed. *Maps of Medieval Thought: The Hereford Paradigm.* Woodbridge, U.K.: Boydell, 2001.
Knudson Jr., C.-A. "Une Aventure d'Antoine de La Sale aux îles Lipari." *Romania* 54 (1928): 98–109.
Kramer, Samuel Noah. "The 'Babel of Tongues': A Sumerian Version." *Journal of the American Oriental Society* 88 (1968): 108–11.
Kristeva, Julia. *Pouvoirs de l'horreur.* Paris: Seuil, 1983.
Labbé, André. *L'Architecture des palais et des jardins dans les chansons de geste: Essai sur le thème du roi en majesté.* Paris: Champion; Geneva: Slatkine, 1987.
Landau, Justine. "Figures of Grammar and Rhetoric in *Las Leys d'Amors.*" *Tenso: Bulletin of the Société Guilhem IX* 19 (2005): 1–18.
Law, Vivien, "Why Write a Verse Grammar?" *Journal of Medieval Latin* 9 (1999): 46–76.
Lecourt, Marcel. "Une Source d'Antoine de La Sale: Simon de Hesdin." *Romania* 76 (1955): 39–83, 183–211.
Lefèvre, Sylvie. *Antoine de La Sale: La Fabrique de l'oeuvre et de l'écrivain.* Geneva: Droz, 2006.
———. "Salade et 'jambon': Deux italianismes chez Antoine de La Sale, ou petites histoires de langue et de bouche." In *Pour acquerir honneur et pris: Mélanges de Moyen Français offerts à Giuseppe di Stefano,* ed. Maria Colombo Timelli and Claudio Galderisi, 539–48. Montreal: CERES, 2004.
Léglu, Catherine. *Between Sequence and Sirventes: Aspects of Parody in Troubadour Lyric.* Oxford: EHRC, Legenda, 2000.
———. "Languages in Conflict in Toulouse: *Las Leys d'Amors.*" *Modern Language Review* 103, no. 2 (2008): 383–96.
———. "Maternal *Consolatio:* Antoine de La Sale's *Reconfort de Madame de Fresne.*" In *The Erotics of Consolation: Desire and Distance in the Late Middle Ages,* ed. Catherine E. Léglu and Stephen J. Milner, 263–91. New York: Palgrave Macmillan, 2008.

———. "A 'New Medea' in Late-Medieval French Narratives." In *Medea: Transformations and Transmutations of a Myth*, ed. Heike Bartel and Anne Simon. Oxford: MHRA, forthcoming.

———. "Rebuilding the Tower of Babel in *Girart de Roussillon*." In *Medieval Historical Discourses: Essays in Honour of Peter S. Noble*, ed. Marianne J. Ailes, Anne Lawrence-Mathers, and Françoise Le Saux. *Reading Medieval Studies* 34 (2008): 137–52.

Le Goff, Jacques. *La Naissance du Purgatoire*. Paris: Gallimard, 1981.

Limentani, Alberto. *L'eccezione narrativa: La provenza medievale e l'arte del racconto*. Turin: Einaudi, 1977.

Liu, Yin. "Incest and Identity: Family Relationships in *Emaré*." In *The Court Reconvenes: Selected Papers from the Ninth Triennial Congress of the International Courtly Literature Society, 1998*, ed. Barbara K. Altmann and Carleton W. Carroll, 179–85. Cambridge: D. S. Brewer, 2003.

Loraux, Nicole. *Les Expériences de Tirésias: Le Féminin et l'homme grec*. Paris: Gallimard, 1989.

Low, Peter. "You Who Once Were Far Off: Enlivening Sculpture in the Main Portal at Vézelay." *Art Bulletin* 85 (2003): 469–89.

Lusignan, Serge. *La Langue des rois au Moyen Âge: Le Français en France et en Angleterre*. Paris: Presses Universitaires de France, 2004.

———. *Parler vulgairement: Les Intellectuels et la langue française aux XIIIe et XIVe siècles*. Paris: Vrin; Montreal: Presses de l'Université de Montréal, 1986.

Mallinger, Léon. *Médée: Étude de littérature comparée*. Geneva: Slatkine Reprints, 1971.

Marguin-Hamon, Elsa. *L'"Ars lectoria Ecclesie" de Jean de Garlande: Une Grammaire versifiée du XIIIe siècle et ses gloses*. Studia Artistarum 2. Turnhout: Brepols, 2003.

Marks, Laura U. *The Skin of the Film: Intercultural Cinema, Embodiment, and the Senses*. Durham: Duke University Press, 2000.

Marshall, John H. "Observations on the Sources of the Treatment of Rhetoric in the *Leys d'Amors*." *Modern Language Review* 44 (1969): 39–52.

Mas i Garcia, Carles. "*Baixa dansa* in the Kingdom of Catalonia and Aragon in the Fifteenth Century." *Historical Dance* 3 (1992): 15–23.

Menache, Sophia. *Clement V*. Cambridge: Cambridge University Press, 1998.

Menocal, Maria Rosa. *The Arabic Role in Medieval Literary History: A Forgotten Heritage*. Philadelphia: University of Pennsylvania Press, 1987.

———. *Shards of Love: Exile and the Origins of the Lyric*. Durham: Duke University Press, 1994.

Milá y Fontanals, Manuel. *Obras de Manuel Milá y Fontanals*. Vol. I, *De los trovadores en España*. Barcelona: Consejo Superior de investigaciones cientifica, Instituto Miguel de Cervantes, 1966.

Minois, Georges. *Suicide in Western Culture*. Baltimore: Johns Hopkins University Press, 1992.

Moisan, André. *Répertoire des noms propres de personnes et de lieux cités dans les chansons de geste françaises et les oeuvres étrangères dérivées*. 6 vols. Geneva: Droz, 1980.

Molle, Jose Vincenzo. "*L'Asnerie:* Un esempio (periferico) di *Sottie* bilingue rinascimentale; Francese e patois borgognone nel repertorio teatrale della *Mère-Folle* di Digione (c.1576–1643)." In *Nuovi saggi sul plurilinguismo letterario*, ed. Vincenzo Orioles, 207–31. Rome: Societa Editrice "Il Calamo," 2001.

Monfrin, Jacques. "*Le Roman de Belris.*" In *Études de philologie romane*, ed. Jacques Monfrin, 451–92. Geneva: Droz, 2001.

———. "*Le Roman de Belris, Le Bel Inconnu, Carduino.*" In *Études de philologie romane*, ed. Jacques Monfrin, 493–511. Geneva: Droz, 2001.

Monga, Luigi. "Translating the Journey: A Literary Perspective on Truth in Cartography." In *Cross-Cultural Travel: Papers from the Royal Irish Academy International Symposium on Literature and Travel, National University of Ireland, Galway, November 2002*, ed. Jane Conway, 11–30. New York: Peter Lang, 2003.

Montoliu, Manuel de. *Un Escorç en la poesia i la novel.listica dels segles XIV i XV.* Barcelona: Editorial Alpha, 1961.

———. *La Llengua catalana i els trobadors.* Barcelona: Editorial Alpha, 1975.

Morf, Heinrich. "Notes pour servir à l'histoire de la légende de Troie en Italie et en Espagne." *Romania* 21 (1892): 18–38, 88–107.

———. "Notes pour servir à l'histoire de la légende de Troie en Italie (suite et fin)." *Romania* 24 (1895): 174–96.

Morse, Ruth. *The Medieval Medea.* Cambridge: D. S. Brewer, 1996.

Muchembled, Robert. *L'Invention de l'homme moderne.* Paris: Fayard, 1988.

Mundy, John Hine. *The Repression of Catharism at Toulouse (the Royal Diploma of 1279).* Toronto: PIMS, 1985.

Noble, Peter. "Anti-clericalism in the Feudal Epic." In *The Medieval Alexander Legend and Romance Epic: Essays in Honour of David J. A. Ross,* ed. P. Noble, L. Polak, and C. Isoz, 149–58. Millwood, N.Y.: Kraus, 1982.

———. "La Disparition de l'occitan en Agenais au XVe siècle." In *Studia Occitanica in memoriam Paul Remy,* ed. Hans-Erich Keller. 2 vols. Kalamazoo: Medieval Institute, 1986.

O'Shea, Stephen. *The Perfect Heresy: The Revolutionary Life and Death of the Medieval Cathars.* London: Profile Books, 2000.

Pagès, Amédée. *Ausias March et ses prédécesseurs.* Paris: Champion, 1915.

———. "La Belle Dame sans merci d'Alain Chartier: Texte français et traduction catalane." *Romania* 62 (1936): 481–531.

———. *La Poésie française en Catalogne du XIIIe siècle à la fin du XVe.* Toulouse: Privat, 1936.

———. "Poésies provenço-catalanes inédites du manuscrit Aguiló." *Romania* 54 (1928): 197–248.

Palès-Gobillard, Annette. *L'Inquisiteur Geoffroy d'Ablis et les cathares du comté de Foix, 1308–1309.* Paris: Éditions du CNRS, 1984.

Pasero, Nicoló. "Sulle fonti del libro primo delle *Leys d'Amors.*" *Studj Romanzi* 34 (1965): 125–85.

Pastoureau, Michel. *L'Etoffe du diable: Une Histoire des rayures et des tissus rayés.* Paris: Seuil, 1991.

Paterson, Linda. *The World of the Troubadours: Medieval Occitan Society, c. 1100–c. 1300.* Cambridge: Cambridge University Press, 1993.

Perret, Michèle. "L'Invraisemblable Vérité: Témoignage fantastique dans deux romans du XIVe et XVe siècles." *Europe: Revue Littéraire Mensuelle* 654 (1983): 25–35.

Perugi, Maurizio. *Trovatori a Valchiusa: Un frammento della cultura provenzale del Petrarca.* Padua: Antenore, 1985.

Pfister, Max. "Observations sur la langue de Girart de Roussillon." *Revue de Linguistique Romane* 34 (1970): 315–25.

Poché, Christian. *La Musique arabo-andalouse*. Paris: Actes Sud, 1995.
Possamaï-Pérez, Marylène. *L'Ovide moralisé: Essai d'interprétation*. Paris: Champion, 2006.
Prevenier, Walter, and Thérèse de Hemptinne. "La Flandre au Moyen Âge: Un Pays de trilinguisme administratif." In *La Langue des Actes: Actes du XIe Congrès International de diplomatique, Troyes, 11–13 septembre 2003*, ed. Olivier Guyotjannin. Editions en ligne de l'École des chartes (ELEC), 7, § 2: "Confins et contacts." Available online: http://elec.enc.sorbonne.fr/document174.html.
Psaki, Regina. "The Play of Genre and Voicing in Boccaccio's *Corbaccio*." *Italiana* 5 (1993): 41–54.
———. "The Traffic in Talk About Women." *Journal of Romance Studies* 4, no. 3 (2004): 13–34.
———. "Women Make All Things Lose Their Power: Women's Knowledge, Men's Fear in Boccaccio's *Decameron* and the *Corbaccio*." *Heliotropia* 1, no. 1 (2003): n.p.
Resnick, Irven M. "Marriage in Medieval Culture: Consent Theory and the Case of Joseph and Mary." *Church History* 69 (2000): 352–71.
Riché, Pierre, and Danielle Alexandre-Bidon. *L'Enfant au Moyen Âge*. Paris: Seuil, Bibliothèque nationale de France, 1994.
Rieger, Dietmar. "'E trait sos meillors omes ab un consel': Emotion, mise-en-scène et *consilium* féodal dans *Girart de Roussillon*." *Zeitschrift für romanische Philologie* 114 (1998): 628–50.
Riquer, Isabel de. "Lo 'Maravilloso' y lo cotidiano en *La Faula* de Guillem de Torroella." *Revista de filología románica* 22 (2005): 175–82.
Riquer, Martín de. *Historia de la literatura catalana*. Barcelona: Ariel, 1980.
Ross, Jill. *Figuring the Feminine: The Rhetoric of Female Embodiment in Medieval Hispanic Literature*. Toronto: University of Toronto Press, 2008.
Roubaud-Bénichou, Sylvia. *Le Roman de chevalerie en Espagne: Entre Arthur et Don Quichotte*. Paris: Champion, 2000.
Rouillard, Linda M. "Rape and Marriage in *Richars li Biaus*." *Medieval Perspectives* 13 (1998): 121–35.
Rubió y Lluch, Antoni. *Documents per l'historia de la cultura catalana mig-eval*. 2 vols. Barcelona, 1908.
Russell, William. "*Transsumptio*: A Rhetorical Doctrine of the Thirteenth Century." *Rhetorica* 5 (1987): 369–410.
Sandler, Lucy Freeman. "John of Metz, *The Tower of Wisdom*." In *The Medieval Craft of Memory: An Anthology of Texts and Pictures*, ed. Mary Carruthers and Jan Ziolkowski, 215–25. Philadelphia: University of Pennsylvania Press, 2002.
Santore, Cathy. "Danaë: The Renaissance Courtesan's Alter Ego." *Zeitschrift für Kunstgeschichte* 54 (1991): 412–27.
Schneider, Robert. *Public Life in Toulouse, 1463–1789: From Municipal Republic to Cosmopolitan City*. Ithaca: Cornell University Press, 1989.
Schulman, Nicole M. *When Troubadours Were Bishops: The Occitania of Folc of Marseille, 1150–1231*. New York: Routledge, 2001.
Shutters, Lynn. "Griselda's Pagan Virtue." *The Chaucer Review* 44, no. 1 (2009): 61–83.
Soriano, Marc. *Les Contes de Perrault: Culture savante et traditions populaires*. Paris: Gallimard, 1968.
Stahuljak, Zrinka. "Jean Froissart's *Chroniques*: *Translatio* and the Impossible Apprenticeship of Neutrality." In *The Politics of Translation in the Middle Ages*, ed. Renate

Blumenfeld-Kosinski, Luise von Flotow, and Daniel Russell, 121–42. Tempe, Ariz.: Arizona Center for Medieval and Renaissance Studies; Ottawa: University of Ottawa Press, 2001.

Stapleton, M. L. *Harmful Eloquence: Ovid's "Amores" from Antiquity to Shakespeare.* Ann Arbor: University of Michigan Press, 1996.

Starkey, Kathryn. "Traversing the Boundaries of Language: Multilingualism and Linguistic Difference in Wolfram von Eschenbach's *Willehalm.*" *German Quarterly* 75 (2002): 20–34.

Stefano, Giuseppe di. *El libro del famoso e muy esforçado Palmerín de Olivia.* Vol. I, *Studi sul "Palmerín de Olivia."* Pisa: Università di Pisa, 1966.

Steiner, George. *After Babel: Aspects of Language and Translation.* 3rd ed. Oxford: Oxford University Press, 1998.

Stern, Samuel Miklos. *Hispano-Arabic Strophic Poetry: Studies.* Edited by E. L. P. Harvey. Oxford: Clarendon Press, 1974.

Stirnemann, Patricia. "Histoire d'amour sans paroles." *L'Art de l'enluminure* 5 (June–August 2004).

Szkilnik, Michèle. "Aroès l'illusioniste: *Perceforest,* 3e partie." *Romania* 113 (1992–95): 441–65.

Tavani, Giuseppe. "Tolosa i Barcelona: Dos consistoris per a una poesia." In *Actes del vuitè col.loqui internacional de llengua i literatura catalanes,* ed. Antoni M. Badia i Margarit and Michel Camprubí, vol. I, 297–324. Barcelona: Abadia de Montserrat, 1988.

Thiolier-Méjean, Suzanne. "Le Motif du perroquet dans deux nouvelles d'Oc." In *Miscellanea Mediaevalia: Mélanges offerts à Philippe Ménard,* ed. Jean-Claude Faucon, Alain Labbé, and Danielle Quéruel, vol. II, 1355–75. Paris: Champion, 1998.

———. "Virgile et Prêtre Jean dans la nouvelle *Frayre de Joy e Sor de Plaser.*" In *Études de langue et de littérature médiévales offertes à Peter T. Ricketts à l'occasion de son 70ème anniversaire,* ed. Dominique Billy and Ann Buckley, 93–105. Turnhout: Brepols, 2005.

Thomas, James. "Fabre d'Olivet and Victor Gelu: Two Responses to the Symbolic Value of Occitan, 1815–1856." M.Phil. diss., University of Bristol, 2005.

Thompson, Stith. *Motif-Index of Folk-Literature.* Copenhagen: Rosenkilde and Bagger, 1956.

Tucker, Holly. *Pregnant Fictions: Childbirth and the Fairy Tale in Early Modern France.* Detroit: Wayne State University Press, 2003.

Uhl, Patrice. "L'Excursion aux îles Lipari d'Antoine de La Sale: Anecdote récréative ou nouvelle fantastique?" In *Colloque International du Centre de Recherche sur la Littérature des Voyages,* Université Paris IV: *L'Imaginaire du Volcan,* December 3, 2001. Audio recording of paper online: www.crlv.org.

Venuti, Lawrence. *The Scandals of Translation: Towards an Ethics of Difference.* New York: Routledge, 1998.

Vernet, André. "Une Version provençale de la *Chronologia magna* de Paulin de Venise." *Bibliothèque de l'École des Chartes* 104 (1943): 115–36.

Vincensini, Jean-Jacques. "Désordre de l'abjection et ordre de la courtoisie: Le Corps abject dans *Paris et Vienne* de Pierre de la Cépède." *Medium Aevum* 68 (1999): 292–304.

Waters, Clare M. "Talking the Talk: Access to the Vernacular in Medieval Preaching." In *The Vulgar Tongue: Medieval and Postmedieval Vernacularity,* ed. Fiona Somerset and Nicholas Watson, 30–42. University Park: Pennsylvania State University Press, 2002.

Watson, Nicholas. "Introduction: King Solomon's Tablets." In *The Vulgar Tongue: Medieval and Postmedieval Vernacularity*, ed. Fiona Somerset and Nicholas Watson, 1–13. University Park: Pennsylvania State University Press, 2002.

Weijers, Olga. *Dictionnaires et répertoires au Moyen Âge: Une Étude de vocabulaire*. Turnhout: Brepols, 1991.

Wilhelm, Raymund. "La lingua poetica nella storia linguistica della Romània medievale." In *Atti del XXI congresso internazionale di linguistica e filologia romanza*, ed. Giovanni Ruffino, vol. VI, 765–77. Tübingen: Niemeyer, 1998.

Willis, Raymond S. *The Debt of the Spanish "Libro de Alexandre" to the French "Roman d'Alexandre."* Elliott Monographs 33. Princeton: Princeton University Press, 1935.

Wunderli, Peter, and Günter Holtus. "La 'Renaissance' des études franco-italiennes: Rétrospective et prospective." In *Testi, cotesti e contesti del franco-italiano: Atti del 1o simposio franco-italiano (Bad Homburg, 13–16 aprile 1987)*, ed. Günter Holtus, Henning Krauss, and Peter Wunderli, 3–23. Tübingen: Niemeyer, 1989.

Yerushalmi, Yosef Hayim. "Inquisition and the Jews of France in the Time of Bernard Gui." *Harvard Theological Review* 63 (1970): 317–76.

Zamboni, Chiara. "Lingua materna, scrittura e politica." In *Lo Spazio della scrittura: Letterature comparate al femminile: Atti del 4. Convegno della Società italiana delle Letterate Venezia, Fondazione Giorgio Cini, 31 gennaio–1 febbraio 2002*, ed. Ilaria Crotti, Luisa Ricaldone, Ricciarda Ricorda, 239–51. Padua: Il Poligrafo, 2004.

Ziino, Francesca. "Una traduzione latina del *Boezio* catalano." *Romania* 119 (2001): 465–82.

Zufferey, François. *Bibliographie des poètes provençaux des XIVe et XVe siècles*. Geneva: Droz, 1984.

Zumthor, Paul. *Langue et technique poétiques à l'époque romane (XIe–XIIIe siècles)*. Paris: Klincksieck, 1963.

———. "Un Problème d'esthétique médiévale: L'Utilisation poétique du bilinguisme." *Le Moyen Âge* 60 (1966): 301–36, 561–94.

INDEX

abjection, 151, 157
Abraham, 59
Adam, 17, 29
Aeneas, 117
Africa, 57
Agamben, Giorgio, 60, 63
Agnes of Bourbon, 183, 186
Agnes (Saint), 155–57
Aigues-Mortes, 160, 168, 169, 174
Alain de Lille, 79
Alegre, Francesc, 146
Alexander de Villa-Dei, 69
Alexander romances, 19–21, 117
Alexander the Great, 185–86
Alexandria, 173
alfaquí, 158
Alfonso II, King of Aragon, 104
Alfonso the Magnanimous, King of Aragon, 145
aljamiado, 28, 144
aljamiado-morisco, 158
allebolus, 66–74
allegory, 13, 111
Allod, 39
allotheta, 68–69, 74
Alonso de Cartagena, 78
Angevin patronage, 144, 175, 182–93
Anjou, René d', 7, 145, 160
Antoni Canals, 78
Antoni Ginebreda, 78
Antwerp, 144
apple, 121, 122, 134–38, 177. *See also* fruit
Aquitaine, 26, 102
Arabic, language, 10–11, 21, 40, 91, 145, 148, 158, 167, 177
Aragon, 144, 145, 158, 169, 175, 178, 179
Ariadne, 163
Aristotle, 60, 81, 185–86

Armagnac, 180, 182
Armenia, 36, 50, 51, 53, 144
Arnau de Vilanova, 12
Arnaut Vidal de Castelnaudary, 35–53
ars dictaminis, 90, 97. *See also* letters
Arthur, King, 177–78, 190
Arthurian literature, 13, 81, 103, 177–78, 190
Augustine (Saint), 191–92
Ausiàs March, 6
Auvergne, 9, 12
Avignon, region of, 62, 63, 64, 74
Avignon papacy, 1–8, 56–60, 64–65

Babel, 13, 17–34, 53, 55, 56–60, 63, 193
Babylon, 21–22, 148, 160, 167
baptism, 41, 125
  and coercion, 41–42
barbarismus, 68, 70
Barcelona, 63, 146, 160, 182
Basile, Giovan Battista, 102
Bel Inconnu, 113–18
Belris, 101, 113–18. *See also* Franco-Italian
Benoît de Sainte-Maure, 162, 166
Bernard Gui, 39, 53. *See also* Inquisition
Bernat de So, 180, 191
Bernat Metge
  Lo Somni, 79–85
  Valter e Griselda, 82
Bertran Boysset, 5
betrothal, 35, 43, 107
birds, as emblems, 92, 93
  as protagonists, 101, 103, 105, 107, 114, 116, 128, 132
  bird of prey, 159, 172
black (color), 86–91, 93–96, 187, 188
Blandin de Cornualha, 36, 101, 103, 109, 119, 127, 128

Boccaccio, Giovanni, 37, 77, 78, 79, 82, 84–85
Boethius, 78, 79, 81, 83, 142–43
border, borderlands, 86, 118, 138
Breton, 1, 4, 7, 21, 26, 73, 122
brothel, 155–57
Brunhamel, Rasse de, 144
builders, 57, 62
Burgundy, 26, 32
    literature of Burgundian court, 162, 164–65, 169, 182

cannibalism, 152, 165–66
cantari, 113–18
Carcassonne, 38
Castilian
    language, 40, 64, 73, 90, 93, 144, 159
    literature, 103
castle, 43, 50–51. *See also* tower
Catalan
    language, 91
    prose literature, 12, 77–78, 86–91, 145, 146
Catharism, 38, 41, 42
Cerverí de Girona, 9
Chaldean, language, 21, 22, 23
chanson de geste, 5, 13, 37
Chartier, Alain, 78
childbirth, 103, 107, 114, 121–22, 129–31, 134, 136, 172
childhood. *See pueritia*
children's literature, 161, 167. *See also* tutors
Chrétien de Troyes, 103
chronicles, 142, 145
Chronologia Magna, 56–64
Cicero, 78, 81
Cixous, Hélène, 112–13, 137–38
Cligés, 103
Coburg, 161
Comminges, 168, 180
commune, 50–51
conception, 130, 132. *See also* Immaculate Conception
conquest, 103
consent, 107–13, 133, 152
Consistori de la sobregaya companhia del gay saber de Tolosa, 12, 64, 65–74, 84
Constantinople, 24, 32, 33
contes de fées, 102–3
conversion, 35, 40, 41
cookery, 167, 172
    and language, 153–55
Corinth, 165
creation, 18, 181

Crete, 144
crucifix, 40–41, 42
Crusade, 93, 147
Cyprus, 179

Danaë, 130–31
dance, 83, 101
Dante, 5, 62, 77
death, 102, 105–12, 122, 133, 148, 149, 153, 154, 172, 189
    "grateful dead," 122
Derrida, Jacques, 141, 177
devil(s), 29, 30, 41, 80
Dido, 25, 117, 162, 164
Diglossia, 74
diplomacy, 30
Dominic (Saint), 41
Donatus, 69
dragon, 114, 164–65
dream, 169
Dry Tree, legend, 117

Eden, 17, 42 122, 125–26
Eiximenis, Francesc, 84, 152, 155
Elissa, 25. *See also* Dido
Elucidari, 4, 8
Emaré, 125
enclosure, 39–40, 44, 120–24, 126–27
    Puella custodita, 130–31. *See also* Danaë, Eracle
endogamy, 118, 120–29, 132–34
England, 36–37, 52, 93
English, 21, 73, 151
entredeux, 113, 138
epistolary writing. *See* letters
Eracle, by Gautier d'Arras, 123
estranh, 50, 66–68
estrangiers, 168–71, 173, 174
ethics, 100, 181
Etna, 177, 178 190
Europe, 57–59
Everhard of Béthune, *Graecismus*, 68, 71
Exemplum, 33, 151
exogamy, 118–34

fable, 99, 100, 180
    as synonym for lies, 40
    Faula, 177–79
fairy mistress, 117
falcon, 116
father, 180
fertility, 153–55

Fillastre, Guilaume, 162
Fin'Amors, 47, 49, 53
fish, 172, 173, 177, 183
flamenca, 36, 101, 123
Flavius Josephus, 17
Flemish, 65, 73, 118, 119–120, 159
Florence, 164
flores rhetorici, "flowers of rhetoric," 33, 70–71
Floridan et Elvide, 144
flors del gay saber, 72
flowers, 93, 114, 126, 136, 184
Foix, county, 4, 8, 146, 180, 182
food, 88, 126, 137
   as body, 125, 152–53, 164, 171–72, 173–74
   denial of, 147
   feast food, 153–55
   foreign food, 168
   as metaphor for incest, 125–26
   as narrative device, 147, 147–48, 151–53, 159, 164
   as writing, 134–38
fool, 129
foreignness. See *estranh, estrangiers*
fortune, 163
Foucon de Candie, 118
Franco-Italian, Franco-Venetian, 14, 101, 113–18, 127
Franco-Provençal, 23, 178
Frayre de Joy e Sor de Plazer, 99–113, 119, 127
French language, 65, 73, 86–91, 99–102, 113, 118, 119, 141–46
   for *devises* and motto, 95
   as second language, 142, 146
Freud, Sigmund, 55
Friar, Franciscan, 147, 149–50
Frondino e Brisona, História del amat, 78, 85–91, 92, 95, 97
Frontinus, Julius, 184–85
fruit, 120, 121, 122, 129–30, 133, 134–38, 172

Galician-Portuguese, 9, 64
Garonne, 180–81, 191
Gascon, 9, 26, 73, 178
Gaston III, Count of Foix (Gaston Fébus), 4, 8, 146, 180
Gautier d'Arras, 123
gender and language, 9, 86–91, 103, 119
genealogy, 8, 20–21, 29–30, 56–61, 63, 70, 99, 121, 127, 131, 134, 136, 167. See also lineage

Genesi de Scriptura, 46–48
Genesis, 46–48, 55–56
Genoa, 146, 147, 160, 169, 189
Genoese, 146
German, 159, 160, 163
Gervase of Tilbury, 178
ghosts, 190
Giant, 109, 125, 181, 193
Girart de Roussillon, 17–34, 35, 37
Gironde, 27, 181
Gloria d'Amor, 144, 145
glossing, 161
go-between, 112, 132, 149, 177–78, 181, 184, 189, 193
Golden Fleece, 162, 173
grafting, 120, 121, 136
grammar, 66–74
grammaticus, 69
Greece, 5, 25, 73
Greek language, 18, 21, 22, 23, 24–25, 27, 28, 41, 59, 69, 71, 82, 167, 185
   "Pseudo-Greek" words, 66–74, 184
Greek literature, medieval, 103
green (color), 93, 187
Griselda, 79, 81, 82, 165
Guido delle Colonne, 162–63, 164
Guilhem de la Barra, 5, 18–19, 35–53
Guilhem de Capestany, troubadour, 145
Guilhem Molinier, 66, 70. See *Leys d'Amors*
Guillem Nicolau, 78
Guyenne, 51, 52, 168

Hagia Sophia, 32
hagiography, 31, 153–57
hallucination, 87
Handless Maiden, 159
Hawthorn, 33
healing, 160–61, 164, 165, 166, 168, 170–74. See also sickness
   healing baths, 182–83
Hebrew language, 10, 17, 18, 21, 22, 23, 28, 29, 41
hell, 183, 190, 193
Henry VII, King of England, 93
heraldry, 93
heresy, 38, 42, 78–79
Histoire d'amour sans paroles, 79, 91–97
Holy Land, 179
honor, 116
Honorius Augustodunensis, 61
hospital, 168, 170–74. See also healing
Hungary, 39

hybridity, 1, 5, 12, 14, 193
   in literature, 18
   in plants, 177

illusion, 188
   smoke as, 187–88
Immaculate Conception, 80
Imago mundi, 61
impropriety of speech, *improprietas*, 68, 71
Incarnation doctrine, 38
   and Jews, 39
incest, 118, 120–29, 132–34
infancy and language, 59–61, 66
Inquisition, 35, 38, 41–42, 53, 68
interpreter, 40, 42, 52, 148, 149–50, 168, 173, 184
intersubjectivity, 101
Irigaray, Luce, 64
Iseut, 145
Isidore of Seville, 17–18
Islamic exegesis, 51
Italian lyric poetry, 6–7, 13
Italy, 5, 12, 65

Jacques Fournier, 41. *See* Inquisition
Jason, 161–66, 169
Jaufré, 36, 151
Jaume (James) I, King of Aragon, 104
Jaume (James) II, King of Aragon, 104
Jean de Calabre, son of René d'Anjou, 144, 185–86
Jean Lemaire de Belges, 93
Jehan de Saintré, 144
Jehan Maillart, 37
Jerusalem, 31, 178
Jeu de Sainte Agnès, 153–57
Jewish exegesis, 51, 52
Jews, 28, 29, 39, 41
Joan de Castellnou, 12
Joan Roís de Corella, 166, 167
Jofre de Foixà, 153
John I (Joan I), King of Aragón, 77, 79, 80, 84
John of Genoa, *Catholicon*, 68–69
John of Metz, 60
John of Salisbury, 74
Jordan, River, 179
Joseph (Patriarch), 36, 46–49, 51
Josephus, Flavius, 55, 56, 59, 61

keys, 93–95, 159, 168, 174
koine, 5, 6, 10, 62, 65, 72, 73
Kornaros, Vitzentzos, 144

La Sale, Antoine de, 144, 182–93
Lacan, Jacques, 63, 64
Lais, genre, 103, 122
Lancelot, 81
Lanfranc Cigala, troubadour, 118
language choice, 62, 99–101, 145
languages, seventy-two, 57, 60
   and lineage, 99–100, 167
   of birds and animals, 72, 101
   of the body, 86–91
   without words, 91–97, 107–8, 147–50, 157–58
Languedoc, 5, 51, 65, 66, 104
Latin, language, 1–10, 18, 21, 22, 24, 41, 61, 65, 71, 78, 91, 112, 146
   auctoritas, 141, 153
   poetry, 153–54
   liturgical, 25–26
   "Latin" of birds, 92. *See* birds
Le Pins, Jean, 144
Leeu, Gherard, 144
Lefèvre, Raoul, 162, 164–65, 169
leprosy, 151, 183
letters, 86–91, 97, 114–17, 164, 167
Levita, Elia, 144
Leys d'Amors, 13, 39, 66–74
Libro de Alexandre, 20
lies, 30, 35, 41, 42, 189, 190
   false accusation, 53, 122, 123
Limousin, region, 1, 9, 12, 26
   language, 1, 9, 10, 12
lineage, 169. *See* genealogy
Lion de Bourges, 119, 126
Lipari Islands, 186–93
Llull, Ramon, 91
Louis III, Duke of Anjou, 182–83
Louis XII, King of France, 93
Lucidarium, 4
Lucretius, *De rerum natura*, 190–91, 193

Macaire, 118
Macaronic poetry, 153
Machaut, Guillaume de, 90, 92
Magi, of Persia, 185
magician, 103, 104, 114, 128
Mallorca, 177, 178
Manekine, 125, 159
mappa mundi, 27, 56, 57–58, 181
   map, 183
Marcabru, 11
María de Luna, 80, 84
Marian poetry, 64, 66

INDEX 235

Marot, Clément, 162, 167
marriage, 42–43, 70, 107–13, 128, 148, 163.
    See consent
Mars, Roman god of war, 131–32
Marseille, 142, 146, 155
Martí I, l'Humà, King of Aragon, 77
martyrdom, 144, 151, 155–57
Mary Magdalen, 22
Mary Tudor, daughter of Henry VII,
    King of England, 93
Matfré Ermengau, 7
Medea, 161–66, 169, 172
medicine, 120
Meditatio, 87–88
Melusine, 179
memory, 60–61, 62
menstruation, 61, 63
messenger-bird, 11. *See* birds, go-between
metaphor, 71, 72
Metge, Bernat. *See* Bernat Metge
milk, 63, 108, 112, 154
minstrel, 149
misogyny, 79–85, 152
monolangue, 141, 177
monolingualism, 55,
Mont Ventoux, 191
Monti Sibillini, 183
"Moorish" language and culture,
    148–50, 167
Morea, 165
Morgan le Fay, 177–78
Morisco community, 158
mother tongue, 1–8, 62–63, 64, 74, 101,
    112, 138, 141, 169–70, 175,
    177–79, 193
  theories concerning, 100–101
  "stepmother tongue," 146
mother, 122, 151, 167, 171, 172
mystery play, 153–57

Naples, 104, 145, 159, 160, 168;
    Kingdom of Naples, 14, 144, 145, 182
Nerbonesi, 118
Nicolas de Clamanges, 144
Nimrod, 55, 56, 60
Noah, 55, 56, 63
"Nomadism," 85
Nompar, seigneur of Caumont, 179–80
Normans, 27, 73
novas, Occitan genre, 99–113
novela sentimental, 90, 145
noves rimades, Catalan genre, 81, 86–91, 97

nurse, 24, 62–63, 120, 122, 123 159,
    168–69, 171
nursing, 62–63, 107–8, 112, 160, 165

Occitan-Catalan, 14, 86–91, 99–113, 119
Occitanisms in French, 143
Oliver, Francesc, 78
orchard, 120–24
Organyà, 7
Orléans, 32
Orosius, 78
Orpheus, 80–82, 83, 85
Ovid, 25, 77
    Amores, 131
    Heroides, 78, 81, 117, 162, 163, 165, 166
    Metamorphoses, 103, 130–31, 169

Palmerín de Oliva, 103
Paolino Veneto (Paulinus of Venice), 56–62,
    63, 64
papal curia at Avignon, 1–8, 56–60, 64–65, 145
Paris and Vienne, 14, 141–58
Paris, 66, 101
Paul (Saint), 33
Pax Dei, 32, 33
peace, 50, 181
Peire d'Alvernhe, 11
Pentecost, 13, 18, 19, 21, 32, 53,
    72. *See also* tongues
Perceforest, 119, 120 128
Pere IV, King of Aragon, 77, 180, 185
Perrault, Charles, 102
Persian, 167
Peter (Saint), 174–75
Petrarca, Francesco, 79, 81, 144, 191
Peyre de Paternas, 1–4, 64
Philip IV, King of France, 39, 65
Philip VI, King of France, 65
Philippe de Voisins, seigneur of Montaut,
    178–79
Philosophy (Lady), 64
Pierre de la Cépède, 141–44, 146, 157–58, 175
Pierre de Provence et la belle Maguelonne, 14,
    159–61, 162, 167–75
pilgrimage, 160, 166, 169, 179–80, 192
Pliny the Younger, 191
Pluto, 190
Polyglot, 62
Pope Alexander III, 107
Pope Clement V, 37
Pope Clement VI, 1
Pope John XXII, 59

Pope, literary character, 33, 148
Potiphar's wife, 37, 38, 46–52
Pozzuoli, 182–83
preaching, 53
pregnancy, 103, 121, 122, 123, 124, 154
Prester John, 102, 104, 105, 148
prison, 134–38, 147–50, 156
Proba, 82
Prosimetrum, 90
Provence, 2, 4, 10, 14, 26, 28, 65, 104, 143, 144, 145
    count of, 143, 144, 160, 168
    as a setting for a narrative, 159
Psalms, 32
Psychomachia, 70–71
pueritia (childhood), 59–61, 66
Puglia, 178, 179
Purgatory, 80
Puy poetry, 12, 66
Pyrenees, 5, 8, 12, 102, 181

Qu'ran, 47, 48

Raimbaut de Vaqueiras, 9
Raimon de Cornet, 7
Raimon Vidal de Besalú, 9, 11–12, 105, 119
Ramon Llull, 12
rape, in literature, 32, 121, 123, 127
    accusation, 47–48, 49–50, 108, 112
    in myth, 190
raptus, 128
razos de trobar, 9
reading for pleasure, 142
religious drama, medieval
René d'Anjou, 7, 145, 160
Requis, 119
rhetoric, 66–74
    personification, 70–71
    in the vernacular, 40
Rhetorica ad Herennium, 71
Richard de Saint-Laurent, 64
Richard li Biaus, 119–28, 129, 138
Rieux, 144
ring, 106, 108, 110–11, 128, 148, 160, 172, 180
Rocabertí, Fra, 144, 145
Rodez, 5
Roís de Corella, Joan, 166, 167
Roman de la Rose, 93
Roman idyllique (genre), 151, 153
Rome, 5, 25, 39, 49, 73, 104, 160, 168, 169, 174, 185
Rondeau, 86–91, 93, 97

Saint-Gaudens, 180
salt, 125, 173
Saracen, 26, 27, 29. See also Moorish
    language, 40
    placename, 174
    protagonists, 40
    religion, 40–41
Sardinia, 12, 104, 189
Satan, 29, 30, 41, 80
Schism (papal), 80
Seneca, 162
Seven Sages of Rome, 39, 49, 52
Seven sleepers, legend, 179
Sicily, 9, 146, 177–78, 184, 186
sickness, 120–24, 132, 147, 148, 149, 160, 164, 165, 167, 168, 183
silence, 148, 157
Simon de Hesdin, *Faits et dits memorables*, 184–86
sleep, 120, 126, 128–29, 131, 132, 134, 159, 164
Sleeping Beauty, 13, 102–103, 119, 127–34
smell, 147–49, 150–58
    and representation in words, 157–58
smile, 105–6, 117–18
Socrates, 69
soloecismus, 69, 70, 71
Soloi, 13, 71, 73
spies, 147, 148, 186, 188–89, 190
starvation, 147–48, 152
stench, as narrative device, 147–48, 150–51, 155–58
stranger, 126, 168–71. See *estranh*, *estrangiers*
stratagem, 151, 158, 184–86
stromboli, 187
suicide, 114–115, 117, 153, 164
Syria, 39

Talmud, 39
teaching, 69–70. See tutors
tears, 87–91
theatre, 153–57
Thebes, 185
theology, 68
Thessaly, 163
Tiresias, 79
tongue, 72, 141. See also Pentecost
Tortosa, 7
Toulouse, 5, 13, 18, 35, 37–38, 53, 64–74, 181
Tournai, 120

tower, in mnemonics, 60
  of Babel, 28, 55, 56, 60–61
  in iconography, 56–57, 93–95
  in literature, 40, 103, 129
  as tomb, 105, 107
translatio, 5, 32, 33, 71, 72, 77, 178
translatio studii, 23
translation, 56–61, 70
  Biblical, 78–79
  between vernaculars, 142, 158, 161, 175
  from Latin, 70, 142, 161, 184
  into Latin, 175
  and metaphor, 77
  putting sense-perception into words, 150–51
  "secondary translations," 162, 175
  theory, 77–79, 80–85, 95
translators, 70, 77–85, 142–43, 161, 184–86, 193
transsumptio, rhetorical device, 71
travel writing, 177–93
  travel in narrative, 167–68
Traveler, 169, 173, 174, 177–93
treason, 28, 30–31
tree, 125, 136
Tristan, 81, 104, 144
Trojan romances, 14, 162–66
troubadours, 5
Tuscan, 5, 60, 78, 144, 145, 146, 163, 164, 175
  Italianisms in French, 184, 187
tutors, 182–93
Tydorel, 122

Uguccione da Pisa, 68
University education, 66–74
Uzeste (Gironde), 37

Valerius Maximus, *Facta et dicta memorabilia*, 192
  in Catalan, 78,
  in French, 184–86
vehicular languages, 64, 149
Venice, 56, 59, 62, 144, 163, 164, 175, 179
Venus, 129–30, 132, 133, 136
Verona, 144
Vézelay, 21, 23, 31–32, 33–34
Villers-Cotterêts, 65
Violant (Yolande) de Bar, Queen of Aragon, 77–79, 82
Virgil
  author of *Aeneid*, 162
  magician, 104, 111, 128
Virgin birth, doctrine of, 103
virginity, 110, 122
Virgin Mary, 61, 64, 80, 163
vulcano, 182, 186–92
Vulgate, 46–47

Waldensians, 38, 157
Walloon, 119
Walter of Châtillon, 20
William IX, Duke of Aquitaine, 11
window, 130–31
wine, 120
wisdom, "Tower of Wisdom," 60, 61.
  See also tower
witchcraft, 157, 164
women and multilingualism, 77–85
women readers and patrons, 1–4, 64, 77–85, 99–101
world, concepts of, 27, 60
  map, 27, 56, 57
  personification, 181, 192–93
writing, 86–91, 115, 117, 135–38

www.ingramcontent.com/pod-product-compliance
Lightning Source LLC
Chambersburg PA
CBHW031549300426
44111CB00006BA/229